The Official Guide for Hikers, Mounta  *ns*

TAHOE RIM
TRAIL

4th
Edition

The Official Guide for Hikers, Mountain Bikers, and Equestrians

TAHOE RIM
TRAIL
4th
Edition

Tim Hauserman

 WILDERNESS PRESS ... *on the trail since 1967*

Tahoe Rim Trail: The Official Guide for Hikers, Mountain Bikers, and Equestrians

Copyright © 2002, 2008, 2012, and 2020 by Tim Hauserman

Manufactured in the United States of America
Distributed by Publishers Group West
Fourth edition, second printing 2021

Editor: Kate Johnson
Maps: Tom Harrison, using mapping information from Jeffrey P. Schaffer
Cover design: Scott McGrew
Interior and cover photos: Tim Hauserman, except the following: page 8: Trevor Fairbank/Shutterstock; page 9: Peter Moulton/Shutterstock (California ground squirrel) and Dominic Laniewicz/Shutterstock (Douglas squirrel); page 10: V Rivers/Shutterstock (golden-mantled ground squirrel) and Tom Reichner/Shutterstock (pika); pages 23, 25, 56, 85, 93, 95, 107, 109, 120, 133, 141, 142, 152, 169, 188, and 212: Joyce Chambers
Paw-print illustrations by Jessica Land
Proofreader: Emily Beaumont
Indexer: Frances Lennie

Library of Congress Cataloging-in-Publication Data

Names: Hauserman, Tim, 1958– author.
Title: Tahoe Rim Trail : the official guide for hikers, mountain bikers, and equestrians / Tim Hauserman.
Other titles: The Tahoe Rim Trail
Description: Fourth edition. | Birmingham, AL : Wilderness Press, 2020
Summary: "This official guide presents the entire 165-mile trail, divided into 8 sections, complete with detailed maps and essential information." — Provided by publisher.
Identifiers: LCCN 2020000466 (print) | LCCN 2020000467 (ebook) | ISBN 9780899979601 (pbk.) | ISBN 9780899979618 (ebook)
Subjects: LCSH: Hiking—Tahoe Rim Trail (Calif. and Nev.)—Guidebooks. | Mountain biking—Tahoe Rim Trail (Calif. and Nev.)—Guidebooks. | Horsemanship—Tahoe Rim Trail (Calif. and Nev.)—Guidebooks. | Tahoe Rim Trail (Calif. and Nev.)—Guidebooks.
Classification: LCC GV199.42.T18 H38 2020 (print) | LCC GV199.42.T18 (ebook) | DDC 917.94/38—dc23
LC record available at lccn.loc.gov/2020000466
LC ebook record available at lccn.loc.gov/2020000467

Published by  **WILDERNESS PRESS**
An imprint of AdventureKEEN
2204 First Ave. S., Ste. 102
Birmingham, AL 35233
800-443-7227, fax 205-326-1012

Visit wildernesspress.com for a complete listing of our books and for ordering information. Contact us at our website, at facebook.com/wildernesspress1967, or at twitter.com/wilderness1967 with questions or comments. To find out more about who we are and what we're doing, visit blog.wildernesspress.com.

Front cover photo: Participants in a 100-mile endurance run on the trail (see Chapter 6, Section 3, page 86)
Back cover photo: Equestrians on the trail (see Chapter 3, page 26)
Frontispiece: Dicks Lake (see Chapter 6, Section 7, page 143)

SAFETY NOTICE Although Wilderness Press and the author have made every attempt to ensure that the information in this book is accurate at press time, they are not responsible for any loss, damage, injury, or inconvenience that may occur to anyone while using this book. You are responsible for your own safety and health. The fact that a trail is described in this book does not mean that it will be safe for you. Be aware that trail conditions can change from day to day. Always check local conditions and know your own limitations.

Contents

Acknowledgments vii
Note for the Fourth Edition viii
Foreword x
Overview Map xii
Map Legend 59

1 **Introduction to the Tahoe Area and the Tahoe Rim Trail** 1

2 **Animals and Plants, Great and Small** 5

3 **Let's All Get Along: A Trail for Everyone** 26

4 **Weather, Water, and When to Go** 30

5 **Fun for All: A User's Guide to the Tahoe Rim Trail** 40

6 **Trail Descriptions** 58

SECTION 1   Tahoe City to Brockway Summit
19.1 miles 60

SECTION 2   Brockway Summit to Mount Rose
20.3 miles 70

SECTION 3   Tahoe Meadows to Spooner Summit
23.1 miles 86

SECTION 4   Spooner Summit to Kingsbury Grade *19.4 miles* 103

SECTION 5   Kingsbury Grade to Big Meadow *23.7 miles* 115

SECTION 6   Big Meadow to Echo Summit
15.7 miles 130

SECTION 7   Echo Summit and Echo Lake to Barker Pass
32.7 miles from Echo Lake
34.9 miles from Echo Summit 143

SECTION 8   Barker Pass to Tahoe City
16.7 miles 161

7 **Other Tahoe-Area Hiking and Biking Trails**   173

APPENDIX A   Resources 189

APPENDIX B   Mileages for the Tahoe Rim Trail 191

APPENDIX C   Tim's Top Five Places on the Trail 195

APPENDIX D   Ways to Save Lake Tahoe 199

APPENDIX E   Leave No Trace Principles 201

Index 203
About the Author 212

Acknowledgments

AN ACKNOWLEDGMENT FOR this fourth edition of the guidebook is really a thank you to all those who have contributed thoughts, assistance, and hiking legs to my telling of the Tahoe Rim Trail story over the last 20 years. I'm profoundly grateful to all of you who lent a hand to my effort on every edition.

This go-round I'd also like to warmly thank the folks at the Tahoe Rim Trail Association (TRTA), including Executive Director Morgan Steel; Office Administrator Laurie Buffington; and especially Deputy Director Chris Binder, the guy in charge of trail operations. He was always patient with all my questions about the latest changes the hardworking TRTA crew has made to the trail. We share a profound love for this big old loop around Lake Tahoe. The TRTA is full of long-term plans for the trail, so I'm sure at some point down the road a fifth edition will be needed.

I'd like to thank the Wilderness Press crew at AdventureKEEN and especially my editor, Kate Johnson, who was able to decipher my gobbledygook and make everything look great. I imagine that as soon as she saw this she was checking the spelling on *gobbledygook*. Can't wait to see the final product.

I'd especially like to thank Joyce Chambers, who joined me over the last two years hiking the trail. Thanks for the laughter and companionship, great photos, and the opportunity to see the trail again through your fresh eyes, which was a great reminder of what a gift the Tahoe Rim Trail has been to me.

Note for the Fourth Edition

HARD TO BELIEVE how fast time travels, but it's been more than 20 years since I first hiked the complete Tahoe Rim Trail and became TRT 150 Mile Club Member #11 (it was changed to the 165 Mile Club once the trail was fully completed and they realized that 150 miles was a bit optimistic). A few of the sections were still under construction when I hiked the trail the first time, and I remember following proposed trail markers from Relay Peak to Gray Lake. The loose rock field on the southern slope of Rose Knob Peak was like a treacherous trek across moving bowling balls. It took about an hour to crawl my way precariously across the rocks. A few years later, that section was a fun little 5-minute saunter across smooth, beautifully built trail. Gotta love the trail builders and the amazing work of art they have created.

The Tahoe Rim Trail changed my life soon after. I was serving on the Tahoe Rim Trail Association board of directors, and at one board meeting Shannon Raborn, who was the associate director of the TRTA at the time, brought up for discussion that with the trail almost complete the organization needed to find someone to write a guidebook for it. For some reason, even though I hadn't written much since my time working on the North Tahoe High School newspaper, I decided I was the guy to write it. And once I finished the challenging task of putting together that first edition, I began the transition to becoming a full-time writer.

The Tahoe Rim Trail is an amazing trail. It provides a wide range of views, ecosystems, and experiences. It's user-friendly with plenty of easy-access points, and because it's a circle it's a perfect candidate for someone who wants to spend two weeks doing a thru-hike. I did my first thru-hike in 2007. It was solo, and it was such a different experience from hiking the trail in segments that I did it again in 2009 and 2011, as a guide for the Tahoe Rim Trail Association's annual thru-hikes. Even though hiking the entire TRT is a walk in the park compared with the 2,600-mile Pacific Crest Trail, for us normal humans, 165 miles is still a long way to walk in one swoop. But it is certainly a worthwhile endeavor.

For this fourth edition, I hiked much of the trail again, with particular focus on the places where trail changes have been made since the last edition. It's been interesting reviewing the text of previous editions and looking at how my eyes saw the trail 20 years ago versus now. I still mountain bike a lot and love to hike and backpack, but I tend not to go as far and as fast as I used to. I do still try to represent the trail for all of the users, from the 20-something who roars down the hills on his bike to the retiree who wants to take a slow stroll through the wildflowers. My mind thinks I still belong to the first group, but my body is starting to steer me closer to the second. I do have one word of warning for the less than expert mountain biker: don't ask an expert whether a trail is difficult or not. What is a piece of cake for some folks is surely a very trying and challenging ride for many others.

I hope this edition gives folks the information they need to be responsible users of the Tahoe Rim Trail. Our beloved trail is more popular than ever, so it is extremely important that we make every effort to leave it just as beautiful as we found it.

Star Lake (see Section 5: Kingsbury Grade to Big Meadow, page 115)

Foreword

LIKE MANY OF US who live in the Tahoe Basin, I have a copy of this guide-book. It is the first edition and has been passed around between family and friends. Its worn and weathered pages are a testament to its many journeys around the trail and the countless epic adventures it has facilitated. As you dive into your copy, I'm excited to welcome you to the Tahoe Rim Trail!

The Tahoe Rim Trail started as a dream—a large loop trail circling Tahoe's rugged peaks, dipping into iconic alpine lakes, and exploring wilderness areas around the Tahoe Basin. Since the late 1970s, this dream has propelled the work of the Tahoe Rim Trail Association (TRTA). The Association was founded in 1981 and, with our partners at the U.S. Forest Service and Nevada State Parks, completed the initial loop trail in the fall of 2001. This world-class trail system now consists of 200 miles of trail [including connectors and other off-the-trail options] and is a showcase for the power of an engaged community. The trail's recreational offerings are available for the public because our community has spent the past four decades providing financial support and volunteering to build and maintain the system. With our organization's

Fontanillis Falls (see Section 7: Echo Summit and Echo Lake to Barker Pass, page 143)

40th anniversary on the horizon, we remain focused on preserving the trail and inspiring stewardship. As in the early years of our association, our work remains a community effort, with TRTA volunteers contributing more than 18,000 hours of service annually to provide this valuable recreational resource to trail users like you.

Whether you are exploring the trail for a few hours or adventuring for weeks, the trail has something to offer. Hoping to catch wildflowers in bloom? Explore north of Showers Lake. Looking for an afternoon bike ride? Visit the Van Sickle Trail. Seeking solitude? Check out Twin Peaks. Hoping for expansive views? Visit Relay Peak. We hope that while you enjoy this incredible trail system you keep in mind that the trail is a shared resource. The trail sees nearly 500,000 annual users, so it is imperative that everyone pitch in to preserve this incredible recreational treasure. This starts with the simplest principle—be nice! The Tahoe Rim Trail is your trail. The majority of it is open to all types of nonmotorized users who each uniquely connect with it. A friendly smile and a "hello" go a long way in avoiding user conflicts and ensures everyone has a great experience.

Practicing Leave No Trace ethics is also imperative to ensure that everyone can enjoy the Tahoe Rim Trail today and in the future. If you aren't well versed in Leave No Trace, make sure to brush up before you head out on the trail (see page 201). These principles help guide outdoor enthusiasts on how to minimize their impact on the trail. This includes standards like staying on designated trails, packing out your garbage, properly doing your business in the backcountry, and camping in appropriate locations. Learn the seven Leave No Trace principles at lnt.org or through one of the TRTA's courses.

Teaching trail users how to best minimize their impact on and around the trail is a big part of our job. We are also busy enhancing the trail system through various reroutes and new trail construction projects. We maintain nearly 200 miles of trail each year, an endeavor that includes everything from removing encroaching vegetation and fallen trees to improving drainage to keep trails dry. We also champion what is best for the trail to ensure everyone can experience Tahoe's world-class recreation today and in the future. Please join us. Visit our website, tahoerimtrail.org, to join the movement by becoming a member or volunteer today!

Happy Trails,
Morgan Steel
Executive Director, Tahoe Rim Trail Association

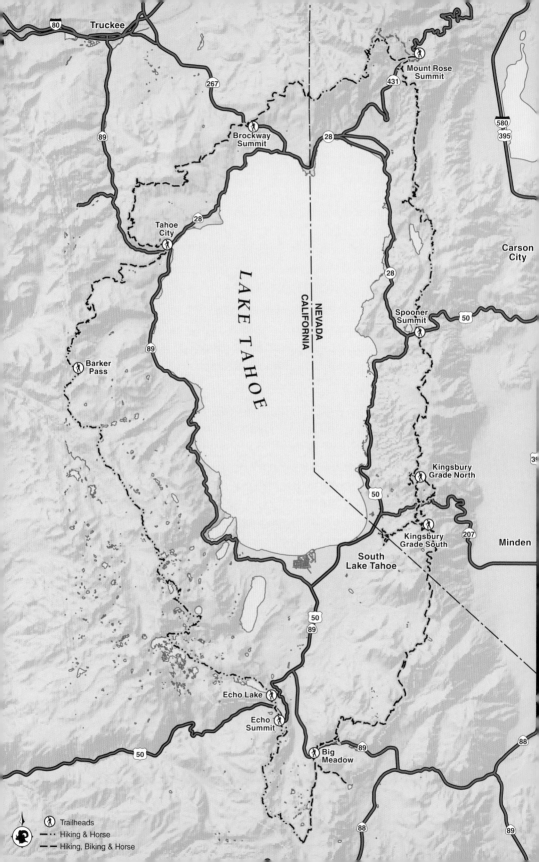

1

Introduction to the Tahoe Area and the Tahoe Rim Trail

Then it seemed to me the Sierra should not be called the Nevada, or Snowy Range, but the Range of Light. And after ten years spent in the heart of it, rejoicing and wondering, bathing in its glorious floods of light, seeing the sunbursts of morning among the icy peaks, the noonday radiance on the trees and rocks and snow, the flush of the alpenglow, and a thousand dashing waterfalls with their marvelous abundance of irised spray, it still seems to be above all others the Range of Light, the most divinely beautiful of all the mountain chains I have ever seen.

—John Muir, 1912

WELCOME TO THE TAHOE RIM TRAIL! This book quickly and easily provides you what you need to know to enjoy your time on this incredibly beautiful route. Having lived at Lake Tahoe most of my life, I've spent countless hours on area trails. While I am not a biologist, a geologist, a naturalist, or an -ist of any kind, I have learned enough about Tahoe plants, animals, and mountains to deepen my interest when I am in the woods. I'd like to help make your outdoor experience just as fun and fascinating.

Picture an enormous, deep-blue subalpine lake surrounded by lofty snow-capped peaks, with lush green forests, dark volcanic peaks, stark granite faces, and hundreds of small jewel-like lakes adorning the wilderness areas above it. Does a place like that deserve a loop trail? Absolutely. Lake Tahoe might be the best place in the world to build a loop trail. In fact, it is quite remarkable that the trail was completed as recently as 2001. The TRT, as it is often abbreviated here, circles one of the world's most beautiful lakes and winds through two states; several wilderness areas; national forest and state park lands; and an incredible diversity of geology, flora, and fauna. The trail accesses both the Sierra Nevada and its Carson Range spur, each of which has a unique personality. It winds through aspen meadows, skirts high mountain peaks, and runs for miles along ridgetops with stunning views. You can walk under a forested canopy or saunter through meadows and can venture above treeline for long stretches. That the trail is a big, circular loop may be its best feature. Wherever you set off, as the days and weeks go by, you can follow the circle back to where you began. Across the big, blue expanse of the lake, you can pick out where you were a week ago, and where you will be again in another week. Much of the multiuse trail was constructed for the pleasure of hikers, equestrians, and mountain bikers, using modern trail-building techniques, with the goal of keeping the grade below an average of 10%.

Geographic Setting

Lake Tahoe is the largest subalpine lake in North America. At 22 miles long and 12 miles wide, it is a beautiful expanse of deep, blue water. What makes it so intensely blue? Its depth. At its deepest point Lake Tahoe plunges to 1,645 feet with an average depth of approximately 900 feet. With its huge surface area, that's a lot of water. Another reason Tahoe is blue is because it is so clear. Its clarity is primarily because the basin around it is fairly small, the water is very cold, and the soils and vegetation have prevented nutrients from entering the lake where they would increase algae growth.

Since the 1960s and 1970s, the population has grown and development has increased dramatically in the Tahoe area, which has had a negative effect on the lake. An increase in algae growth has reduced Tahoe's legendary clarity. A substantial investment of energy and money is now underway to protect the lake. For information on how you can help, see page 199.

Trail History

During the 1970s, when Glenn Hampton was a recreation officer for the Lake Tahoe Basin Management Unit of the U.S. Forest Service (USFS), he first had the idea of completing a trail, with volunteer labor, around the rim of Lake Tahoe. He forged a partnership between the USFS, Nevada State Parks, and a newly created nonprofit volunteer organization called the Tahoe Rim Trail Fund. The purpose of the partnership was to plan, construct, and maintain a Tahoe Rim Trail. While the Tahoe Rim Trail uses the existing Pacific Crest Trail in the section that overlaps from Meiss Meadows to Twin Peaks, the vast majority of the trail was built after 1984 by volunteers from the Tahoe Rim Trail Association.

The Tahoe Rim Trail Fund (now the Tahoe Rim Trail Association) is administered by a volunteer board of directors and has a small professional staff. The trail has been built partially by professional crews hired by the USFS or Nevada State Parks and partially by volunteers who have contributed thousands of hours. For many it has been a labor of love. Construction of the trail began in July 1984 from Grass Lake, on the north side of CA 89 near Luther Pass, toward Kingsbury Grade. In 1985 two additional construction projects began at Spooner Summit and Tahoe City. In 2001 the last section of the trail was completed, between Rose Knob Peak and Mount Baldy. Since that time, sections of the trail have been removed from roads and replaced with singletrack trail, loops have been added, and much of the trail has been improved or rerouted.

In 1999, then–First Lady Hillary Clinton and the White House Millennium Council designated the Tahoe Rim Trail as the Millennium Trail for the state of Nevada, an honor bestowed upon only one trail in each state. Today the TRT is destined to become one of the most popular trails in the United States, taking its place beside the Appalachian, Pacific Crest, and John Muir Trails.

The Tahoe Rim Trail Association (TRTA)

The mission of the TRTA is to maintain and enhance the Tahoe Rim Trail system, practice and inspire stewardship, and preserve access to the natural beauty of the Lake Tahoe region. Funded through contributions, memberships, fundraising, grants, and the sale of merchandise, the association coordinates about 1,000 volunteers to work more than 15,000 hours on the trail annually. Over the past 39 years, the TRTA and its government partners have not only built and improved the trail itself but also built several major trailhead facilities and a 1.3-mile wheelchair-accessible interpretive trail. The TRTA is also the prime source of information for people interested in hiking, biking, or horseback riding on the Tahoe Rim Trail.

The TRTA also administers the Tahoe Rim Trail 165 Mile Club. Those who hike, ride their horses, or bike (where allowed) the entire trail can become members of the club. The TRTA also has an active guided-hiking program that leads thru-hikes and segment hikes throughout the summer.

There is always much to do to maintain and improve the trail, including repairing damaged sections, removing downed trees, and making changes to prevent future damage. Volunteers add switchbacks, change routes, add connecting trails, and do whatever is necessary to improve the trail.

The TRTA is key to the future of the trail, and anyone can become a member. Members receive newsletters; an invitation to the annual meeting; discounts on merchandise; and the opportunity to attend TRTA-led hikes, trainings, and events—not to mention the satisfaction of knowing that you are doing your part for this wonderful trail. For more information, contact the Tahoe Rim Trail Association info@tahoerimtrail.org, 775-298-4485, or tahoerimtrail.org.

Regulations and Permits

The Tahoe Rim Trail travels through three wilderness areas, which are managed by national forests: Mount Rose Wilderness, Desolation Wilderness, and Granite Chief Wilderness. Much of the rest of the trail is on national forest lands in California and Nevada, and some lies in Lake Tahoe Nevada State Park. The only areas with limitations on hiking or camping are Desolation Wilderness and Lake Tahoe Nevada State Park. These two include the following sections, described in greater detail in Chapter 6:

SECTION 3: TAHOE MEADOWS TO SPOONER SUMMIT This section travels through Lake Tahoe Nevada State Park, where camping is limited to two primitive but developed campgrounds with picnic tables and pit toilets. A hand-operated well providing drinking water was installed at the Marlette Campground in 2010. Permits are not required here. In this area, several charming log cabins close to the TRT are available for rental year-round. For more information, contact Lake Tahoe Nevada State Park at 775-831-0494.

SECTION 7: ECHO SUMMIT AND ECHO LAKE TO BARKER PASS This section travels through Desolation Wilderness. Permits, obtained at the trailhead, are required to enter the wilderness. If you are staying overnight, you must get a camping permit online or at the Taylor Creek Visitor Center, located on CA 89, 0.5 mile northwest of Camp Richardson. The wilderness is divided into zones, and a limited number of permits are available for each zone, so you may not be able to get one for the more popular areas (which tend to be lakes close to trailheads) in midsummer, particularly on weekends. Permits may also be obtained for thru-hikers who are traveling through the wilderness and may spend several days in different zones. For more information, contact the USFS Lake Tahoe Basin Management Unit on College Drive in South Lake Tahoe at 530-543-2600 or fs.usda.gov/ltbmu.

2

Animals and Plants, Great and Small

THE LAKE TAHOE AREA has a tremendous variety of interesting flora and fauna. You will enhance your enjoyment and experience of this beautiful region by getting to know some of them. This chapter gives a quick summary of what you may encounter as you journey along the Tahoe Rim Trail.

While many of these animals are a rare treat to encounter, smaller animals such as squirrels and birds are found in abundance. Among the highlights of traveling in the Tahoe woods are the fascinating trees and wildflowers that you pass along the way. This book provides a quick, easily understood introduction to the most common animals and plants in the Tahoe Basin area; it is not intended as a substitute for a good field guide.

The Largest Animals in the Tahoe Region

BLACK BEARS The largest omnivores in the Sierra are black bears, but often their fur is cinnamon brown, dark brown, reddish, and sometimes even off-white. Bears are common near developed parts of the lake, where they have learned to gain access to the garbage and food supplies of humans. Whether you live in the Tahoe area or are just visiting, you can do your part to protect bears—and yourself—by keeping your garbage away from where they can get to it, and by keeping your house and car locked. If you are camping or backpacking in bear country, follow these simple rules:

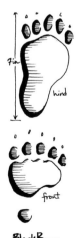

- Don't leave any food or clothes that smell like food in your tent. When they come to get it, you don't want to be sleeping in the path of a hungry and determined bear.

- Put your food (all your food!) in a safe place at night and when you are not in camp. If a campground has a bearproof container, use it. In the backcountry not only are you advised to put your food in a bearproof canister, but in some areas, including several wilderness areas in the central and southern Sierra, you are required to do so. The next two best methods are to hang your food high in a tree, suspended from a rope, or to put it on a 15-foot-high rocky ledge where bears can't reach it.

- Keep a clean camp so that bears or other animals won't be attracted to the site. Put food, cleaning, and fragrant hygiene supplies, such as shampoo, toothpaste, and soap, away soon after you are done with them.

- If you see a bear, make lots of noise. Bang pots and pans together, stand up and shout, and throw your arms around to scare it away. (Note that this approach doesn't always work!)

- Be smart. If a bear is chomping down on your food, it has already won, so don't try to take the food away from it.

- If you startle a bear, make eye contact, but do not stare at it. Instead, slowly back away and wait for the bear to amble off. Be sure not to block its escape route.

- Don't forget that bears are good runners and can climb trees.

- Treat bears with respect. Remember that you are in their territory.

While it is important to be cautious, bear attacks are extremely rare. In those very unusual circumstances where black bears have injured people, it was usually the result of human error. Be careful and enjoy them from a safe distance.

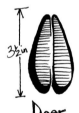

3½ in

Deer

DEER The most common deer in the Sierra are mule deer, named for their large, floppy ears that resemble those of a mule. Mule deer also sport a small white bob of a tail. Deep snow and lack of forage keep them away from the area during winter months. At that time, you are more likely to find them in the warmer climes of the Carson Valley, a short jaunt over the Carson Range from the east shore. As the season warms up, these animals are commonly spotted on the east slopes and in other areas of the Tahoe Basin.

MOUNTAIN LION OR COUGAR The rare and elusive mountain lion or cougar has been seen occasionally in the Tahoe area, especially in lower-elevation open areas such as the east shore and around Truckee. While I have not personally seen one on the TRT, I have seen tracks, which were following close behind a set of deer tracks. Someone once brought a pet mountain lion to my office; its power and grace were awe-inspiring. We had the feeling that it could dispose of any one of us in half a minute. These large cats range in size from 6.5 to

8 feet long (including the tail), and can weigh up to 200 pounds. Each animal has a vast range and can cover many miles of territory in one night. Mountain lions hunt deer primarily, although they also prey on raccoons, birds, mice, and even skunks and porcupines. Porcupines?! That would have to be one hungry mountain lion.

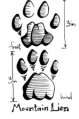

Mountain lions can jump 12 feet up a tree from a standstill. If you do encounter one, experts recommend that you do not run. Instead try to look as big as possible by standing tall, opening up your jacket, and waving your arms. Once the cat perceives that you don't behave like prey, it will probably back off. Also, a mountain lion leaves the remains of a kill and returns later to eat; needless to say, it is not wise to hang around a lion kill.

Medium-Size Animals

BOBCAT You are more likely to hear the loud scream or howl of this elusive member of the cat family than to see it. With an average weight of about 20 pounds in adulthood, it is a good deal larger than an average domestic cat. A bobcat has a short, stubby tail that is black toward the end and tipped with white. A nocturnal predator, the bobcat likes to dine on squirrels and mice. These cats seem to have become more common recently. They have been sighted throughout the Tahoe region and Truckee and are regular visitors to residential areas.

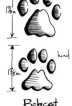

COYOTE These adaptable creatures are common in the Tahoe area. While I've seen them in many locations, they seem to prefer woodlands and meadows. They can often be heard yipping and howling at night in Ward and Blackwood Canyons, Squaw Valley, Alpine Meadows, and throughout the Tahoe region. Though coyotes resemble medium-size dogs, they are much more graceful and lissome when they run, a sight to behold. It is not uncommon for a dog to chase a single coyote, only to discover that the coyote is leading him back to his teammates. Although many people believe that coyotes do not hunt in packs, I have seen them several times in groups of three or four adults. If you live in the mountains, take care with your domesticated animals, even around your home. Many a lost cat or small dog has become a coyote's dinner.

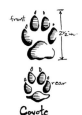

MARTEN It is a rare treat to spot a marten, also called a pine marten. At about 1.5–3 feet long, including its tail, the marten is about the size of a housecat but longer and sleeker. Martens have beautiful, lush brown to reddish fur and long, bushy tails. They are agile climbers and sometimes live in a cavity high up in a tree. They are elusive animals but can occasionally be seen in pursuit of squirrels or chipmunks, their favorite dinner. The grace and stealth of the marten is unmatched.

WEASEL Seven members of the weasel family are found in the region, including long- and short-tailed weasels, river otters, and mink. I've spotted the reddish-furred, long-tailed weasel several times in Desolation Wilderness. They are similar in size to the marmot but a bit sleeker in appearance.

MARMOT If you hear a high-pitched squeak when walking past a big rock pile, there's a good chance that rock pile is harboring a yellow-bellied marmot. Related to squirrels, these rodents are approximately the size of a large housecat, are dark brown and cinnamon in color, live in groups, and love to sun themselves on rocks. I have often seen marmots in Desolation Wilderness, on the Pacific Crest Trail near Twin Peaks, and in the Mount Rose area.

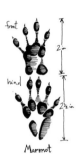

Marmot

PORCUPINE These large rodents are sometimes seen on roads or sitting in trees. About 2–3 feet long, they are large and round with short legs. They have light-brown to yellowish fur and numerous hollow, sharp quills up to 3 inches long. Porcupines walk in a slow, lumbering fashion—if no one wants to eat you, why hurry?—and enjoy a diet of succulent bark and herbaceous plants. No other animals, except cougars perhaps, want to have anything to do with these quill-covered critters. Interestingly, although their quills can cause others, especially overzealous dogs, a great deal of pain, it is a myth that they can "shoot" their quills.

RACCOON Identified by its distinctive white face with masklike black band across the eyes, this carnivorous little burglar is one of the most interesting animal species in the Sierra. They range in size but can get as big as a medium-size dog. Raccoons are nocturnal— all the better to wake you in the middle of the night while they are knocking over garbage cans in pursuit

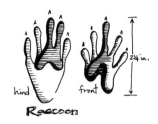

of food. It is common to see them on house decks but rare to see them in the wild. Often the best evidence of a raccoon is the handlike tracks they leave.

Small Animals

These ubiquitous rodents inhabit the ground, the trees, and perhaps even your attic and represent a fair percentage of local roadkill. A recent census reported 178 million in the Tahoe Basin (give or take based on today's road-kill number).

CALIFORNIA GROUND SQUIRREL This squirrel has a large body like the gray squirrel but has a much smaller tail. They have a mottled brown coat and a silver saddle over the shoulder. They spend most of their time on the ground and are very busy all summer getting fattened up to hibernate through the winter.

California ground squirrel

DOUGLAS SQUIRREL This medium-size, dark-brown squirrel, also called a chicka-ree, has a reddish tinge on its back, a white belly, and a bushy tail with a silver tip. It stays active all winter and makes a short, explosive *quer-o* sound. If you hear fir cones crashing down to the ground and see mangled remnants of the cones sitting on a stump, you'll know you are in chick-aree country. These squirrels love to climb trees and drop the cones for later, when they disassemble the entire cone, piece by piece, in order to get to the tasty seeds.

Douglas squirrel

GOLDEN-MANTLED GROUND SQUIRREL AND CHIPMUNK What's the difference between a chipmunk and the golden-mantled ground squirrel? A chipmunk is smaller and has dark lines on its back that go all the way over its head. The golden-mantled, the Tahoe area's most common squirrel, has a lovely black-bordered white band running up each side of its back and ending at its shoulders. To complicate matters, there are a number of different chipmunk species with minor differences in appearance. Both chipmunks and ground squirrels eat seeds, grasses, and fruit.

Golden-mantled ground squirrel

WESTERN FLYING SQUIRREL These small brown squirrels (smaller than a chickaree) are very friendly and social, but because they are nocturnal most people will not have the opportunity to see one. They don't fly but rather glide through the air from branch to branch. Like the western gray squirrel, the flying squirrel remains active all winter.

WESTERN GRAY SQUIRREL Larger than the chickaree and the ground squirrel, the gray squirrel also lives in the area but in smaller numbers. It has a uniform gray body and a long, broad tail. Like the chickaree and unlike the ground squirrels and chipmunks, the gray squirrel is active all winter. It loves to sit in trees and "laugh" at cats and dogs, which stare at it with evil intent.

PIKA OR CONY The pika is smaller than a chipmunk, is light brown in color, and lives primarily in high, rocky areas. It looks like a cross between a chipmunk and a small rabbit (and is in the same animal order as the latter) with shorter ears. It makes a peeping noise. They are rare in the Tahoe region and apparently, because they depend on a cold climate, are vulnerable to climate change.

American pika

Birds

AMERICAN ROBIN Slightly smaller than the Steller's jay, the robin has a similar physique and is a frequent summer visitor to Lake Tahoe. With its brick-red breast, yellow bill, and gray back, the robin cheerily hops through the understory of local woods or meadows, looking for insects or worms.

BALD EAGLE A very large, majestic black bird with a white head, the bald eagle is occasionally spotted flying near water, perched on a large tree, or riding updrafts. I remember watching an eagle fly along the lakeshore, when suddenly two ospreys began to chase it. The three completed some incredible acrobatic stunts before the ospreys gave up. Perhaps the eagle had ventured too near the osprey nest. Count yourself lucky if you see one of these rarer raptors.

BLUE GROUSE You are more likely to hear a blue grouse than to see one. Males vocalize a very low, bass-drum *brrrm, brrrm, brrrm* sound. Females are large, plump birds about the size of a pheasant or chicken. Their plumage is brownish gray with some white feathers near the neck. They can sometimes be seen in trees or brush. Breaking cover, they startle you as they suddenly take flight with a loud *wap, wap, wap* of their wings. This bird can commonly be seen or heard in heavily wooded sections on the west shore, including Desolation Wilderness and areas north of Tahoe City.

CANADA GOOSE Commonly seen along Tahoe beaches and in parks, this large, grayish-tan goose has a black head and neck and a prominent white chin. Though geese are known to steal food from unsuspecting small children, they are beautiful when flying in their A-line formations. Less beautiful are the copious amounts of droppings they leave. Similar to but rarer than Canada geese, snow geese can occasionally be seen flying in large groups above the Sierra. It is a sight to behold, but you will hear their raucous cries long before you see them.

CLARK'S NUTCRACKER Similar in shape and sound to the Steller's jay, this light-gray bird has black wings with white patches. Seen at treeline along high ridgetops—very much Tahoe Rim Trail country—Clark's nutcracker makes a loud and slow *flap, flap, flap* with its wings as it flies from tree to tree. They have a symbiotic relationship with whitebark pines: a single bird can bury thousands of whitebark pine seeds in a summer season, and then some of the seeds that they forget become whitebark pine trees.

JUNCO This smallish member of the sparrow family looks a bit like a chickadee. The light-gray bird is often seen or heard rustling in the undergrowth looking for seeds.

MOUNTAIN BLUEBIRD A rare and beautiful treat, the mountain bluebird is sky blue and startling in its soft beauty. About the size of a robin, it is a lighter blue than the much more common Steller's jay. Look for it in grassy meadows or at the edge of the forest hunting insects. I have seen it in Ward Canyon and near Truckee.

MOUNTAIN CHICKADEE Perhaps the most common bird in the Tahoe woods, the small chickadee (about 5 inches long) is light gray with a black cap and a white line over each eye. Usually quiet, this active bird may be best known for its call, which many people say sounds like *cheese, burrr, gerrrr;* others claim its call sounds more like *tsick-a-dee-dee-dee.* You be the judge. Maybe it just sounds like the voice of a chickadee.

MOUNTAIN QUAIL This subspecies of California's state bird is small to medium in size and slightly chunky. You can identify it by the little standard issuing from the top of its head, its gray to brown coloring, and the way it scurries away into nearby brush. It stays close to the ground under bushes near sunny, open areas and water sources. Because quail convene in coveys, once you spot one, you will likely hear and see others.

OSPREY The osprey is best known for its ability to swoop down and catch fish in its talons. It's a little smaller than an eagle, with brown feathers on its back and white feathers on its breast. When flying above you, it appears mostly white, but while sitting in a nest with wings tucked, it can appear mostly brown. The osprey makes a high-pitched squeak and can be seen along the lakeshore or high up in large nests it has built out of sticks at the top of dead trees. I have watched an osprey dive into Dicks Lake and Fontanillis Lake and remove fish that were feeding in the evening. It has become more common along Lake Tahoe's shore, with nearly a dozen nests occupied on the south side of Emerald Bay.

OWL Various species of owls inhabit the Tahoe area. Primarily nocturnal, they live in the deep woods and are more likely to be heard than seen. While the calls of owls vary with the species, in general you can hear a deep *who, who, who.* Owls have large, round faces with piercing, front-facing eyes perfect for late-night hunting. Some species have catlike ear tufts that stick straight up.

Headwaters of Gray Creek just above Gray Lake (see Chapter 6, Section 2, page 70)

STELLER'S JAY The seemingly ubiquitous Steller's jay is most often found at lake-level elevations and in campgrounds. It is medium-size with a dark-blue body and a black mantle, throat, and crest. Its aggressive, raucous cry or squawk is distinctive. It will eat your potato chips and raid your snack packs, yet many Eastern birders delight in seeing this bird for the first time.

WESTERN TANAGER Though somewhat uncommon, the tanager is one of the most colorful birds in the Tahoe area. The male has a red head, a bright-yellow body, and black wings. The female is also bright yellow but has a less dramatic, greenish-yellow head. Try to spot this small to medium-size bird (bigger than a chickadee, smaller than a Steller's jay) flitting from tree to tree.

Amphibians and Reptiles

PACIFIC TREE FROG These tiny frogs can be heard in many Sierra locales. They are especially common in the grassy area around Twin Lakes, so if you are walking to these lakes, be careful not to step on them. About 1 inch long, the frogs are brown or green with black eye stripes. Though called tree frogs, they have no special preference for trees and are just as comfortable on the ground or in the grass.

SNAKES Several snakes live in the Tahoe area. Happily for area hikers, the rattle-snake is not common among them. The most common snake in the Tahoe area is the garter snake. It is about 2 feet long or less and slender, with a tail tapered to a sharp tip. The garter snake has a black or gray upper surface with a yellow line along its back. While for the most part it is harmless, if handled it may discharge a foul-smelling liquid. Less common to this area is the rubber boa. A wonder to behold, this docile, harmless small brown snake is usually less than 2 feet long. With its smooth skin, it looks like a worm on steroids.

WESTERN FENCE LIZARD This 6- to 9-inch lizard is often found in dry areas lounging on a rock or running to escape your big feet. The scaly skin of the lizard is gray, and they are often seen doing "push-ups" on the rocks, exposing their blue bellies.

Insects

BEES, YELLOW JACKETS, AND WASPS Honeybees and bumblebees quietly go about their business of pollinating flowers and rarely sting people. Yellow jackets, even though they look like bees, are actually a form of wasp. After an above-average winter snowfall, especially in a season with a lot of spring moisture and cold temperatures, yellow jackets are found in small numbers. In drought conditions, however, yellow jackets multiply, and by late summer and fall they can be a nuisance. They are ferocious predators and carnivores, and their stings can be painful and cause swelling. These wasps can nest in the ground or in a trailside log. If you get too close to their nests, they will come out in force to sting you. Wasps are most active from midday to just after sunset.

MOSQUITOES These pesky little critters are usually a problem from mid-June through mid-July throughout the Tahoe area. The timing of their emergence from the shadows of spring, however, depends on the quantity of precipitation that fell during winter and how quickly the snowpack melts. Mosquitoes are active at dusk and dawn and are prevalent in shady forest areas; in and near meadows; and near lakeshores, creeks, or any body of standing water or moist area. They especially like small, shallow bodies of water, where they breed. To avoid mosquitoes, either pack a lot of insect repellent (or lemon eucalyptus), take to a granite mountain or ridgetop area, and pray for wind.

Fish

Fish have not been seen recently on the Tahoe Rim Trail itself, but there are some in the streams and lakes that you might pass. Here are the few to look out for:

BROOK TROUT Not a true trout but a char, the brook trout is distinguished by lighter-colored spots on a dark green-gray background. It also has a yellow- to ruddy-colored underbelly. It can be found in any Sierra water source but is especially common in small creeks and streams.

BROWN TROUT Hugging river bottoms, the brown trout sports olive-green to cinnamon-brown coloring with reddish spots along its sides. These fish were imported into the Sierra from Germany and Scotland.

CUTTHROAT TROUT The most common fish in mountain lakes and streams, the cutthroat can be identified by its red, orange, or yellow "slash" marks under each jaw. It is sometimes called the spotted trout.

KOKANEE SALMON Introduced into Tahoe-area lakes in the 1940s, the kokanee can still be found here. It has a robust body and dusky olive to bluish coloring. It is silvery on its underside and nests in bottom gravel like the rainbow trout. During their fall spawning run, they turn bright red and can be found in large numbers in Taylor Creek, on Lake Tahoe's South Shore. Sometimes they are also found in smaller numbers spawning up Eagle Creek, right next to Vikingsholm Castle near Emerald Bay, as well as close to where the TRT passes through Tahoe City, a few hundred yards downstream from the Truckee River dam.

MACKINAW OR LAKE TROUT Incorrectly blamed for eliminating the cutthroat from Lake Tahoe, the mackinaw trout is also a char family member like the brook trout mentioned above. Gray with some yellow speckles that brighten during spawning season, it is the least colorful of all the Sierra fish. It grows to a large size; every year 20- to 30-pounders are caught in Lake Tahoe and Donner Lake, and 10-pound fish are common.

RAINBOW TROUT With a bluish-gray to gray-green back, silvery belly, and dark-black speckles, the rainbow's most distinctive mark is a red streak down each side. Mountain men and prospectors introduced rainbows into the Sierra in the 1800s.

Trees

ASPEN OR QUAKING ASPEN The Sierra's most colorful deciduous tree derives its name from the appearance of its leaves quaking in gentle breezes or windstorms. With white bark and oval-shaped leaves, aspens are common in wet and moist areas, along creekbeds, near springs, and in meadows. Their presence can indicate a groundwater source. Aspen trees spread by cloning themselves via root suckers, which grow up into more aspens around the base of their trunks; a single tree may put out dozens of shooters, and thus a whole grove may have started with one tree. This tree provides most of the Sierra's fall yellow and gold color.

INCENSE CEDAR These trees can grow to a height of 150 feet. Incense cedar is commonly found near the lake (6,200′) with an upper elevation of around 6,500 feet—a little higher in sunny locations. Incense cedars have red to cinnamon-brown, flaky bark and dark-green, short needles that lie in flat, feathery groupings.

JEFFREY PINE This is the dominant pine tree in much of the Tahoe Sierra and, though it is especially prevalent near lake level, it can grow at elevations of up to 8,000 feet. The Jeffrey pine can reach a height of 180 feet. It has thick gray to reddish bark, which turns redder as the tree matures, and

Humongous hemlocks in Blackwood Canyon (see Chapter 6, Section 8, page 161)

smells like butterscotch, vanilla, or pineapple, depending on what kind of nose you have. It also has large, roundish cones with upturned prickles and long needles of three.

LODGEPOLE PINE This usually straight tree (hence its value as a lodgepole for American Indians) is very common in a variety of soil conditions from below 6,000 feet to higher than 9,000 feet in elevation. It has thin, scaly, light-gray, sappy bark and small cones. The needles are in bunches of two; a single pair resembles the letter *L* (as in "lodgepole"). The tree prefers wet areas, and its presence often signals mosquito territory.

MOUNTAIN HEMLOCK Preferring high snow areas above 7,000 feet, mountain hemlock is common above 8,000 feet in many north-facing areas along the Tahoe Rim Trail, generally in areas of maximum snowpack. A beautiful and majestic tree reaching heights of 25–100 feet, with smaller trees at the highest elevations, mountain hemlock has short, dark-green needles on branches that cover the tree from bottom to top. The branches have a gentle sloping appearance; the cones are small and dark brown. What makes the mountain hemlock especially magical is the way the top of the tree droops over like a wizard's hat. Some hemlocks have wide skirts reaching out from the tree just above the ground, with some skirts wider than the tree is high.

PONDEROSA OR WESTERN YELLOW PINE A member of the same yellow pine family as the Jeffrey pine, the ponderosa prefers lower elevations, usually below 6,500 feet, and grows in smaller numbers near Lake Tahoe. It has yellowish to reddish-brown bark and often reaches heights of 100 feet. Like the Jeffrey pine, the ponderosa also has long needles of three. Ponderosa pine cone prickles stick up and out, while the Jeffrey's turn up and in (remember "gentle Jeffrey" and "prickly ponderosa"). Ponderosa cones also tend to be smaller than Jeffrey cones. Some areas have a hybridized combination of Jeffrey and ponderosa, making identification difficult.

RED FIR White fir's red cousin dominates the landscape in some areas above 7,000 feet, often living in dense stands. The red fir needle bunches are tighter than those of the white fir, curve inward, and grow to longer than an inch. The bark is reddish brown to gray, and the tree sprouts medium-size light-green cones of 6–9 inches, whereas the cones of the white fir are only 3–5 inches. Red fir cones point straight up from branches near the top of the tree.

Trees and Elevation

Trees in the Sierra tend to find their niche at a particular elevation. By knowing how far above sea level you are, you might be able to identify the tree; conversely, if you can identify a tree, it might help you determine your elevation. The one exception to the rule is the lodgepole pine, which seems to be found at nearly any mountain elevation. The chart below details where trees are dominant. Be aware that you may find a few outliers above and below the listed ranges. But if, for example, you see a lot of western white pines and no sugar pines, you will know that you are above 7,000 feet in elevation.

6,000–6,500 FEET Jeffrey, ponderosa, and lodgepole pine; white fir; aspen; and incense cedar

6,500–7,000 FEET Red fir, Jeffrey and lodgepole pine, and aspen

7,000–8,000 FEET Hemlock, western white and lodgepole pine, red fir, and mountain juniper

8,000–9,000 FEET Hemlock; western white, lodgepole, and whitebark pine; and juniper

ABOVE 9,000 FEET Whitebark pine

SUGAR PINE These beautiful, majestic trees can reach a height of 250 feet. They are rarely seen above 6,500 feet elevation and only occasionally seen in lower elevations because most were cut down for lumber at the end of the 19th century. The sugar pine has long, cylindrical cones that grow 10–16 inches downward from the tips of long, graceful branches. John Muir said of the sugar pine that it "is the noblest pine yet discovered, surpassing all others not merely in size but also in kingly beauty and majesty."

WESTERN (SIERRA) JUNIPER These trees are often found in dry, rocky areas at higher elevations—particularly in the Desolation Wilderness. Junipers more than 1,000 years old have been found in the Tahoe area. They have an appearance similar to that of incense cedars with reddish-brown bark, but the junipers are generally smaller, rarely exceeding 50 feet in height. Those growing in windy, exposed areas may be twisted and gnarled. The best way to tell the difference between juniper and incense cedar is that juniper has blueberry-like berries and is usually found at higher elevations. Scratch and smell one of these berries, and you will quickly discover that they are used to make gin.

WESTERN WHITE PINE These trees grow at elevations of 7,000–9,000 feet and can reach 150 feet in height, although they are usually much smaller because of the harsh conditions in which they live. Like the whitebark pine, the western white pine has needles that come in clusters of five. Its cone resembles that of the sugar pine, though it is shorter (6–8 inches) and narrower. The upper branches of a western white pine, also known as silver pine, turn upward at their tips. Mature trees have a distinctive checkerboard pattern on their bark.

WHITE FIR Probably the most common tree in the Tahoe Basin, the white fir typically grows below 6,500 feet in elevation (although they are sometimes seen up to 7,500 feet). They have gray bark and short, bunched needles that have an average length of 1.5–2 inches and a flat appearance. The bark of younger trees is somewhat smooth; as the trees age, the bark gets rougher and more like that of other pine and fir trees. The light-green upright cones are soft and found scattered about the woods—the work of chickarees. They grow rapidly and in thick stands, and contribute significantly to fire danger.

WHITEBARK PINE This high-elevation tree is usually found near mountaintops and is easily mistaken for lodgepole pine. The whitebark has short, stiff needles clustered in groups of five (lodgepole needles are in groups of two). The bark is gray-white, and the cones are small and dark brown. Near the tops of peaks, it is also common to see whitebark pines only a foot or so high, a phenomenon called krummholz. Krummholz whitebark pines can be found on Mount Rose, on Freel Peak, and in other high-altitude, windy locations.

Wildflowers

Wet Areas: Meadows, Stream Banks, and Springs

CORN LILY This poisonous plant looks somewhat like a stalk of corn but smells like cabbage. Not only is its poison deadly, but it has been reported to turn its victims green. The corn lily starts out like a big cigar popping out of the moist meadows in the spring, which by late summer grows to 3–6 feet tall. At the top of its broad-leaved stalk, it shows a large grouping of cream-white flowers.

COW PARSNIP A large wildflower with huge, maple-shaped leaves, cow parsnip stalks can reach up to 10 feet tall but average 4–5 feet. It is often found in meadows, along creeks, or in other moist areas. It has several tall stalks with tight white button flowers that look like miniature cauliflower heads at the top.

CRIMSON COLUMBINE The most commonly seen columbine of the Tahoe area has numerous bright red-orange flowers that look like miniature Chinese lanterns hanging off tall, thin stalks. It grows to about 3 feet high in moist meadow areas and along streambeds.

DELPHINIUM OR LARKSPUR Towering larkspur or larkspur delphinium have tall, narrow stalks with beautiful small purple flowers that bloom all along the stalks. They are found in large numbers in some meadow and stream areas and provide a dramatic display, especially when they reach their maximum height of 6–8 feet. Nuttall's larkspur is a smaller variety at only about 1 foot high; it is found in limited numbers in dry or wet areas.

ELEPHANT'S HEADS Sprouting off the foot-tall green stalks of this plant are numerous tiny pink flowers shaped like elephant trunks and ears. While not as showy as other meadow plants like columbine and tiger lilies, elephant's heads are often seen in spring and early summer in Tahoe Meadows and especially in Meiss Meadows.

Elephant's heads

MONKEYFLOWER There are 11 species of this plant in the Tahoe area, all having flowers that vaguely resemble little monkey faces. The most common are the pink Lewis's monkeyflower and the yellow common monkeyflower. They favor the banks of small streams or seeps throughout the Tahoe area.

Monkeyflower

MONKSHOOD A relatively uncommon plant, monkshood is found in moist areas. Its large, deep-purple flower resembles a monk's cowl. This tall plant can reach 6 feet and grows amongst the tremendous variety of flowers found near Marlette Lake as well as in the Page Meadows area.

REIN ORCHIS This orchid is a profusion of small bright-white flowers hanging from a straight bright-green stalk of between 8 inches and 2 feet. They are found at a wide range of altitudes near seeps and meadow areas.

SHOOTING STARS Found in moist meadow areas, shooting stars have delicate petals that bend back to expose their darker stamens, thus making them like stars streaking across the night sky. The alpine shooting star has pink flowers, while the Jeffrey's has a purple to pink flower with a black point and a small band of yellow just above the black.

TIGER (ALPINE) LILY Often found with columbine in wet or marshy areas, the tiger lily can grow 4–6 feet tall and is a wonderful visual treat, with bright-orange flowers speckled with brown.

Dry and Sunny Areas

CHECKERMALLOW Along with mule-ears, this is perhaps the most common flower in dry, volcanic areas. It is found from lake level up to more than 9,000 feet and is a low-lying flower with small pinkish-purple cups threaded by white veins.

DEEP FOREST PINEDROPS The pinedrop is a saprophyte, which means that the plant obtains its nutrients from decaying vegetation in the ground rather than through photosynthesis. Pinedrops grow to 4 feet tall and have orange-red to reddish-brown stalks with numerous little curlicues coming off the sides of each narrow stalk. After they die, they often remain standing for years, turning darker as years go by.

DOUGLAS OR SIERRA WALLFLOWER This bright-yellow-flowered plant is common in dry areas and on rocky slopes. A member of the mustard family, it has a big cluster of little yellow petals forming a ball atop a straight green stem. It reaches a height of 1–3 feet.

FIREWEED This wildflower grows in pro-fusion along old road cuts and areas that have been recently burned or disturbed, or where most of the plant cover has been removed. It seems to be most prolific after drier-than-normal winters. The plants are 3–4 feet high and have bright-pink flowers.

HORSEMINT Occurring in abundance in dry meadows and on rocky flats (Tahoe Meadows is one example), horsemint is identifiable by its purple corn-cone group

Fireweed

of flowers situated on top of a green stem with many green leaves. It is related to pennyroyal.

MARIPOSA LILY The beautiful, round, white flowers of the Mariposa lily have a purple to black center and a delicate appearance. Three cream-white petals form a small bowl. This plant is usually shorter than 6 inches and prefers dry or sandy soil on sunny, open slopes.

MOUNTAIN PENNYROYAL OR COYOTE MINT This common flower grows in open forests and along volcanic slopes. A member of the mint family, penny-royal has white or pink flower clusters atop upright stalks. It provides a strong mint smell as you walk by.

MULE-EARS In areas with open, south-facing slopes, and particularly ones with volcanic soils, mule-ears are often the dominant flower species. They can cover acres of land with very few other plants in view. When you see a field of mule-ears, you will also smell them, as they have a strong odor. Big yellow sunflowers and large leaves that resemble the ears of a mule lend the plant its name. In the fall, the leaves dry up, turn brown, and make a rustling noise in the wind.

Lava rocks and mule-ears

PRETTYFACE These relatively common flowers grow close to the ground and have six light-yellow petals at the end of each flower stem. Each petal has a small dark-purple line extending toward its tip. Large groups of "pretty faces" can be found looking at you from dry soil.

SCARLET GILIA The bright red-orange beauty of scarlet gilia is startling to behold when it appears in dry, sandy forest and on open slopes. It can get up to 3 feet tall and has many bright trumpet-shaped flowers.

SNOWPLANT Like pinedrops, snowplants are saprophytes and do not require sunlight to grow. Appearing near trees or in dense forest areas, they are long and cylindrical (from 6 inches to 1 foot high) and a bright red color. Snowplant shoots straight out of the ground like a huge asparagus stalk, adding a splash of color to the shade of the forest. They get their name because they pop up just after the snow melts.

Mixed Wet or Dry Areas

ASTERS AND DAISIES There are several species of these sunflowers that have pale purple petals circling a disk of yellow or gold. The western aster and wandering daisy are both quite common in the Tahoe area. Both plants grow up to 2 feet tall, although they are usually shorter, and occur up to 9,000 feet. They prefer moist settings over dry.

EXPLORER'S GENTIAN This late-season bloomer has deep blue or purple tubular flowers. Light dots speckle the inside of the petals. Found in moist or rocky terrain, gentian provides a bit of bright color when many summertime flowers have come and gone.

LUPINE One of the Tahoe region's most common flowers, lupine comes in a number of different varieties. The feature they have in common is that the leaves, no matter how small or big, are palmate, which means they form groups like a hand. In the Sierra, most lupines show off deep-purple flowers. Tall large-leaf lupines are found in abundance in

Explorer's gentian

wet areas, such as between Meiss Meadows and Showers Lake. Other large lupines include Torrey's and Tahoe lupine. Brewer's lupine is a high-altitude, low-lying lupine with tiny leaves and dark-purple flowers.

PAINTBRUSH The orange-red Applegate's paintbrush and the giant red paintbrush are the two species most commonly seen in the Tahoe area. Both have flowers that look like the brush end of a bright orange-and-red paintbrush. Often they are called Indian paintbrush. These and other species can be found on dry slopes to wet meadows, up to 9,000 feet.

PRETTY YELLOW FLOWER (PYF) A large variety of different yellow flowers that I can never remember the names of dot the Sierra landscape.

Shrubs and Bushes

BUCKTHORN, SNOWBUSH, OR MOUNTAIN WHITETHORN This plant with many names grows along disturbed areas, such as trails, and has lots of narrow white branches with spiny, thorny tips; when flattened by the snow, these branches lay down over the trail. I call it "mountain bikers' menace" because its thorns can puncture tires. Whitethorn is about 3–4 feet tall and spreads out over 5–10 feet. It has small, ovate (egg-shaped) whitish or green leaves. Often the plants are so dense it is difficult to determine where one plant ends and another begins.

CHINQUAPIN This common plant was named after a condominium project north of Tahoe City (or was it the other way around?). Chinquapin is a bushy shrub related to oaks that inhabits dry slopes and rocky ridges and frequently grows near manzanita bushes. The narrow leaves of this 2- to 4-foot-tall plant are up to 3 inches long, yellow-green on the top, and yellow-brown underneath. Chinquapin produces yellow-green seedpods in spring.

HUCKLEBERRY OAK One of the most common plants in this area, huckleberry oak typically gets up to about 3 feet high and grows on dry, south-facing slopes. It has small, leathery, ovate leaves of medium to dark green. At the end of the narrow stalks, you may see a light-green acorn.

MANZANITA While there are five species of manzanita in the Sierra, only two are commonly seen in the Tahoe area. Greenleaf manzanita is widespread in drier areas over a wide elevation range. Its smooth bark is dark red or reddish brown with shiny, bright-green leaves, and it grows to about 3–5 feet tall. Manzanita has lots of rigid, crooked, thick branches. In the spring they put out tiny pink flowers that supposedly look like little apples (*manzanita* is Spanish for "little apple"). Pinemat manzanita, with smaller leaves and stalks, is a smaller plant that grows to about a foot tall; it likes to form a carpet along the ground or over the top of granite rocks. Pinemat manzanita usually grows at a higher altitude than its greenleaf cousin. It is especially common between South Camp Peak and Kingsbury Grade.

RED MOUNTAIN HEATHER This dwarfish bush has dark-green, coniferlike needles and clusters of small bright-pink or red flowers on short stalks. It grows

Rabbitbrush, one of many pretty yellow flowers (PYF) on the trail

at high elevations throughout the Tahoe area, along some lakeshores, and in the Desolation Wilderness. This fragile plant is a thick ground cover running alongside the trail—take care not to step on it.

SQUAW CARPET OR MAHALA MAT Thick patches of this plant as wide as 10–20 feet across are made up of hollylike leaves carpeting the ground. In the spring, clusters of small blue to violet flowers grow among the sharp-edged leaves.

THIMBLEBERRY They may not keep you from starving in the woods, but thimbleberries are edible and quite tasty when they ripen in late August and September. They are in the same family as blackberries and raspberries, and you will not be surprised to hear that the berries look like little thimbles. This bush is usually found in large groups, lying close to the ground near streams and in other shady, moist areas. Thimbleberry has large leaves that resemble a maple leaf, with three to five pointed lobes. The showy white flowers bloom in early summer.

TOBACCO BRUSH This plant is also called snowbrush ceanothus and curl-leaf ceanothus. Some say the pungent aroma of tobacco brush is sensuous and aromatic; to me, it smells like tobacco. With large, shiny, dark greenish-blue leaves, the plant grows up to 5 feet tall and has numerous small white flowers. In early summer it can be covered with lightish-yellow flowers. Tobacco brush likes dry, disturbed areas along road cuts and trails and can become the locally dominant plant.

Let's All Get Along: A Trail for Everyone

THE GOAL OF THE TAHOE RIM TRAIL ASSOCIATION and for the governmental land managers is for all users to safely enjoy the trail while working to maintain and protect it. It is important that all trail users pleasantly coexist. Doing so comes down to understanding and being courteous to one another and recognizing that we are all out there to have fun. The only way to continue to have good relations between the user groups and to keep the TRT well maintained is for users to follow some simple rules.

Rules for Mountain Bikers

When the Tahoe Rim Trail was first constructed, mountain biking was a new sport, and the governmental agencies controlling the land under the TRT had to develop regulations for it. Now, most of the trail is open to bike use, with the primary exceptions being land located in designated wilderness areas where mechanical devices are not allowed and on land shared with the Pacific Crest Trail. Cycling is a legitimate use of backcountry trails, but there are responsibilities that all bikers are expected to assume. Hikers have complained about encountering bikers on sections of the trail closed to biking, while many hikers, trail runners, and horseback riders have been surprised or threatened by bikers speeding past.

The Tahoe Rim Trail Association has published the Dirt Users' Hints, the rules of the trail for bikers (see "Dirt Users' Hints," opposite).

Hikers, Take Note

It is also the responsibility of hikers to make an extra effort to get along with other trail users. If hikers use common sense and follow the basic rules of courtesy, everyone will benefit and more fully enjoy the trail. If hikers don't reciprocate, they may turn into the dreaded inconsiderate backcountry blockhead (see page 29). Don't let this happen to you!

Sharing the Trail with Horses

While horseback riding can cause more damage to trails than any other use, equestrians account for a smaller percentage of trail users. Many equestrians are actively involved in trail maintenance and construction too. In my experience, horseback riders are courteous and willing to work with other users to share the trails.

Depending upon individual circumstances and as a practical matter, all users should yield to each other. In general, hikers should yield to horses, while mountain bikers must yield to both hikers and horses. In other words, horses have the right-of-way on the trail. In the mid-1990s an article written by Sonja Willits, a woman with years of experience riding horses on Sierra trails, appeared in the Tahoe Rim Trail newsletter. Willits did a good job of explaining trail use from the horse's point of view. With her permission, I've summarized the main points below.

- *A horse believes that everything will eat it until proven otherwise.* The first instinct of many horses is to run away, which can endanger both horse and rider, as well as anyone in the flight path who could get trampled or knocked off the trail. It is the job of all humans—equestrians, hikers, and mountain bikers—to assure the horse that no harm is intended.

Dirt Users' Hints

PRESERVE THE DIRT

- Skidding destroys trails. Use both the front and rear brakes like the pros do.
- Stay on the trail! Snowbanks? Deadfall trees? Hurdle them. You're tough.
- Stay in the center of the trail. Preserve a singletrack trail as a singletrack.
- Do not cut new trails. You need written approval from the governing land agency to build your dream trail.
- Join maintenance crews that are helping to preserve the integrity of the trail.

RESPECT OTHER USERS

- Pass others at an acceptable velocity—for them! Be courteous and ring a bell, smile, and say hello when passing.
- Horses think you want to eat them. Act accordingly: wait on the lower side of the trail.
- Wear a helmet, or others will have to drag your body back to your loved ones.
- Ride only trails open to bikes. The Pacific Crest Trail, wilderness areas, and certain other portions of the TRT are closed to bikes. It's up to you to find out whether the trail you want to ride on allows bikes.
- Leave nothing behind—that includes trash, skid trenches, and off-trail tracks.

A tip of the hat from a TRT cowboy

- *When you are approaching a horse from behind, be sure to talk to the rider.* Talking calmly lets the horse know that you are not something that will hurt it. A bike that comes speeding up from behind a horse can severely frighten it. Be particularly cautious when rounding blind corners—horse riders often can't hear you coming.

- *When you see a horse coming toward you on the trail, talk to the rider.* Again, this soothes the horse and assures it that you are not a threat.

- *When approaching a horse going down a hill, pull over to the downhill slope of the trail and allow it to pass.* Spooked horses often want to go uphill.

- *If you are in a group of more than one biker or hiker, encourage everyone to move to the same side of the trail when you encounter horses.* Horses can feel trapped between you if you are standing on either side of the trail. A horse that feels trapped is not a good thing.

- *Wait to change clothes, repack your backpack, or make any sudden moves until the horses have passed.* It may seem perfectly fine to take off a shirt or rearrange things while you are waiting for a horse to go by. However, as far as the horse is concerned, your movement and changed appearance may add to its feelings of being threatened.

Most horseback riders will move off the trail when it is easy for them to do so. They don't expect hikers and bike riders to give way all the time, particularly when the trail is especially narrow or precarious. However, it is the job of bike riders and hikers to step to the side first, and it is important to have a basic understanding of horse-and-rider psychology in order to be a conscientious sharer of the trail.

Tim's Quick Tips for How to Be an Inconsiderate Backcountry Blockhead

✔ Make a lot of noise.

✔ While people are relaxing and enjoying the quiet at a mountain lake, yell at your friends on the other side.

✔ Let your dogs bark; when they take a swim, let them shake off on people you don't know.

✔ While you are walking along on the trail, talk loudly so that everyone within a half mile can hear you.

✔ If you are camping, make lots of noise late at night and again early in the morning. When you are in the quiet woods, it's party time!

✔ Loud stereos especially appeal to your average nature lover.

✔ Camp or sit close to other people. When you encounter a solitary person at a beautiful mountain lake, they obviously need some companionship and nonstop chatter.

✔ Don't worry about your garbage; someone else will pick it up. Anyway, it should biodegrade in a couple thousand years. Leave things in your campsite so that everyone knows you were there. It's a way to mark the good spots.

✔ Stay on the trail in people's way when they are trying to get by. If people are riding up a hill, stand in their way so that they have to get off their bikes; they will enjoy struggling to get back in their pedals on a steep hill.

✔ When you are walking or riding along the trail, ignore someone else who wants to pass. What's the hurry?

✔ Wash your dishes and clean your fish in streams and lakes. Fish thrive on detergent and consider bits of processed cheese great delicacies.

✔ Feed the animals. That way you help train them to get food from the next hiker who comes along. Backpackers get to practice the art of keeping animals out of their packs in the middle of the night. You can train some chipmunks and squirrels so well that they will practically jump into your lap to get a snack. While they can carry bubonic plague, the risk is a small price for well-trained squirrels.

✔ Leaving food out at night for bears is even more fun. The sound of a bear rampaging through your camp gives you a better rush than a double espresso.

Weather, Water, and When to Go

4

SOME BASIC KNOWLEDGE about the weather and water availability in the Lake Tahoe area and along its Rim Trail will help you plan a safe and enjoyable trip. All outdoor recreational activities in the Sierra are greatly affected by weather conditions. Of particular relevance is how much precipitation, usually in the form of snow, occurred the previous winter. In some years, it begins to snow in October and doesn't stop until June. After a year like that, hiking on dry land is out of the question until mid-July in most areas. The following winter may not see snow until late January and will then make up for it by dropping a lot of snow through May (a great year for late-fall hiking). One season might have early heavy snow, followed by light snow, and then warm temperatures after February. This seasonal shift bodes well for those who want to get into the woods early to enjoy great wildflower displays and decent water availability.

Snowpack

The areas of highest elevation around Lake Tahoe often receive more than 600 inches of snow annually. Several factors determine whether the place you want to go will be out of the snow in the spring or summer, and some general rules govern the area's snowpack. Winter storms arrive primarily from the west, leaving lots of snow near the Sierra Crest. There is less snow as you travel farther east from the mountaintops. The west side of Lake Tahoe gets considerably more snow than the east does. (The east shore gets about 30% less snow on average at the same elevations as the west shore.)

Elevation

The amount of snow is greatly determined by elevation. As cold air lifts and passes over higher terrain, the likelihood and amount of precipitation increase. Storms progress across landforms, and temperatures drop as you go up in elevation; the higher you go, the more likely it is that the precipitation will be snow. Over the course of a season, high elevations receive considerably more snow than lower elevations.

Which Way the Mountain Faces

Snow melts at different rates depending on which direction the mountain is facing and which side of the mountain you are on; north-facing slopes get less sun and stay cooler, which means the snow melts more slowly. The difference between the snowpack on a north- or south-facing slope can be quite surprising; it is not unusual to see 5 feet of snow on a north-facing slope while on the south-facing slope the ground is bare and wildflowers are coming up.

Although the difference between north and south is more pronounced, east-facing slopes are also cooler and have more snow than west-facing slopes. A classic example in the Tahoe area of the north–south difference is Emerald Bay. The Vikingsholm Trail and the trail along Emerald Bay toward Bliss State Park on the south-facing side of the bay are free of snow in most years at least one month before the trails on the north-facing side of the bay.

Trail-Use Tip

Early in the season, your best bet for a hike or ride is close to the lake or in the Truckee area (lower elevations and in the lee of the mountains), on the east side of the lake (Carson Range), and at lower elevations. As the season progresses, other areas become available for snow-free travel, moving from east to west, and south-facing to north-facing.

Lee of the Mountains: Away from the Wind and Rain

The farther east you travel away from the western face of the mountains, the less likely it is that snow will fall. The mountains block and capture the snow and rain, leaving little moisture for the areas to the east. Consequently, the area around Serene Lakes on Donner Summit gets more snow than almost anywhere else in the United States, while just 40 miles to the east, and behind several mountains, Reno frequently receives less precipitation than any other major city in the United States.

The Wind, It Doth Blow

Winter winds create huge snowdrifts that resemble desert sand dunes. What does this mean to a hiker? There are areas where these winter dunes take longer to melt (most commonly on the lee side of ridgetops where cornices form) than other snow-packed areas do. These cornices can last well into the summer, while all around them wildflowers grow.

Winter Wonderland

The winter landscape of the Sierra Nevada is both serene and pristine, with a beauty that you rarely find in the summer. In the winter, a soft white blanket covers the world with cold sparkles reflecting the blue sky. Walking or skiing through new-fallen snow, you will find the rarest of gifts—peace and true quiet. In addition to the heavy snowfall in winter, you will also have some sunny winter days that provide wonderful opportunities to get out and enjoy all that deep white powder.

Although many people prefer to enjoy the mountains and woods in winter, it can be a more challenging and dangerous time. Unpredictable weather, unsigned trails, and other snow-related hazards are among the risk factors with which you should become familiar. Observe the weather and snow conditions. If the weather is getting bad, be smart: turn around and get out. Continually check your surroundings, observe familiar peaks, creeks, and other landmarks that will allow you to get back to your starting point if you are in a blizzard. Some of the most powerful blizzards can quickly become life-threatening. If you learn about mountain winter conditions and take a few simple precautions, much of the trail and areas in the Lake Tahoe area are great for winter snowshoeing or cross-country skiing.

Land Without Visible Trails

The fact that the Tahoe Rim Trail is not signed for winter creates challenges for even the most experienced traveler. Much of the trail traverses along steep slopes, making winter travel following the trail potentially dangerous. Many popular winter spots may have tracks from the people who were there before you, but there are no real trails. You must follow landforms and head for saddles, mountaintops, or flats. Often, you may be heading in a general direction instead of to an exact spot. Know where you are and where you have been, and don't hesitate to follow your own tracks back out to where you began. In

Dicks Lake (see Chapter 6, Section 7, page 143)

winter, it becomes even more important to have a map and follow it. Learn how to use a compass.

Dehydration

Drinking too little water is another serious risk when you are hiking, snowshoeing, snowboarding, or cross-country skiing. With all that snow around, you still need to remember to drink. When the weather is colder, people tend to drink less even though they may actually need as much water as they would on a hot day. While you are at it, eat. You'll need the energy.

Hypothermia and Frostbite

When the body's core temperature is seriously reduced as a result of exposure to cold and moisture, hypothermia can result. It is a serious condition, aggravated by cold wind and sudden climate changes. The symptoms of hypothermia include shivering, loss of coordination and the ability to do simple tasks, disorientation, and confusion. The treatment is based on common sense. First, get the victim out of the wind and elements, then prevent heat loss by getting them into warm, dry clothes (you should be carrying extra clothing in your pack). Next get the victim into a sleeping bag, if you have one, and climb in to add your body heat (be careful, as this approach may lower your own body temperature). Finally, provide warm liquids and high-carbohydrate foods.

Frostbite is the freezing of body tissues because of prolonged exposure to cold. The most susceptible areas are the feet, hands, ears, and face. Prevention is key for both hypothermia and frostbite. Remember a few simple rules: Eat high-energy foods and drink plenty of liquids. Stay rested. Wear the right clothing and bring layers. Don't do something that will get you wet, and get out of the woods if you do get wet on a cold and windy day. Bring an extra set of clothes in case you get wet.

Avalanches

Understanding how avalanches occur and how to avoid them is too big a topic for this book, but a few words of warning can help you avoid a tragedy. Remember that you are most vulnerable to an avalanche when you are on moderately steep slopes (very steep slopes may not hold enough snow to avalanche), the lee side of mountains, or in gullies. Unstable snow conditions most often occur during or right after a storm; the bigger the storm, the bigger the risk. If you plan to do a lot of backcountry travel, take a Level One avalanche-awareness course, which will teach you how to determine avalanche risk and how to work with beacons and probes to rescue those who have been caught in an avalanche. For more information or to obtain an updated avalanche danger report, go to avalanche.org or sierraavalanchecenter.org.

Tim's Quick Tips for Avoiding Winter Weather Risks

❆ Keep an eye on the weather forecast until right before you leave. Be sure to look for the National Weather Service's detailed weather discussion, and don't rely on the quickie "chance of snow" forecast put out by your phone. You need to zero in on when it might happen, how much, and how windy it will be.

❆ Before setting out, let someone know where you are going and when you plan to return.

❆ Bring extra layers of clothing. The weather may change for the worse even if the forecast calls for nice weather.

❆ Do not venture out unless you know how to navigate without a visible trail.

❆ Use a compass and map.

❆ Bring your survival kit!

❆ Drink lots of water.

❆ Avoid situations that cause hypothermia and frostbite.

Sunburn

The bright sun makes the snow even more beautiful and white. At the end of the day, you might have beautiful memories and one heck of a sunburn. Snow reflects the sun's rays like water does and can burn your skin quickly. Use sunscreen and wear sunglasses to protect your eyes.

Guided Winter Hikes

The Tahoe Rim Trail Association runs a program of guided snowshoe hikes during the winter months. Past trips have included full-moon jaunts in Tahoe Meadows and daytime hikes into Page Meadows. For more information go to tahoerimtrail.org.

Packing and Dressing for Winter Weather

Aside from sunscreen, be sure to carry a basic survival kit. Your kit should include the following items:

- Two large plastic garbage bags (to be used as a poncho or emergency shelter in bad weather)
- Waterproof matches
- Candle
- Metal cup for melting snow
- Duct tape for repairs (can be wrapped around a ski pole)
- Cocoa or other powdered mix
- Cell phone (but don't count on having service)

You have three goals when it comes to clothing yourself for outdoor winter adventures: keep dry, keep warm when it is cool, and keep cool when it is warm. To accomplish these goals, wear or pack clothing items made of synthetic fibers. They are lightweight and wick moisture away from your body, which will help keep you warm. Bring several lightweight layers of clothes, including a waterproof outer shell; it will help you stay dry but allow you to remain cool if the temperature turns warm. Wear a sturdy pair of waterproof boots with wool or synthetic-fabric socks. Wear water-resistant pants, such as those designed for cross-country skiing; carry a waterproof shell to wear over them if you are snowshoeing or traveling through deep snow. A hat is essential, whether it is a baseball cap on a warm day or a warm fleece hat on a cold day.

And don't forget gloves; the style depends on the conditions and activity you are doing. If it is warm and you will be strenuously cross-country skiing, lightweight ski gloves are fine. If you are out hiking or snowshoeing on a cold snowy day, bring a thicker, warmer pair of gloves.

When (and Where) to Go

Winter to Spring

For those who love the snow and winter sports, there are a number of places that are especially attractive and challenging for winter activities. Here are a few of the best spots:

KIRKWOOD CROSS-COUNTRY SKI AREA

Kirkwood is located 30 miles south of South Lake Tahoe on CA 88. It has a network of more than 30 miles of trails with spectacular views of the Carson Pass and Kirkwood area. For more information, call 209-258-7248 or visit kirkwood.com/explore-the-resort/activities-and-events/cross-country.aspx.

PAGE MEADOWS

The easiest way to access Page Meadows in winter is through the Talmont Estates subdivision. Where CA 89 meets CA 28 in Tahoe City, go 2 miles south on CA 89 to Pine Avenue. Turn right, and then right again on Tahoe Park Heights Drive. Go 0.9 mile to the top of the hill, and continue straight on Big Pine Drive. Follow Big Pine 0.25 mile to Silvertip Drive and turn left. There is limited parking available at the end of Silvertip. From the end of the road, head west a few hundred yards to the first of several meadows. The area around Page Meadows is especially popular for cross-country skiing and snowshoeing. The terrain is mostly level, perfect for beginners. The meadows are beautiful on a sunny day or at night when the moon is full.

TAHOE MEADOWS

Located on the south side of NV 431, the meadow is great for a beginner on either skis or snowshoes. From the intersection of NV 28 and NV 431 in Incline Village, drive 7 miles up NV 431, the Mount Rose Highway. Here, you will see a large treeless area on your right. Park along the road. Both the large open meadow and its surrounding forest are very popular for winter sports; in fact, on a weekend you might find this area too crowded. Head south up through the trees to Chickadee Ridge for extraordinary lake views. You could well be dazzled by lodgepole and whitebark pines covered with hoarfrost.

On the north side of the highway at Tahoe Meadows, the TRT climbs toward the radio tower and Mount Rose, another excellent area to ski or snowshoe. While this route can get quite steep and difficult near the top, the views of Mount Rose and Lake Tahoe from the radio tower are inspiring. Snowmobiles are allowed on this side of the highway.

TAHOE CROSS-COUNTRY SKI AREA

Located on Dollar Hill about 2 miles northeast of Tahoe City along CA 28, Tahoe Cross-Country (Tahoe XC) is the venue for the Great Ski Race from Tahoe City to Truckee, which crosses the TRT. This wonderful area provides 40 miles of trails through the forests between Mount Watson and Tahoe City. Many of this Nordic center's trails are popular with mountain bikers and hikers in the summer, and Tahoe XC also rents bikes from the lodge in summer. Contact Tahoe Cross-Country at 530-583-5475 or visit tahoexc.org.

The Tahoe Nordic Search and Rescue (TNSAR) team has all kinds of valuable information, and they are the guys and gals you will be really happy to see if you get lost in the snow. Some of the information in this section comes from the TNSAR team's winter-awareness brochure, *A Guide to Winter Preparedness and Survival*. To obtain a copy, visit tahoenordicsar.com/TSARsml.pdf. For more information about TNSAR and winter awareness, visit tahoenordicsar .com. Above all else, if you have a phone, call 911 in an emergency.

Summer to Fall

Summer and early fall at Tahoe are mostly sunny, warm, and glorious. Nevertheless, afternoon thunderstorms do come up. Some summers may have no thunderstorms, while in other years, storms may occur almost daily. Usually storms are scattered, developing—sometimes out of a clear blue sky—during mid- to late afternoon when the temperatures are warm and a great deal of tropical moisture has moved in from the south. Keep your eye on any large, high, darkening clouds moving rather quickly in your general direction. Better yet, check out the weather information channel or local weather broadcasts, and plan accordingly. You can also visit wunderground.com.

The chance of a thunderstorm need not thwart or curtail your plans, but do bring your rain gear. Sometimes a storm moves swiftly through a specific area and drops only a little rain before it passes. However, if it gets exciting and lightning starts to flash, get out as quickly as possible, especially if you are on an exposed peak, near bodies of water, or under tall trees. Avoid areas of high exposure, such as the top of a pass. I can tell you from personal experience that Dicks Pass, for example, is not a good place to be in a thunderstorm. When one does occur, however, you will discover that you are capable of hiking to safety much faster than you thought. Avoid the urge to take shelter under a solitary tree in open lands. If you cannot get out of the woods in time, stay in the forest in an area of similar-size trees. While lightning can be scary and dangerous, it is also important to remember that people are rarely struck by a lightning bolt. Absent a bit of very bad luck, if you take reasonable precautions you should be fine.

Water

Much of the Tahoe Rim Trail is located along ridgetops, a perfect situation for enjoying the sublime views of Lake Tahoe and the surrounding mountains. However, its rim location results in a shortage of water along many sections of the trail, especially those along the east shore. Plan ahead and make sure you have enough water to get you through the section you will be hiking. On hot summer days, you will need at least 2–3 quarts of water per day. Water is an especially important issue to consider if you plan to thru-hike the entire TRT.

Be sure to avoid drinking any untreated water in the Sierra Nevada. Giardia, a microorganism that occurs in many bodies of water here, can wreak havoc in your intestines. To prevent giardia or other bugs from getting into your system, be sure to filter, boil, or chemically treat any water that you draw from a natural source.

In each section of the trail described in Chapter 6 (page 58), additional specific water information is provided.

Fear of Heights (FOH)

Fear of heights is one of those things that you either have or you don't. If you don't have it, you might be confused why that person in front of you seems to be shaking with fear as they slowly work their way across a cliff-edged section of trail. If you have it, it can be temporarily unnerving and quite stressful to get across a section of trail. I have it, but I still hike just about everywhere, just sometimes with a lot of focus and sweating. Fortunately, there are probably only about 2–3 total miles on the entire Tahoe Rim Trail that will cause most people with FOH to get the heebie-jeebies.

Here are the locations on the TRT where my FOH is heightened:

SECTION TWO: Brockway to Mount Rose Trailhead The narrow section below the Radio Tower about 1 mile north of Relay Peak. Fortunately, it's only about 0.5 mile.

Dicks Lake and Fontanillis Lake from Dicks Pass (see Chapter 6, Section 7, page 143)

SECTION FIVE: Kingsbury Grade to Big Meadow A portion of the new trail just before Mott Canyon and for several miles north of Mott Canyon headed toward Monument Pass.

SECTION EIGHT: Barker Pass to Tahoe City The short cliff traverse just before the volcanic knobs about a mile and a half east of Barker Pass, and the traverse from the bottom of the North Blackwood Creek drainage for about 0.25 mile.

Fun for All: A User's Guide to the Tahoe Rim Trail

DURING SPRING, SUMMER, AND FALL, many types of users enjoy the Tahoe Rim Trail. Each has particular needs, but all have the same general goal of having fun, enjoying nature, and challenging themselves on the trail. Because one user's mode of transport on the trail—whether it is a pair of legs, a pair of wheels, or four strong horse hooves—can affect another's, this chapter focuses on the different types of users and offers tips and suggestions for a mutually safe and pleasant journey.

A Hiking Paradise

Most people who buy this book probably enjoy hiking already and know the basics: Carry plenty of water; wear comfortable boots or shoes; take a map, guidebook, and sunscreen; and bring extra clothes in case of a change in the weather. Chapter 6 (page 70) has complete descriptions of each section of the TRT, plus information about short spur trails that hikers can add to customize their outings. Every section of the trail offers something unique, whether it's the scenery or the specific challenge of the route.

To get the most out of your journey, take care of a few simple things before you leave. Most important, tell someone where you are going and when you expect to be back, and then check in when you return. Although the TRT is not as isolated as a lot of backcountry areas, you may still be alone on many parts of it. It is only common sense to leave information with a friend or family member about your general whereabouts. Much of the Tahoe Rim Trail is used primarily in the daytime, so late in the day is when you are most likely to be alone on the trail. The checklist of key things to remember (see sidebar, page 55) will help you plan your Tahoe Rim Trail trek.

Backpacking and Camping

Why not hike the whole Tahoe Rim Trail? Depending on how strong a hiker you are, it takes anywhere from 10 days to three weeks to circumnavigate Lake Tahoe on this route. (Such a hike is called a thru-hike.) Two weeks would be a comfortable period (although "two weeks of backpacking" and "comfort" are not usually used in the same sentence). Since the TRT is a loop trail, you could start anywhere and end up right back where you began.

A backpacking trip of this length requires some logistical planning. Your primary concerns will be where to camp and where to get water and additional food. Camping is allowed without restrictions everywhere on the Tahoe Rim Trail except in Desolation Wilderness, where you must obtain a

Camping at the top of the ridge between Armstrong Pass and Freel Meadows looking toward Hope Valley

permit. For more information, call 530-573-2674. Although permits are not required in Lake Tahoe Nevada State Park, camping there is limited to two primitive campgrounds, each with a pit toilet and picnic tables. The Marlette Campground also provides water through a hand-operated well. For more information, call 775-831-0494.

To find out where else you can camp, refer to the trail descriptions in Chapter 6 (page 70). For details on water availability, review the Heads Up! section found at the beginning of each trail description. If you are hiking in late summer or fall, keep in mind that some of the water may have dried up. If you come to a major water source in the fall, fill up, but be sure to boil, filter, or treat the water before drinking it.

The good news (or bad, depending on your perspective) is that a lot of people live at Lake Tahoe, and they have built communities with stores that carry every amenity you could possibly need.

Road Crossings and Drop-Off Points

You can design your backpacking trip so that you can pick up food and supplies at various locations and trailheads along the way. Between the stops where you may have arranged to meet friends, you will need water. Alpenglow Sports in Tahoe City will accept packages shipped to their shop. They are a great backpack supplier as well, so you could kill two birds with one stone by mailing a package there and then stopping in to get your backpack goodies. They do have size requirements and would like to be notified in advance. Contact them at 530-583-6917 or alpenglowsports.com. Following is a summary of the road crossings and communities along the TRT.

TAHOE CITY (Sections 1 and 8)

The trail route goes right through Tahoe City, a good midway stopping point if you started your trip at Echo Summit or Kingsbury Grade. As you cross the road from one section of the trail to the next, you will be within 100 yards of a supermarket and within half a mile of several motels. The latter are often booked in the summer, so call ahead and warn them to have the showers ready. Tahoe City is loaded with outfitters that will be happy to sell you any equipment you may have forgotten or need to replace. Check out Alpenglow Sports, located near the trail at 415 N. Lake Blvd., the main road that goes through the center of town.

Tim's Top Tips for Backcountry Hikers

❀ Bring more water than you think you will need.

❀ Don't drink the water in lakes and streams unless you boil, filter, or treat it.

❀ Carry a first aid kit. If you take something out, don't forget to restock it.

❀ Dress in layers. Avoid wearing cotton except on hot, dry days in the middle of summer.

❀ Wear good hiking boots or comfortable athletic shoes. Some hikers prefer high-quality hiking sandals.

❀ Wear hiking socks made of synthetic material or wool, *not* cotton.

❀ Bring enough clothes, including rain gear; weather can change quickly in the Sierra.

❀ Carry and use sunscreen.

❀ Start out early in the day, when it is still cool and there are fewer people on the trail.

❀ Bring a map and this guidebook. A good field guide is also useful.

❀ Tell someone where you're going and when you expect to return. Check in when you return.

❀ If your knees hurt when you hike, try using trekking poles. They can make a significant difference when you hike downhill and help to balance you when you need to scramble over a rocky section of trail.

❀ If you have recently come from a much lower elevation, take time to acclimate to a higher elevation before you set off.

KINGS BEACH (Sections 1 and 2)

The trail crosses CA 267 at 2.75 miles northwest of Kings Beach. A supermarket, with most of the supplies you may need, is located near the intersection of CA 267 and CA 28. This road crossing is a good place for a friend to drop off food or water. Very little water is available on the section of trail between Tahoe City and Brockway Summit; when you cross CA 267, the next water source is a spring beyond Mud Lake or Gray Lake, both more than 10 miles away. *The spring may run dry by fall, so don't count on it.*

INCLINE VILLAGE (Sections 2 and 3)

The TRT crosses NV 431 at 8 miles above Incline Village, another place to meet your wonderful friends who have brought you fresh supplies. Be sure to load up on water at Ophir Creek, about a mile along the trail after you cross NV 431. The next reliable water source is at the Marlette Campground, 14 miles south.

SPOONER SUMMIT TO US 50 (Sections 3 and 4)

There are no towns nearby, but this first road crossing in 23 miles may be a good place to stop and get replenished by those now-great friends of yours (your "trail angels").

DAGGETT PASS (Sections 4 and 5)

There are no amenities where the road crosses NV 207 (Kingsbury Grade), but you can access the Tramway Market by crossing North Benjamin Drive to the North Daggett Loop and then walking up the Daggett Summit Connector to Tramway Drive. After visiting the market you can continue up the Tramway Market paved road to the Stagecoach Kingsbury Grade South Trailhead. At 2.6 miles south of Kingsbury Grade, you meet a junction where the Van Sickle Trail takes you past beautiful lake views in 3.3 miles to South Lake Tahoe, just above the casinos. Here you will find Heavenly Village with a supermarket and a host of other amenities, including lodging.

CA 89, BIG MEADOW TRAILHEAD (Sections 5 and 6)

You have just hiked 23 grueling miles when you get to the road where there is nothing except a bathroom. Use it. This crossing is another good drop-off point where your loyal friends can bring you food acquired in nearby South Lake Tahoe or Meyers. If your friends don't show up or you have an emergency, Meyers is about 5.3 miles downhill from the trailhead.

ECHO SUMMIT AND RESORT (Sections 6 and 7)

About 18 miles past Big Meadow Trailhead, you reach the Echo Chalet (530-659-7207, echochalet.com), which has a store. Stock up because Barker Pass Road is 33 miles north. Echo Chalet sells excellent sandwiches and ice cream, both highlights when I arrived there on day 11 of my first TRT thru-hike.

BARKER PASS (Sections 7 and 8)

This remote road crossing is more than 11 miles from Tahoe City via Barker Pass Road and CA 89, but it could work as a drop-off point in a pinch. The road is closed in the winter and remains closed until the snow has melted.

WARD CREEK BOULEVARD (Section 8)

The trail crosses this road 11 miles from Barker Pass and 5 miles from Tahoe City. If necessary, you could ask someone to meet you at this road crossing to supply moral support and give you the news of the day. This crossing is also just about a mile and a half from CA 89 at Sunnyside, where there is a market, several restaurants, a campground, and a public beach. There is also bus service into Tahoe City, which is 2 miles away.

Although depending upon your friends to assist with your thru-hiking plans is certainly desirable, if that doesn't work out, you may have to make arrangements yourself. This might mean mailing food packages to yourself or picking up food along the way. Tahoe City or South Lake Tahoe, with great outdoors stores and several supermarkets a short distance off the trail, are your best bets for resupplying on the trail.

What to Bring in Your Backpack

My good friend and hiking buddy Shannon Raborn hiked all 2,100 miles of the Appalachian Trail, which runs between Georgia and Maine. When she told me what to bring on a spring, summer, or fall backpacking trip in the Sierra, I listened. I thank Shannon for her helpful contributions to the following list, which we wrote together.

First, you will want to organize your pack by the object's use. Remember, the less weight and space taken up, the better off you will be as you carry it down (and up and down again) the trail.

CLOTHES

Pack hiking shorts; lightweight wool or synthetic shirts; a warm fleece shirt; a rain shell; several pairs of socks; Tevas, Crocs, or water socks (for around camp); a baseball hat; and warm pants or convertible pants that can be shorts during the day and pants at night. If it will be very cold or you are cold-natured, bring a fleece hat and gloves.

TOILETRIES

Bring a toothbrush; toothpaste; vitamins and medications; sunscreen; toilet paper; biodegradable all-purpose soap; and a scrubby sponge for cleaning pots, pans, and your hands. Pack any scented products in a scent-proof container, and remember to store them in a bear canister when you sleep at night.

CAMPING SUPPLIES

Bring a first aid kit; a tent; rope; a lightweight sleeping pad; a sleeping bag (lightweight is best); a backpacking pillow (a luxury, but it feels *soooo* good!); a camp stove (I like Jet Boil's all-in-one pot and stove with gas canisters); gas for your stove; a water filter and/or iodine tablets; water bottles, a Camelbak, or other water-storage container that allows you to carry large amounts of water, necessary on the drier sections of the trail; a trowel (pooper-scooper); a lighter and/or matches; a pot-and-pan kit; a bowl; a cup; utensils (spoon or fork); a small sharp knife; a compass; a headlamp or flashlight; a map; heavyweight garbage bags (to keep things dry in case of rain); duct tape; field guides; this book, of course; and a camera.

If you are camping light, the weather forecast does not call for rain, and it is past mosquito season (late summer), you could forgo the tent and rain fly. If you do not mind going without cooked food, you can also eliminate the stove, fuel, and pots and pans. Keeping your clothes to a minimum is another technique to lower weight, but be sure not to cut out something you may need to stay warm and dry.

BEAR CANISTERS

In areas with lots of bears (anywhere near Lake Tahoe), bear canisters are essential. Canisters work well at keeping out small animals such as squirrels and marmots, too, and can serve as a chair or as a washtub for doing your laundry.

FOOD

Pack what you need, but keep it light. Remember that John Muir took only a pocket full of biscuits with him! Freeze-dried dinners are tasty, but they can be expensive for a long trip. I especially like the ones that require only hot water. Some recommended food items are: instant oatmeal, pasta, couscous, soup, energy bars, gorp or trail mix, bagels, salami, hard cheese, avocados, tortillas with fillings such as cheese or cooked chicken, crackers, hot chocolate or coffee, dried fruit packages, cereal, powdered milk, cookies, and tea.

Yippee! Mountain Biking

It is important to understand that the Tahoe Rim Trail is really only suitable for intermediate and advanced riders. Most sections are quite difficult and technical, so riders should make sure they are capable of riding the section before setting out. I have found that getting accurate information on the difficulty of a trail is a problem. One person's piece of cake is another's miserable and potentially unsafe day on the trail.

More than half the trail is open to mountain bikers. The areas closed to bikers include the approximately 50 miles of the route that overlap with the Pacific Crest Trail. Bikes are also forbidden in the wilderness areas (Desolation Wilderness and Mount Rose Wilderness). Also, bikes are prohibited on a section of trail going north from Spooner Summit past Snow Valley Peak to Hobart Road, and on the trail to Galena Falls from the Mount Rose Trailhead, but both of these sections have alternate routes that riders can take. Bikes are permitted on the rest of the TRT.

For detailed descriptions of each section of the trail, directions to trailheads, and special sidebars applying to bikers, refer to individual trail descriptions. Here's a summary of which sections you can and cannot ride on (these are also shown on the maps).

SECTION 1: Tahoe City to Brockway Summit Riding is allowed throughout.

SECTION 2: Brockway Summit to Mount Rose Mountain biking is allowed between Brockway Summit and the Mount Rose Wilderness boundary, a distance of about 7 miles. If you start from the Tahoe Meadows end, there are two trails, one that allows mountain bikes and one that does not. Follow the instructions for that section. Either way, you can go only 4 miles to the Relay Peak Tower on your bike.

SECTION 3: Tahoe Meadows to Spooner Summit Mountain biking is allowed between Tahoe Meadows and Hobart Road, which is 14.3 miles (for the section between Tahoe Meadows and Tunnel Creek Road, which is 9.2 miles, mountain biking is allowed only on even days of the month). At Hobart Road, a detour is available down to Marlette Lake and then out to Spooner Lake via North Canyon Road.

SECTION 4: Spooner Summit to Kingsbury Grade This entire section is open to bikes.

SECTION 5: Kingsbury Grade to Big Meadow This entire section is open to bikes, but much of it is very difficult.

SECTION 6: Big Meadow to Echo Summit Bikes are allowed from the Big Meadow Trailhead for about 5 miles, to where the Tahoe Rim Trail meets the Pacific Crest Trail in Meiss Meadows. Bikes are prohibited on the PCT.

Tim's Top Tips for Mountain Bikers

🚲 To preserve the trail, ride only where bicycles are permitted.

🚲 Wear your helmet.

🚲 Speed is your friend. Hitting the brakes too hard or going too slowly over a rocky section can send you flying over the bars. With a little speed you can bounce right over the rocks. Of course, if you fall, the rule has now changed to "Speed is your friend, until it isn't."

🚲 To prevent undue erosion, avoid wet, muddy areas.

🚲 Spring and fall temperatures, which are bearable when you're hiking, get bone chilling as you cruise downhill at 20 miles an hour. When it's cold, wear a thin hat under your helmet, warm socks, and several layers of clothing. Your legs will be pumping, so they won't get as cold, but the wind will go right to your neck and through those bike shoes. Perhaps not being in a mad rush to get to the trail on a cold morning is a good idea.

🚲 Wear bike shoes, bike shorts, and bike shirts; they are designed to make your ride more enjoyable.

🚲 Wear a Camelbak or other similar hydration system. Mountain biking is strenuous exercise, and a water bottle isn't sufficient on a warm day. A Camelbak also allows you to drink without making a stop and keeps the water colder throughout the whole ride.

🚲 When riding downhill, lift your bottom slightly off the seat, lean back gently, don't grip the handlebars too tightly, and flow down that awesome singletrack. (Don't forget to yippee!)

🚲 Bring a spare inner tube, and learn how to fix a flat and do minor repairs on your bike.

🚲 Scrapes and cuts are common while biking, so always carry a small, light first aid kit in your pack. One brand I like is Adventure Medical Kits.

SECTION 7: **Echo Summit and Echo Lake to Barker Pass** Bikes are not allowed on this section, which overlaps with the PCT.

SECTION 8: **Barker Pass to Tahoe City** The first 5 miles are on the PCT, where bikes are prohibited. From Twin Peaks to Tahoe City, bikes are allowed.

Getting Horsey on the TRT

Much of the Tahoe Rim Trail is challenging to ride. Equestrians and their horses should be experienced. Water is a concern on much of the trail, especially on the east shore. If you plan to ride on the TRT, be sure to read through trail descriptions for detailed information. While on the trail, watch out for other users. Horses are supposed to be given the right-of-way, but be alert and cautious just the same. Horses are fairly rare on the TRT—other users may not expect to see them. Many experts suggest equestrians always wear helmets. Learn the trail ahead of time, and be sure to maintain a comfortable pace for yourself and your horse. Stay on the trail to protect the fragile environment. Two other issues that equestrians must consider before embarking on a ride along the TRT are where to park and where to camp.

Where to Park the Trailer

TAHOE CITY

There is one parking lot available in Tahoe City. It's located at the 64 Acres (Truckee River Access) parking lot located on CA 89 where it intersects with CA 28 in Tahoe City. From here, you can ride along a paved bike trail for a short distance, then ride under the new bridge across the Truckee River and meet the TRT heading toward Page Meadows.

From here you could also ride across busy CA 89 and up Fairway Drive to the section of the TRT heading toward Brockway Summit. Be aware that this parking lot and the highway are extremely busy in the summer with bike riders and Truckee River rafters. Perhaps a better bet, if you have a friend, is to drop the horses off at the trailhead on Fairway Drive, then return the trailers to 64 Acres.

BROCKWAY SUMMIT

Parking at the busy trailhead is extremely limited. Your best parking spot is 0.9 mile past Tahoe Rim Trailhead, just a short distance past the top of Brockway Summit toward Truckee. On the right is Martis Peak Road, leading up to Martis Peak. This is a great spot for horses, and from here you can ride your horse up the lightly traveled Martis Peak Road about 4 miles until you meet the TRT.

MOUNT ROSE AND TAHOE MEADOWS

The Tahoe Meadows Trailhead parking lot was designed for horses, but it may be congested on a busy day. Be sure to use the parking lot next to the road; the one down by the bathroom is too congested. If the roadside parking lot is full, the meadow side of the road has a wide shoulder. After you park, follow the sign toward Brockway Summit or Spooner Summit. If you are heading toward Brockway Summit from this trailhead, use extreme caution because you will have to ride parallel to and then cross the very busy road to the trailhead. There is also limited parking at the Mount Rose Trailhead.

SPOONER SUMMIT

Neither of the two trailheads on Spooner Summit is a convenient place to park your trailer. The south side has more parking possibilities. For the north side, park farther down the road toward Carson City, near the Nevada Department of Transportation Building, and follow a use trail to the TRT. Trying to cross busy, four-lane US 50 with your horse is not recommended.

KINGSBURY GRADE NORTH

The north trailhead of Kingsbury Grade has room to park your trailer.

KINGSBURY GRADE SOUTH

The large Heavenly Ski Area Stagecoach parking lot should provide plenty of room to park your horse trailer.

BIG MEADOW

The Big Meadow parking lot has parking spots designed for horse trailers, but the access is quite narrow, and often the horse-trailer spots have been taken by cars in this crowded parking area (if you do not have a horse, give those with horses a break and park in the other spaces if they are available). The parking lot also has some challenging, winding, sharp turns. If you are heading toward Freel Peak, you can park along the road near the Grass Lake Trailhead, 1.8 miles east of the Big Meadow Trailhead, and then use the connector trail there to reach the TRT.

ECHO SUMMIT

At the top of the summit on the south side of the road, there is a large snow park that makes for a great spot to park your trailer. From here, you can ride across the parking lot and head south or follow the trail north to Lower Echo Lake. There is also parking at Lower Echo Lake, although it can be full to overflowing on summer weekends.

BARKER PASS

There are limited parking spaces available at the top of Barker Pass. From here, you can head in either direction on the Tahoe Rim Trail. The paved road up to Barker Pass is a good one but has a few narrow, twisting turns.

Places to Horse Camp

When looking for a place to camp when you are backpacking, your primary considerations are finding water and finding a pretty spot. When you have a horse, another concern enters the picture: where do you find grass for your horses without destroying a beautiful meadow? Equestrians should bring their own horse feed instead of relying on unpredictable and fragile grass and meadowlands.

Some of the good camping spots for horses include:

- **Watson Lake**

- **Ophir Creek** Go straight at the TRT–Ophir Creek Trail junction to a nice spot near the creek but out of Tahoe Meadows. You are now on Ophir Creek Trail but still close to the TRT.

- **Star Lake**

- **Armstrong Pass** Take the Armstrong Pass connector down to the dirt road and a nearby stream. The dry meadow is known as Horse Meadow.

- **Meiss Meadows and the area near Showers Lake**

- **Desolation Wilderness** See permit information in Chapter 1 (page 16).

- **Ward Canyon, below Twin Peaks**

- **Robie Equestrian Park** This special 160-acre wilderness equestrian park serves as the staging area for the annual Tevis Cup 100-mile horse ride from Tahoe to Auburn. Although not on the Tahoe Rim Trail, the equestrian park is 3 miles from Watson Lake and has two trails with direct access to the TRT. Accessible by vehicle, it is a convenient place for horse camping or setting out for day rides. Livestock water, outhouse facilities, and ample parking are available. The park is open to day use throughout the summer. Reservations for overnight camping are needed in advance. Contact The Wendell & Inez Robie Foundation at robiefoundation.org.

Goin' Fishin'

Rainbow trout, brook trout, brown trout, and cutthroat trout are the most common fish in the mountain lakes and streams around Lake Tahoe. In a few lakes, including Lake Tahoe itself, you will also find kokanee salmon and mackinaw trout (which has edged out the cutthroat in the lake). Most mountain lakes are stocked with fish on a regular basis, although there has been talk of ending the stocking program, especially in wilderness areas, which could greatly affect the mountain fishing experience.

Fishing on the TRT is just like anywhere else: anyone older than age 16 must have a fishing license. To obtain one, contact your local sporting goods store. If you have questions about fishing regulations in California, contact the California Department of Fish and Wildlife at wildlife.ca.gov/licensing/fishing. In Nevada, contact the Nevada Department of Wildlife at www.ndow.org/fish.

Much of the TRT lies along the ridgelines surrounding the Lake Tahoe Basin, generally above the lakes and major streams that support fish. However, several locations along the trail are good for fishing, and a number of spur trails take you to fishing sites. In general, since most of the lakes and streams are above the west shore, that is where the best fishing is. Half the fun is discovering your own secret hole, so I reveal only the more popular places below.

The best way to make sure that Tahoe area waterways continue to have fish is to practice catch-and-release fishing. Create barbless hooks by smashing the barb on your hook with a pair of pliers. Once you catch the fish, treat it gently. Remove the hook while the fish is still in the water, and release it back into the environment where it belongs. If you are camping and really would enjoy a fish dinner, go ahead, but be sure to only take the fish you will eat. After you decide to keep the fish, you face a dilemma with no easy answer: cleaning the fish in a lake leaves fish body parts that can be unsightly, but burying the remains can attract wildlife like bears. If it is just one fish, perhaps the best strategy would be to take the remains back out with you.

For more details about fishing in the Sierra, refer to these time-tested titles. The *Sierra Trout Guide* by Ralph Cutter (Amato Publications, 1991) provides a list of every lake in the Sierra and what kind of fish may be found there. Another informative source is the *Lake Tahoe's Desolation Wilderness Fishing Guide* by Jerome Yesavage (Talmont Trout Publications, 2008).

Desolation Wilderness and Western Rim

The area between Echo Lakes and Barker Pass has some fishable lakes. In recent years several lakes in the Sierra have had fish removed in order to help the frog habitat. Explore the area, and you will find the best spots to fish.

Truckee River

In Tahoe City, the TRT meets the Truckee River, a popular fishing spot. During summer months, this area is also popular with rafters. It is best to fish in early morning or late afternoon, or you may catch a big raft instead of a trout.

North Shore

Watson Lake, a fairly shallow lake, is pretty much your only choice in this area. Two others, Gray Lake and Mud Lake, do not have fish and are sometimes not even lakes.

East Shore

Only a few lakes of any size exist on the east shore. Close to the trail and right off the highway is Spooner Lake, which allows catch-and-release fishing only. Marlette Lake is also catch and release. Because the shallow Twin Lakes often dry up in late season, they lack fish, but Star Lake, at the base of Jobs Sister, has trout.

South Shore and Meiss Meadows Areas

In this area, the Upper Truckee River, Meiss Lake, Dardanelles Lake, Round Lake, and Showers Lake provide opportunities for fishing. In recent years Tahoe's native fish, the Lahontan cutthroat trout, has been reintroduced to these waters, and a zero-limit, catch-and-release policy (meaning no fish can be retained) has been instituted.

Hiking with Kids

The Tahoe Rim Trail is a challenging trail even for grown-ups because it traverses terrain that has lots of elevation gain. For this reason, much of the trail is simply not suitable for younger children. There are, however, a few great destinations for family outings. Here are a few suggestions on my favorite places to take the kids. The complete route descriptions can be found in Chapter 6, starting on page 70.

Mount Rose and Tahoe Meadows Area

Near the top of the Mount Rose Highway at Tahoe Meadows, the Tahoe Rim Trail has two TRT trailheads, one with an interpretive loop trail. All three of these trails provide an opportunity for kids to learn about and enjoy the mountains. Each of these trailheads is located above 8,000 feet elevation, about 7.5–8 miles up NV 431 from the intersection of NV 28 and NV 431 in Incline Village. They are all in the same vicinity or across the street from each other.

Tahoe Meadows Interpretative Trail

If you are coming from Incline Village on NV 431, you will see a parking area and a building set down below the road on the right side after 7.4 miles. This area has a very easy, wheelchair- and stroller-accessible, 1.3-mile loop. The trail starts on the eastern edge of the lower parking area and winds through the meadow. It is a great spot for early-summer wildflowers and a place where the little ones can stretch their legs. This is the easiest segment of the Tahoe Rim Trail and is suitable for very young children.

Tahoe Meadows to Spooner Summit

This hike starts from the western edge of the same parking lot described above. First, the trail traverses Tahoe Meadows and passes a display of wildflowers, a few small streams, and larger Ophir Creek—a playground for kids. Once you have crossed the meadow, the trail levels out and heads uphill, not too steeply, to the top of a saddle 1.7 miles from the trailhead. From the saddle, the trail levels off again and remains mostly level for several miles with only a few gentle up-and-down passages. The views of the lake are incredible, and numerous flat-rock "armchairs" invite you to enjoy your lunch or a snack. Walk as far as you want, and then turn around. This area is also a great spot for someone who is learning how to cross-country ski or snowshoe.

Tahoe Meadows and Mount Rose to Brockway Summit

From Incline Village on NV 431, drive past the main Tahoe Meadows Trailhead, on your right in 7.4 miles, and go another 0.7 mile, where you reach the Mount Rose TRT Trailhead. As you hike up the trail, Lake Tahoe, Tahoe Meadows, and the mountains around the lake quickly come into view. In 2.5 miles of fairly easy walking, you reach lovely Galena Falls and a junction. A left (west) turn takes you up to the top of the falls, where you can turn left and head to Snow Pond or keep straight toward Relay Peak. From Snow Pond you can either turn around and retrace your steps, or turn left and follow the dirt road and mountain biking–friendly TRT section back to the trailhead for a 6-mile loop.

If you take the right (north) turn at the Galena Falls junction, toward the Mount Rose Summit, at the bottom of the falls you will quickly cross two streams and find great midseason wildflower displays.

Big Meadow Area

Drive 5.3 miles south of Meyers on CA 89 to the Tahoe Rim Trail Big Meadow Trailhead. This trail heads northeast toward Kingsbury Grade, or south 5 miles to where the Tahoe Rim Trail intersects the Pacific Crest Trail. If your children are hearty, they may enjoy the hike south where, after about 3 miles and approximately 800 feet of elevation gain, you will reach Round Lake. Along the way, you traverse lovely Big Meadow. You will also encounter some huge volcanic rock formations. The lake itself is a great respite for the kids. (You could also take the spur trail to Dardanelles Lake, a beautiful lake 3.4 miles from the trailhead).

Echo Lakes Area

At Lower Echo Lake (see directions in Chapter 6, Section 7, page 143), you will find a store, a small marina, and a large parking facility. From the lake, your trail is the combined Tahoe Rim, Tahoe-Yosemite, and Pacific Crest Trails; it heads north. The first 2.5 miles are along the Lower and Upper Echo Lakes and provide great views of them. This trail has some fun up-and-down passages and rocky scrambles, perfect for almost any 10-year-old.

After 2.5 miles, you can continue on the trail, turn around, or take the water taxi back to the Echo Lakes parking lot. The water taxi operates seasonally, so be sure to check ahead to make sure it is running. The taxi pier is a great place for a swim while you are waiting for the boat. Late in the summer, the lake level drops too low to allow the taxi to pass between Lower and Upper Echo Lakes. For more information about the taxi, contact Echo Chalet at 530-659-7207 or echochalet.com.

Another option is to take the taxi to the end of the two lakes and cut out 2.5 miles of a trip to Lake of the Woods or Lake Aloha. If you take the water taxi, it is only about 3 miles to Lake of the Woods and 3.5 miles to the eastern edge of Lake Aloha. I found Lake Aloha to be a perfect spot to take my child on a backpacking trip. Be prepared for a hearty climb of about 1,000 feet through rocky terrain.

Page Meadows Area

The Page Meadows area can be approached from several different directions and is an excellent and easy place to take the kids on a hike. The easiest way into the area is through the back of the Talmont Estates and Twin Peaks subdivision. Where CA 89 meets CA 28 in Tahoe City, go 2 miles south

Watson Lake

on CA 89 to Pine Avenue. Turn right, and then right again on Tahoe Park Heights Drive. Go 0.9 mile to the top of the hill, and continue straight on Big Pine Drive. Follow Big Pine 0.25 mile to Silvertip Drive and turn left. Follow Silvertip to the end of the road, and park where you see a sign that reads SKI PARKING. A dirt road heads west from the end of the road. Follow it down the hill straight ahead until you pass a sharp left turn. Just after the turn, a singletrack trail heads off to the right and arrives at the first meadow in about 100 yards. Follow the edge of the meadow until you see a trail heading left (west) through the meadow. From here you can start exploring. The trail goes by several big meadows. The meadows provide tremendous mountain views, great wildflowers in the summer, and lots of aspen trees, making it prime for fall colors. Bring a picnic lunch and a Frisbee, and have at it with the kids. Avoid trampling the fragile meadow at least until late summer or fall, when it has had a chance to dry out.

Ward Canyon Area

On CA 89, drive 2.4 miles south of Tahoe City, past Sunnyside Resort to Pineland Drive on the right. In 0.4 mile it becomes Twin Peaks Drive. Stay on the left at the Y, and in about 0.1 mile the road becomes Ward Creek Boulevard. Take this about 1.5 miles to a TRT sign on your left, where the trail begins. Follow the old road as it parallels the largely unseen Ward Creek for the next 3 miles. Go as far as you want, and then turn around. The trail eventually leads rather steeply up to Twin Peaks, but that would be a long haul for the little ones. The first 3 miles, however, are a gentle uphill with lots of wildflowers in season, Ward Creek nearby, and wonderful views of the Sierra Crest above. A good turnaround point is McCloud Falls, which is where it begins to get pretty steep.

For more information about hiking and backpacking with children, pick up a copy of my book *Monsters in the Woods: Backpacking with Children*, published by the University of Nevada Press.

What About Fido?

While dogs are allowed on all of the Tahoe Rim Trail, restrictions do apply at several state parks, including Lake Tahoe Nevada State Park. In fact, regulations governing dogs on trails completely depend on what county you are passing through. It is your responsibility to know what the specific regulations are under each county's jurisdiction. I'm sure many dog lovers would disagree with me, but in general, it is best to leave the pups at home or at least keep them on a leash. Off-leash dogs chase and interfere with wildlife and trample the understory of forests. Your chances of encountering wild creatures will increase without a dog, and you'll have the satisfaction of knowing that you are limiting your effect on the trail. If you do hike with your pooch, be sure to have it on a leash or under voice command at all times. Letting dogs jump on other hikers, chase mountain bikers, run beyond your sight line, or harass horses is a big no-no.

Trail Descriptions

6

THESE TRAIL DESCRIPTIONS list point-to-point mileages. The mileage figures are based on several sources; the primary sources for the maps you see in this book are Tom Harrison's *Lake Tahoe Recreation Map*, which has been enhanced with information generously provided by Jeffrey P. Schaffer, whose *Tahoe Sierra* and *Pacific Crest Trail: Northern California* set the standard for guidebooks in this area. These figures give you distances between certain locations. However, you should realize that when it says 0.9 mile, another source might report it as 1.1 miles. If this difference really bothers you, perhaps you need to relax a bit. I have found the best way to relax is to spend time walking in the woods.

Before each description, I recommend when the section can be hiked without encountering large amounts of snow. These dates are estimates based on an "average snow year," but there is no such thing as an average year. It either snows more than average or less than average—usually way more than average or way less than average,

Wildflowers gone wild north of Showers Lake

unfortunately. The dates should give you a rough idea of when you can hike. If it has been an especially mild winter and a warm spring, you could expect to hike the trail sooner than the dates stated here. After a really big winter, it can be late July before you can access many parts of the TRT. Refer to Chapter 4 (page 30) for more detail about snow seasons.

Finally, the Tahoe Rim Trail is constantly evolving. Minor trail changes for maintenance and realignment are planned and implemented on a regular basis. Although this book attempts to be up-to-date, changes to the trail may have been made since this book was published. For more information about any recent changes to the trail, contact the Tahoe Rim Trail Association at 775-298-4485 or visit tahoerimtrail.org.

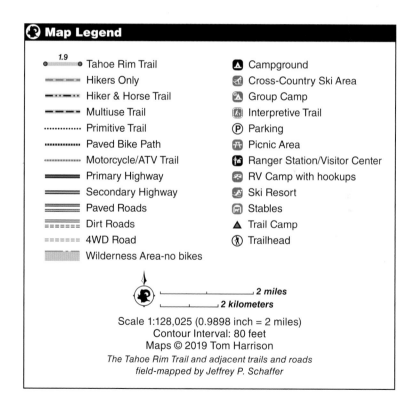

Map Legend

1.9 ●——● Tahoe Rim Trail	▲ Campground
—— —— Hikers Only	Cross-Country Ski Area
—·—··— Hiker & Horse Trail	Group Camp
— — — Multiuse Trail	Interpretive Trail
············ Primitive Trail	Ⓟ Parking
▪▪▪▪▪▪▪▪ Paved Bike Path	Picnic Area
·············· Motorcycle/ATV Trail	Ranger Station/Visitor Center
━━━━ Primary Highway	RV Camp with hookups
═══ Secondary Highway	Ski Resort
▤▤▤ Paved Roads	Stables
═══════ Dirt Roads	▲ Trail Camp
═══════ 4WD Road	Ⓧ Trailhead
▨▨▨ Wilderness Area-no bikes	

├————————┤ **2 miles**
├————————┤ **2 kilometers**

Scale 1:128,025 (0.9898 inch = 2 miles)
Contour Interval: 80 feet
Maps © 2019 Tom Harrison
The Tahoe Rim Trail and adjacent trails and roads
field-mapped by Jeffrey P. Schaffer

Tahoe City to Brockway Summit

19.1 miles

DIFFICULTY This section is strenuous. It is long, requires a good deal of climbing, and can be quite hot in the summer, when it is also mostly waterless.

BEST SEASONS While portions of the trail at lower elevations are accessible from late May to early November, higher-elevation areas have snow until later. The snow melts first along the first several miles north of Tahoe City.

HIGHLIGHTS This section includes a several-mile jaunt along the edge of the Truckee River Canyon with excellent views of Lake Tahoe and the Truckee River. Much of the area has been logged extensively over the years, so you will see mostly smaller, newer-growth trees and a wide variety of species as you move through the different elevations. The section above the Truckee River has several incredibly large sugar pine and Jeffrey pine specimens. The trail has outstanding views of Alpine Meadows and Squaw Valley. Watson Lake, while not the most beautiful lake along the Tahoe Rim Trail, is a pleasant, shallow lake nestled among the trees two-thirds of the way through your hike.

HEADS UP! This is a long stretch, and water is in short supply. Year-round water sources do not exist, except for Watson Lake, which is 12.4 miles from Tahoe City and 6.7 miles from Brockway Summit. Watson Lake is shallow, and its water looks unenticing to drink. (These days, you should treat water from even the most sparkling lakes.) A stream east of Watson Lake may be available in the early season. Bring lots of water if you're hiking this section!

With many road crossings and much off-highway-vehicle (OHV) use, don't be surprised to hear or see cars close to the trail. Watson Lake can be accessed via a paved road and is heavily used by car campers and occasionally by late-night partiers.

For mountain bikers, the rocky terrain can be challenging, even frustrating. While overall this section is not recommended for beginner riders, there are some stretches that are easier for beginners. If you plan on mountain biking this section, it is best to head south from Brockway Summit toward Tahoe City, although either direction will challenge you with steep, rocky terrain that includes technically challenging sections.

GETTING THERE, TAHOE CITY TO BROCKWAY SUMMIT From the Y intersection at CA 89 and CA 28, go 0.2 mile west on CA 89 toward Truckee. Just past a gas

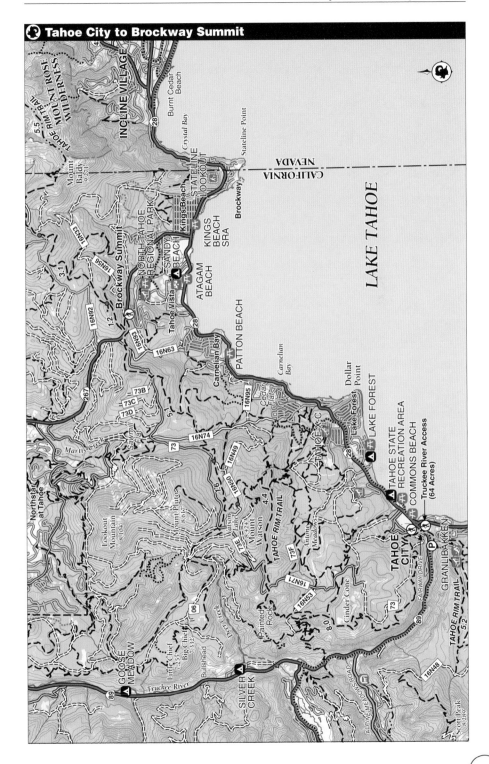

Tahoe City to Brockway Summit

LAKE TAHOE

Truckee River from a clifftop viewpoint

station (a Chevron at the time this book was published), turn right on Fairway Drive. Drive another 0.2 mile to a parking lot and the Fairway Community Center on the right. If this parking lot is full, you can park (on weekends only) at the Tahoe City Public Utility District offices about 0.1 mile back toward CA 89. Your trailhead is across the street from the center.

GETTING THERE, BROCKWAY SUMMIT TO TAHOE CITY From the intersection of CA 28 and CA 267 in Kings Beach, drive 2.75 miles north on CA 267 to the TRT trailhead. Look carefully—it is easy to miss. Limited parking is available at the road pullout on the left, 0.5 mile before Brockway Summit. Get there early on summer weekends to get your spot. The trail starts at the downhill edge of the parking area.

Trail Description

FROM THE TAHOE CITY TRAILHEAD with rock terracing and a trailhead map, the trail starts out as a moderate grade and passes through thick sections of manzanita, patches of squaw carpet, and a forest of white fir, Jeffrey pine, sugar pine, and incense cedar. Note the large volcanic boulders just above the trail, and the ancient, rusted pickup trucks below. Several views of downtown Tahoe City and the lake open up beyond. After about 0.7 mile you cross a dirt road; for a little history lesson, detour right and climb steeply uphill about 100 yards, and then turn right. You will see a white cross that sits above Tahoe City (see Side Trip "Boyle's Last Ride," opposite).

Back on the Tahoe Rim Trail, a gentle climb brings you to the first of many crossings of what locals call the Fiberboard Freeway (also Forest Service Road 16N73 or Forest Route 73), after the company that was once the principal landholder in the area. The term *freeway* is derived from the fact that while at this point it is a narrow dirt road, later in our hike when we cross it several times, it becomes a wide gravel road and the main backcountry route linking Tahoe City and Brockway Summit (and via another connection, Truckee). After crossing the road, you quickly reach a seasonal stream, followed by a small climb to your first major lake view. Here you see, in addition

SIDE TRIP
Boyle's Last Ride

William Boyle was an easygoing codger with a dry sense of humor who lived in Tahoe City in the early 20th century. According to the local legend, he once asked his drinking buddies to bury him above the town so he could keep an eye on them. True to their word, when he died, his friends pulled Boyle's body up the hill on a sled and buried him above Tahoe City on February 4, 1912. Shortly afterward, the cross was erected at the site. Photos from that time depict a clear, treeless view down to the lake. Now, however, trees and brush have grown so thickly that much of the view from the cross has been obscured.

to a healthy swath of Lake Tahoe, the tiny Granlibakken ski area and its surrounding neighborhood, as well as the Truckee River. For folks in Tahoe City looking for a quick workout and access to a great view, you can hike to this point and back to the trailhead in less than an hour.

Boyle's cross above Tahoe City

Squaw Valley through a forest of red firs

You have been heading west, and now the trail heads north, following the ridgetop of the Truckee River Canyon for the next 4 miles. The ascent is steady but not overly strenuous, and the views are some of the most unique on the entire Tahoe Rim Trail. After a saunter along the ridgeline, the trail takes a brief foray into a thick forest of white fir, where you may find some of the biggest pinedrops you will ever encounter. Soon enough, you are back on the canyon edge, marveling at the majestic sugar pines and Jeffrey pines as you meander along the lava-topped ridge. After another section of climbing through thicker forest, you gently descend to an open field of green, a seasonal creek crossing, and a short climb at about 3 miles from the trailhead to a stunning viewpoint: a cliff's-edge lava flat bordered by gnarled junipers overlooking the Truckee River, where summertime rafters can be heard and seen. If you can look up from the river view, Twin Peaks looks pretty impressive as well.

The good stuff continues for the next 0.5 mile as the trail follows the ridge, with views of Squaw and Alpine a constant companion. Alas, all things must come to an end, and you leave the ridgeline and head into the forest for a sustained mile-plus climb. Your trail switchbacks through sections of thicker forest and recently thinned sections before passing waves of pinemat manzanita where the forest canopy changes from white to red fir. Springtime hikers will likely discover snow on this section in the thick forest.

A last traverse brings you to nifty trail work through a pile of volcanic rocks and the first of two awesome lunch spots, both with plenty of rocks to sit on to enjoy the views. This first vista includes Lake Tahoe, Twin Peaks, and parts of Alpine Meadows. The next one, just 200 yards farther, looks directly into the entrance to Alpine Meadows and a good portion of Squaw Valley. The second view sits on a big pile of fractured basalt; when you walk over it, it sounds like broken glass, which apparently is enough for many mountain bikers to refer to this popular section of trail as Glass Mountain.

> **SIDE TRIP**
> **Cinder Cone**
>
> Leave the trail and walk east onto the mostly flat, red surface of the Cinder Cone. The dearth of plant growth and the evidence of filled-in ditches clearly show that the site was once used by humans. It has been a long time, however, since this area was used for water treatment, and it is recovering nicely.

Next the trail follows the ridge, and you soon see to your right the dark-red volcanic rock of the Cinder Cone. Longtime Tahoe locals will tell you that this cinder cone area was the repository for Tahoe City sewer water before the Tahoe Truckee Sanitation Agency treatment plant was built along the Truckee River east of Truckee in the 1970s. Does that change your mind about where you planned to stop for lunch? As the trail skirts the Cinder Cone, you see the remnants of an old fence (see Side Trip "Cinder Cone," above).

Squaw Valley from Glass Mountain Viewpoint

Past the Cinder Cone, the trail heads north for 0.5 mile and then descends rather steeply through a small north-facing section of thick forest (which will hold snow into summer) to an open saddle at the end of a former dirt road, which has become the now popular Powerline mountain bike trail, which goes from here to the Fiberboard Freeway. Here you begin heading gently uphill through an open forest of fir trees and manzanita. Quickly the trail proceeds downhill again, and the forest becomes thicker and your hike shadier.

Like most of the northern and western shores of Lake Tahoe, this area has been logged heavily in the past. The most extensive logging occurred in the late 1800s, when much of the Tahoe Basin was logged to make braces in the silver mines of nearby Virginia City to keep them from collapsing (as well as for lumber and fuel). Loggers at that time focused on the best trees for their purposes—the pine trees, especially the majestic sugar pine—and left most of the fir trees. During an extended wet period, the red and white firs took over the territory from the more drought- and disease-resistant Jeffrey and sugar pines, creating an unnaturally dense forest made up primarily of firs. If nature had been allowed to revert to its own natural process, periodic forest fires would have thinned the population of fir. Instead, the federal and state governments, under heavy pressure to prevent forest fires and limit tree cutting, had a policy of preventing major forest fires by putting out all fires as quickly as possible. In the short term this policy saved the forest, but it led to a denser forest and increased the likelihood of a catastrophic fire. We now know that this

> **SIDE TRIP The Wall**
>
> A left here would quickly take you 300 yards northwest to a minor saddle and the start of a steep downhill known as The Wall by biking enthusiasts. It leads to the Western States Trail and, in a few steep downhill miles, to the bike trail at the bridge across the Truckee River between Squaw Valley and Alpine Meadows. The bike trail leads back to Tahoe City and the beginning of the TRT; it makes a nice loop for experienced bikers.

historic policy excluded the ecological role of frequent natural fires. Expansive stands of dead trees in an overly thick forest are a recipe for disaster. The U.S. Forest Service and the state park departments of both Nevada and California have begun an aggressive effort of salvage logging and controlled burning to reduce the danger. As you walk or ride on the Tahoe Rim Trail, you may see evidence of this effort in the form of brush piles waiting to be burned and stumps from recent logging in many locations.

About 1 mile past the last dirt road, you cross another dirt road (see Side Trip "The Wall," above). This one is in a dry gully above the headwaters of

Alpine Meadows from Painted Rock

Burton Creek. Those desperate for water can head 0.75 mile southeast down the road to its end at the Fiberboard Freeway (FR 73). Turn left there, and head briefly north to the creek, which may dry up by early summer after a mild winter.

To continue on the TRT, cross this second dirt road to enter prime mountain biking terrain. The amount of trail traffic will increase dramatically. The trail here is part of a network of trails providing great biking opportunities out of Tahoe City and the Tahoe Cross-Country Ski Area, located in the Highlands subdivision. The next stage is a mostly moderate climb through soft volcanic dirt and mixed forest 0.9 mile to the east edge of Painted Rock (7,754'). Along the way you pass some impressive volcanic boulders. After the climb to Painted Rock, you're rewarded with two viewpoints. The first, and less dramatic, of the two offers a view southeast toward Lake Tahoe; a little farther you reach an awe-inspiring view into Squaw Valley backed by the Sierra Crest.

After all the uphill work you've done in the last 8 miles, you get a break with a mostly shady descent (or if on a bike, a really fun downhill) to another crossing of the Fiberboard Freeway at about 9 miles from the Tahoe City Trailhead. The Great Ski Race passes this point on its way to Truckee, usually on the first Sunday in March. This 30K (18.4-mile) cross-country ski race, from the Tahoe Cross-Country Ski Area on Dollar Hill to Truckee, attracts more than 1,000 people, making it one of the biggest cross-country ski events in the western United States. For the next 0.8 mile you cover a smooth, gentle incline over hard-packed sandy soils. (Mountain bikers should ride it back

SIDE TRIP
Mount Watson

A left turn at the Fiberboard Freeway will take you back to Tahoe City, while a right turn leads to Truckee, Brockway Summit, or the top of Mount Watson. Should you want to climb or ride to Mount Watson, follow the freeway uphill from where it meets the dirt road for 0.7 mile to a junction with a major dirt road that turns sharply right (southeast). Turn onto this road, and follow it for 1 steep mile on a 640-foot ascent to the top of Mount Watson (8,424'). Kudos if you can ride up this steep route without getting off your bike. Views from the top are glorious; you can see most of Lake Tahoe and its surrounding mountains as well as Squaw Valley and Alpine Meadows to the west.

down to enjoy one of the best biking stretches on the whole TRT, especially for beginners. Mountain bikers call this fun section Fire and Ice.) Where the trail levels off and runs into an old narrow dirt road, a left will take you 100 yards north to the Fiberboard Freeway (see Side Trip "Mount Watson," left).

Just south of the Fiberboard Freeway, take the TRT; it turns right and follows an old abandoned dirt road, now overgrown with manzanita and tobacco brush. This gentle, mostly downhill stretch continues 1.6 miles, providing several excellent lake views before a left turn heads you back uphill. (Straight ahead here leads to the Lakeview Ridge Trail, a switchbacky mountain bike trail that in about a mile leads down to Kevin's Crest. Here, at an excellent viewpoint of Lake Tahoe, you meet the winter location of Tahoe Cross-Country Ski Area's Lakeview Trail and

View of North Tahoe High School and Lake Tahoe seen from the slopes of Mount Watson

are now connected to a great network of summer trails that head out from the ski area's lodge parking lot.)

You now wind uphill, northeast, between lava boulders and cliffs for the next 0.75 mile to a wonderful stopping place among several especially large boulders, with enticing views of the lake to the south between the boulders. That large white-roofed building in the foreground is my alma mater, North Tahoe High School. Beyond the viewpoint, the trail levels off and turns right before it reaches another junction, 1 mile short of Watson Lake. (A left turn here would take you steeply uphill to the top of Mount Watson.)

Continue straight ahead on the TRT on a moderately steep downhill toward Watson Lake. Just before the lake, you reach a gravel road; turn left on this road and follow it uphill. In a short distance, the TRT takes off to the right and skirts the east shore of Watson Lake. While little Watson Lake is pleasant enough, it is shallow, surrounded by trees, and visited by numerous mosquitoes. It can also be heavily used in the summer because it is the only lake between Brockway Summit and Tahoe City and is accessible by car along a paved and gravel road. Be sure to filter any water you get from Watson Lake.

After you pass the lake, with about 12.4 miles under your belt and 6.7 miles to go, the TRT heads about 0.25 mile north to a shallow gully. The trail now descends gently 1.25 miles east, through beautiful wildflower meadows and forested areas, to a road, down which you can head 0.3 mile to usually reliable Watson Creek. You pass several small seep streams that provide water until midsummer. Because these are the last water sources along this section, take advantage of the opportunity if it's still available. Just 0.25 mile east beyond the road, a short (90-yard) spur trail leads off to the right to a large rock pile with another pretty view of Lake Tahoe, specifically Carnelian Bay. Enjoy the view—it's the last full lake view you get before you reach the Brockway Summit Trailhead in about 4.5 miles.

The trail turns north and in 0.8 mile switchbacks down through a thick forest of white fir and Jeffrey pine to a crossing of FR 74, and 100 yards farther crosses FR 75. After a gentle descent northeast for about 0.7 mile, you cross another road, then traverse about 200 yards to yet another. Now you have a fairly gentle climb for 1 mile as the trail takes you through manzanita and chinquapin before it crosses FR 73 (Fiberboard Freeway). There is still more climbing for 1.3 miles until you cross the Fiberboard Freeway one more time. The next 0.7 mile gently descends to the trailhead, located next to CA 267. At this point, you are about 0.5 mile east of Brockway Summit.

Brockway Summit to Mount Rose

20.3 miles

DIFFICULTY With much of this section of the trail rising above 9,000 feet and some of it higher than 10,000 feet in elevation, it is relatively strenuous, especially considering that you start at around 7,000 feet. If you are day hiking this section, it might be easier to begin on the Tahoe Meadows side and hike to Brockway Summit, where your starting elevation is approximately 8,800 feet. As they say, 1,800 feet here and 1,800 feet there, and eventually you are talking about some real elevation gain.

BEST SEASONS The entire trail can be hiked between late July and mid-October. The first 5 miles from the Brockway end can be hiked as early as June, but most of the trail is not free of snow until mid-July. The highest sections of the trail are among the first places to be covered with snow in the fall.

HIGHLIGHTS The middle part of this section is mostly exposed, south-facing volcanic slopes with sandy soils. This wide expanse at a high elevation features tremendous panoramic views of the lake and a wonderful feeling of remoteness. Two small lakes are found on the trail or close to it: small Mud Lake and Gray Lake, a prettier, knee-deep lake that is 0.6 mile off the Rim Trail via an access trail. A lovely waterfall, several streams, awesome high-elevation views, and prolific wildflower displays await you along the last 6 miles of your route.

HEADS UP! Because much of this hike is at high elevation, the air is quite thin, which can cause problems for those unaccustomed to the altitude. If you feel faint, it may be because of reduced oxygen rather than the beauty of the views. Much of the trail is also exposed to cold and wind or to the hot sun. The first 5 miles can be tedious, but the remainder is a wonderful high-altitude experience.

Though you can collect water from several seasonal streams, as well as from Gray Lake and sometimes Mud Lake, the supply is severely limited. There is a small seasonal spring about 50 feet below where the TRT meets the old Western States Trail and Incline Lake Trail after Mud Lake. Gray Lake is about 0.9 mile downhill from a saddle just past Mud Lake, and Mud Lake itself lives up to its name by becoming a mud puddle by late summer. About 2.5 miles from the end of the trail, you'll find water cascading down from Galena Falls.

Those with a fear of heights may find the half mile of trail north of the Relay Peak radio tower quite unnerving.

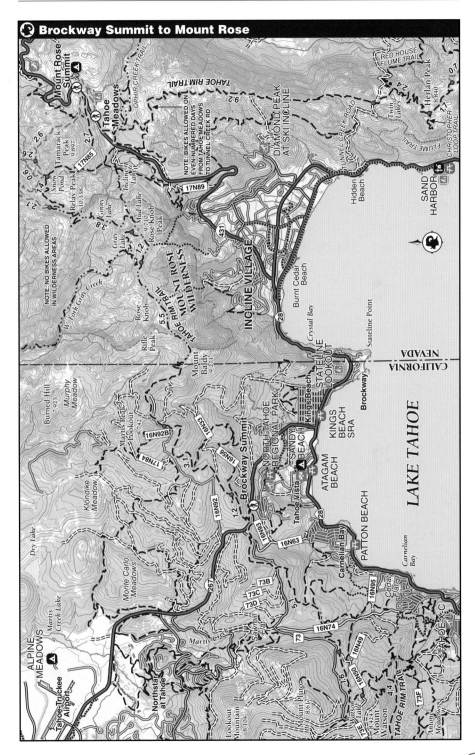

Brockway Summit to Mount Rose

RED HOUSE FLUME TRAIL

Mount Rose Summit

TAHOE RIM TRAIL

OPHIR CREEK TRAIL

Tahoe Meadows

Herlan Peak 8,840'

CHRISTOPHER LOOP TRAIL

FLUME TRAIL

Twin Lakes

Tamarack Peak 9,897'

NOTE: BIKES ALLOWED ON EVEN-NUMBERED DAYS FROM TAHOE MEADOWS TO TUNNEL CREEK RD

17N85

17N89

DIAMOND PEAK AT SKI INCLINE

TUNNEL CREEK ROAD

SAND HARBOR

Hidden Beach

Snow Pond

Relay Peak 10,338'

Incline Lake

Mud Lake

Ginny Lake

Rose Knob Peak 9,710'

431

Gray Lake

W. Fork Gray Creek

MOUNT ROSE WILDERNESS

INCLINE VILLAGE

Burnt Cedar Beach

NOTE: NO BIKES ALLOWED IN WILDERNESS AREAS

Rose Knob

TAHOE RIM TRAIL

28

Crystal Bay

Stateline Point

Rifle Peak

NEVADA

CALIFORNIA

Mount Baldy 9,271'

Burned Hill 7,935'

Murphy Meadow

Martis Peak Lookout 8,742'

STATELINE LOOKOUT

Kings Beach

16N92B

16N93

NORTH TAHOE REGIONAL PARK

Brockway

17N84

16N56

Brockway Summit

SANDY BEACH

KINGS BEACH SRA

LAKE TAHOE

Klondike Meadow

3.1

ATAGAM BEACH

Monte Carlo Meadows

16N92

Tahoe Vista

28

1.2

16N93

PATTON BEACH

Dry Lake

16N63

Carnelian Bay

Carnelian Bay

267

73B

16N95

Cedar Flat

Martis Creek Lake

73C

73D

Sawmill Flat

73

16N74

16N49

ALPINE MEADOWS

Martis Creek

16N50

TAHOE XC

Northstar at Tahoe

Mount Pluto 8,617'

73

16N50

TAHOE RIM TRAIL

73F

Tahoe-Truckee Airport

Lookout Mountain 8,104'

Mount Watson 8,424'

Watson Lake

73E

Antone Meadows

TIPS FOR MOUNTAIN BIKERS If you are looking for a good section of the Tahoe Rim Trail to ride, this is probably not the one to choose. Please do not ride on the portion of this trail that does *not* allow bikes! The soil on that stretch is quite fragile and easily damaged.

From the Brockway Summit side, bikes are allowed for the first 7.6 miles. It begins with a steady, technical, and sometimes steep climb of 4.3 miles to a dirt road. From here you can take a left turn and head back to a quick junction with paved Martis Creek Road. From here, a right turn heads up to the Martis Peak Fire Lookout, with spectacular views north. A left turn on the road heads toward CA 267, which is reached in about 3 miles. Back on the TRT, you could continue to ride, but it gets even steeper and more technical for most riders and may not be worth the effort.

The TRT from the Mount Rose Summit Trailhead has two alternate routes. The first parallels NV 431 for 0.5 mile to a dirt road, where you turn right and ride 2.1 miles to Snow Pond. This route allows mountain bikers and horses. The second route, which begins to the right and above the bike route, allows only hikers. From Snow Pond, it is a moderately steep and rocky uphill ride for 1.5 miles on dirt road to the radio tower, which is the end of the trail for bikers.

GETTING THERE, BROCKWAY TO MOUNT ROSE SUMMIT TRAILHEAD (TAHOE MEADOWS) From the intersection of CA 28 and CA 267 in Kings Beach, drive 2.75 miles northwest up CA 267 toward Brockway Summit to the Tahoe Rim Trail Trailhead. At this point, you will see a parking pullout on the left and a steep dirt road on the right (Forest Service Road 16N56). Park on either side, but this trailhead is on the right (uphill) side. If you reach Brockway Summit at the top of the hill, you have gone 0.5 mile too far.

GETTING THERE, MOUNT ROSE SUMMIT TRAILHEAD TO BROCKWAY From the intersection of NV 431 and NV 28 in Incline Village, take NV 431 (Mount Rose Highway) north past the Tahoe Meadows TRT trailhead and then on to the trailhead just at the summit of the Mount Rose Highway on the left. The Mount Rose Summit Trailhead is 8 miles from Incline Village, and 0.7 mile from the main Tahoe Meadows TRT Trailhead. It is directly across the highway from Mount Rose Campground, which can be a great camping spot for thru-hikers or a way station the night before you begin your TRT hike.

ALTERNATIVE ROUTES The Mount Rose Trailhead also accesses the popular trail to the top of Mount Rose, as well as the lightly used but beautiful Rim to

Reno Trail (see sidebar, page 85), which allows hikers to travel from the outskirts of Reno through the Mount Rose Wilderness to the Mount Rose Trail and the Mount Rose Summit Trailhead.

Trail Description

FROM THE BROCKWAY TRAILHEAD, cross the busy road carefully if you are parked on the south side of CA 267, and follow the dirt road uphill (east) 300 feet to the trail and trailhead sign. The trail leads left into the trees. This first section is no-nonsense, fairly steep, with occasional views of the lake as you switchback through a forest of newer-growth Jeffrey pines and white firs. Walk quickly to escape the drone of automobile traffic from the road below. After about 0.5 mile, the views get better as you pass through an area of manzanita and squaw carpet. In early summer you will also encounter numerous wildflowers. Listen closely and you may hear the mating call of a blue grouse; it sounds like a bass drum: "*brrrm, brrrm, brrrm.*" After about 1 mile of steady climbing, you reach a junction at 1.2 miles from the trailhead (see Side Trip "View from a Rock," right).

The TRT continues northeast on a ridge, descending briefly before leveling off. Here the path becomes more open, with fewer, more scattered trees, along with mule-ears. About 0.7 mile past the spur trail, you cross a gravel road (Forest Service Road 16N33) about 450 feet east of its junction with paved Martis Peak Road. You head up again gently and then go downhill briefly to a small grassy opening with early-summer flowers and a streamlet providing water in the springtime.

Next, head steeply up again through a forest that is transitioning from Jeffrey pines and white firs to the higher-altitude lodgepole pines and red firs. The air is thick with the pungent cinnamon aroma of tobacco brush. Your climb eases, and you come out of the forest into a huge field of equally aromatic mule-ears. Continuing uphill, you leave the thick forest, and the scenery changes dramatically. You reach an open rock pile, almost 4 miles from

SIDE TRIP
View from a Rock

On your left is a short spur trail, which heads 0.3 mile up to a pile of rocks that looks as though it was part of a set for *The Flintstones*. From atop the rocks, you get great lake views to the south and mountain views to the north and west. This is a very popular summertime spot to catch the last rays of the sun, and if you are camping, it's a good spot to see the sunrise.

the trailhead, that hosts dramatic views to the south of Lake Tahoe. Looking south across the lake, you can see (clockwise from east to west) Snow Valley Peak (9,914'), the highest peak above the east shore; Jobs Sister (10,823'); Freel Peak (10,881'); South Lake Tahoe; Mount Tallac (9,735'); Desolation Wilderness and the Crystal Range; Twin Peaks (8,878') above the west shore; and finally Squaw Valley and Northstar. Freel Peak and Jobs Sister are the two highest peaks in the Tahoe Basin. (If you continue on the TRT another 70 miles, you will walk just below Freel Peak as you cross a saddle at 9,730 feet.) If you enjoy sitting in the sunshine while eating your lunch, this south-facing spot may be just the ticket. On September 22, 2001, this viewpoint was the location for the official opening dedication ceremony for the TRT. It also starred as the cover photo for the first edition of this guidebook.

SIDE TRIP
Martis Peak Lookout

A left turn on this dirt road takes you to the Martis Peak (8,742') lookout. To get there, go 0.2 mile and then turn right and take the paved road 0.7 mile up to the lookout at 8,656'. To the south, you will see excellent views of most of Lake Tahoe and the crest that rims it, and to the north, most of the lands from the Donner Pass and Lake environs east into western Nevada.

When you can drag yourself away from the panoramic views of the lake, continue up rocky terrain along the edge of a ridge. You will have a clear view of Mount Baldy to the east and the beautiful aspen groves along its flanks. With Mount Baldy as your goal, you pass a rocky viewpoint to your right and a field full of mule-ears to your left, before heading back into the woods again briefly and reaching an access trail to a major dirt road at 4.3 miles in from your trailhead (see Side Trip "Martis Peak Lookout," above).

This dirt road makes a good alternative trailhead for those who would like to hike 16, instead of 20, miles. Because it sits at 8,400 feet, you can also eliminate 1,400 feet of climbing by beginning here. To access the road from CA 267, turn right on Martis Peak Road, which is about 0.5 mile north of Brockway Summit. Follow this paved but somewhat potholed road as it climbs up and up, and at a big left turn 3 miles in, the dirt road heads straight ahead. Go about 0.2 mile to the trailhead on your right.

From this road-access junction, the TRT turns right and follows new singletrack trail built in 2018. Hikers used to have to hike about a half mile on that dusty dirt road. Now the trail gently descends east through a thick forest of red fir, passes over a rocky OHV road, and then reaches a junction with the old trail at 0.6 mile from the access trail.

Here the TRT turns right and continues east through forest and alternating open rocky sections and in 0.5 mile reaches a saddle with views north. The tree composition is transitioning again, with more red firs and occasional junipers, western white pines, and the first hemlocks you see on this section. Your climb becomes steeper as you switchback 0.3 mile up to a ridgeline that has views into a large U-shaped valley, the drainage area for Juniper Creek, which empties into the Truckee River.

After about a 300-yard traverse southeast on the ridgeline, the trail angles south for a 0.4-mile traverse of gentle slopes to a road; from here, the trail ascends 0.2 mile south to the road's end and the resumption of trail tread. In less than 0.5 mile you climb first moderately southeast and then moderately northeast up to the ridgeline. There's a great view here, but even more superlative ones lie ahead. Just 0.2 mile south you reach a low rock pile immediately west of the trail that has dramatic views of almost the entire lake to the south and of the mountains to the west and east. In addition, there are great views to the north; you can see Castle Peak, Donner Lake, the town of Truckee, and Boca and Stampede Reservoirs. This is one of the best views on the entire Tahoe Rim Trail and is just the beginning of an extravaganza of Lake Tahoe views over the next 4 miles.

Lake Tahoe

From this view, you are now about 6.8 miles from the Brockway Summit Trailhead. The TRT goes briefly east to the ridgeline, where you cross into Nevada. (This is a good place to turn around if you are on a bike.) As the trees get smaller and fewer, and you get higher, now above 9,000 feet, the ridgeline area opens up. Only the hardiest trees, such as lodgepole, western white, and whitebark pine, grow here. On the north-facing slopes below and also east of you, snow may last well into the summer.

After climbing moderately southeast 0.5 mile up the ridgeline, the TRT angles northeast, traversing just under a minor summit on a high ridge, which is 9,271-foot Mount Baldy. Just past it, you enter the Mount Rose Wilderness. At about 7.6 miles from the trailhead, this is the end of the section of trail permissible to mountain bikes. Bike riding is not allowed in the wilderness. (A better place to turn around is the viewpoint you just passed or where the trail met the dirt road, 4.3 miles from the Brockway Trailhead.)

Now you traverse the side of an open, southeast-facing slope with incredible expansive views to the south and east of Lake Tahoe, Incline Village, and beyond. For the next 2 miles, with the exception of a brief uphill foray into

SIDE TRIP Gray Lake

While the old Gray Lake Trail began on a steep, north-facing, potentially dangerous slope, a new trail built in 2011 starts out on a level section of ridge and descends gently through a grove of hemlocks—great job, trail builders. It then makes a meandering, gentle descent 0.6 mile northeast down to clear but knee-deep Gray Lake, where a loop trail around the lake provides access to excellent campsites above its north shore. A beautiful mountain stream leads past lush wildflowers into the lake from the huge rockfall below Rose Knob and then drains out of the lake near the lake's biggest campsite.

Although in early and midsummer the lake can be a haven for mosquitoes, in the fall it is a pleasant and quiet place to relax. At 9,043 feet, this lake with marshy surroundings is quite fragile; take extra care not to damage the plants near the water. Note the especially large lodge-

pole and whitebark pines and hemlocks in this idyllic setting. Also of note, with its very shallow depth and location in a high-altitude bowl, Gray Lake sometimes has ice on its surface well before you would see ice anywhere else—one time when I visited on a cold August morning. As the only dependable lake between Watson Lake and Star Lake, Gray Lake is well worth a stop.

From Gray Lake a rebuilt trail takes you back to an intersection with the TRT above Mud Lake. The former very steep 0.5-mile trail has been replaced by a well-laid-out 0.9-mile climb that takes full advantage of the views by climbing through the enormous talus field below Rose Knob. Why not visit Mud Lake, which is just below us to the right from the Gray Lake Trail junction with the TRT? Here's why: Mud Lake lives up to its name. In late summer it gets quite small before sometimes disappearing altogether.

Lush meadows surround Gray Lake.

the forest, you walk beneath a volcanic ridge eastward on a gentle ascent over wonderful light-brown, sandy soil through huge open fields of mule-ears. Views of the lake are truly glorious, with almost the entire lake displayed before you. It is a real highlight of the Tahoe Rim Trail, and considering how far you are from either the Tahoe Meadows or Brockway Summit Trailheads, you may even have it all to yourself.

About midway on your northeast traverse, you pass just beneath a steep-sided 9,499-foot summit, behind which lies unseen, flat-topped Rifle Peak. In 0.5 mile you traverse beneath pyramidal Rose Knob, and then in another 0.7 mile reach a junction. At about 10 miles from the Brockway Summit Trailhead, you have reached the access trail to Gray Lake (see Side Trip "Gray Lake," opposite).

From its first junction with the Gray Lake Trail, the TRT stays high and continues straight ahead (east) across south-facing slopes toward Rose Knob (9,710'), an impressive pile of volcanic rock with three distinct pointy peaks. After a 0.5-mile traverse across slopes, the TRT crosses a saddle with clusters of whitebark pines and then soon climbs 0.25 mile southeast, where it passes beneath the southernmost summit of Rose Knob. Then the trail rounds the bend and travels northeast across talus on the south-facing side of the mountain.

This rocky section was one of the last parts of the trail to be completed, and one of the most difficult to build. The trail builders have constructed formidable rock walls and created a fairly smooth trail through the talus field. As you go around the mountain, you once again enjoy magnificent views of almost the entire lake. After a 0.3-mile traverse mostly across talus, the trail

High above Lake Tahoe between Mud Lake and Relay Peak

angles north and contours over to a saddle above Mud Lake; this stretch has a few scattered mountain hemlocks. At the east edge of the saddle is a junction with the Gray Lake Trail, about 11.2 miles from the Brockway Summit Trailhead and 9 miles from the Mount Rose Summit Trailhead.

From the saddle between Mud Lake and Gray Lake, the Tahoe Rim Trail goes right (southeast) and descends gently 0.25 mile on an open slope above Mud Lake, with additional spectacular views all the way to Fallen Leaf Lake at the far end of Lake Tahoe, in the distance to the south. The TRT then traverses 0.25 mile northeast, exchanging volcanic tread for granite (to be followed shortly by more volcanic tread briefly before returning to granite). You reach a junction with the Incline Lake Trail and former Western States Trail (see Side Trip "Incline Lake Trail," opposite).

About 50 feet below this junction, near some willows, is a small spring that can provide water for most of the season. After the snow melts, this is your last source for water until you get to Galena Falls, about 6 miles away. You could also head downhill steeply about a half mile for water on the Incline Lake Trail.

With about 8 miles remaining, start up the TRT on a series of short switchbacks. You soon traverse just below a dramatic, large red-and-black volcanic rock at the top of a ridge. The trail passes just below and to the east of this rock and climbs slightly to the north-facing side of the mountain about 0.75 mile past the Gray Lake junction. Below is Ginny Lake, and in the distance are Tahoe Meadows, the Mount Rose Highway, and Mount Rose itself. You now

SIDE TRIP Incline Lake Trail

Incline Lake once was a small lake visible from the old TRT (road) to Snow Pond, which headed up from Tahoe Meadows. Access into the area of private homes, however, was prohibited. More important, access to this trail, which in just 2 miles goes from Tahoe Meadows to the Tahoe Rim Trail near Gray Lake, was private as well. Now the U.S. Forest Service owns the land, which opens up lots of wonderful opportunities for hiking in the area. After acquiring the property, the Forest Service removed the dam, so Incline Lake is more likely to be a meadow than a lake when you see it (although after big winters it can still look lakelike).

The Incline Lake Trailhead is on the north side of NV 431, across the busy highway from the Ophir Creek Trail, right at the edge of Tahoe Meadows. You begin by walking past the gate to an aspen-lined, paved road, which in a half mile leads to a big left turn where the trail begins on the right with a short downhill to a creek crossing. Then a 1.5-mile ascent begins. While the trail is quite steep at times, you walk through some of the largest ancient western white pines, hemlocks, and lodgepoles that I have seen. In the last half mile you cross another stream, pass the Mount Rose Wilderness boundary, and reach a saddle with great views of Lake Tahoe. A short, easy descent brings you to the TRT at its low point between Mud Lake and Relay Peak.

Via the Incline Lake Trail, you can hike to Gray Lake, loop around Rose Knob, and return to your car at Tahoe Meadows in just 8 miles. You can also turn right where the Incline Lake Trail meets the TRT, climb up to Relay Peak, follow the trail past the waterfall to the Mount Rose Summit Trailhead, and then cross Tahoe Meadows back to the Incline Lake Trailhead. This 12-mile loop provides a tremendous amount of hiking bang for your buck.

traverse slightly uphill across the north-facing slope to a saddle just below a granite ridge. Here you have crossed a steep slope that is covered in snow most of the year—take care if the pathway is icy. The terrain is spectacular, with several large craggy volcanic rocks towering above and a hemlock forest below.

At the saddle, you now face your second 800-foot climb; the first was up to the wilderness boundary below Mount Baldy. The imposing massif straight ahead would be formidable if tackled head-on, but fortunately the TRT avoids that, and the climb is exceptionally well graded. From the saddle the TRT has several short switchbacks up among granite boulders, and then it jogs east then west. Here it climbs 0.6 mile north with abundant views to a switchback just above the east end of a west-trending ridge that climbs to the summit of Relay Peak. Along this ascent, Clark's nutcrackers flit between the scattered gnarled whitebark and western white pines.

From the switchback, huge panoramic views open up to the west of Castle Peak, Donner Lake, and the Truckee area and to the south in the distance of Freel Peak above Lake Tahoe. From your vantage point, you also have closer views: west down the gaping West Fork Gray Creek Canyon, a close-up of the

Mount Rose through the hemlocks

nearby Slab Cliffs, northwest down equally gaping Gray Creek Canyon, and northeast to a radio-towered peak.

From this switchback, where snow can linger well into July, you are about halfway up your major ascent. The TRT climbs 0.5 mile southeast up volcanic slopes, and you surpass 10,000 feet in elevation before you reach a switchback that has poor views. You now have two shorter switchback legs to Relay Peak, the highest point on the entire Tahoe Rim Trail, at 10,338 feet in elevation. On a clear day you can see all the way to Lassen Peak and, rumor has it, Mount Shasta if the day is crystal clear. The panorama seems unlimited as dozens of narrow valleys and ridgelines unfold before you. Much of what you see in the foreground is the Mount Rose Wilderness. Mount Rose (10,776') itself stands out to the northeast in its full volcanic relief. At sunset, the mountain certainly lives up to its name as it takes on a beautiful rosy hue. To the east-southeast, beyond Tahoe Meadows and the Ophir Creek Canyon, lies large Washoe Lake.

From Relay Peak your trail now merges with an abandoned dirt road that heads downhill steeply north along the ridgeline to a relay microwave tower developed by AT&T. Although the top of the ridgeline provides an excellent location for receiving radio waves, it is unfortunate to see a large, ugly tower in this incredibly beautiful location. Near the tower you reach a junction with a broad gravel road, which is still used by vehicles for administrative purposes. Over the next 5 miles you will encounter a number of junctions and trail options. The good news is that recent trail building in the area has provided some great options for loops in the Mount Rose and Tahoe Meadows area.

The bad news is that it may be a bit of a challenge to keep track of it all. Listen closely and use a map.

OLD TRT: If you turn right on this broad utility road you will be on the old Tahoe Rim Trail and the section that allows bikes. You descend 0.3 mile south to a switchback and then 0.5 mile north to a bend east, where you pass an old equipment lift. Before the road to the top of the ridge was built, this lift was constructed as a means to bring the building materials necessary for the relay tower to the top of the mountain; later the lift was used to access the tower during extreme winter periods when snowcats were unable to make the trip to the top. The road descends into a big open bowl with scattered stunted white-bark pine trees. In the winter this area is quite popular with skiers, snowshoers, and snowmobilers.

Now, after 1.4 miles of moderately steep downhill on the road, you reach a small pond, known both as Snow Pond (because it is covered in snow much of the year) and as Frog Pond. Off to the left a trail quickly accesses the main TRT (or new TRT), which allows only hikers. On the Old TRT/Bike Route about 1 mile past the pond, you get full views of the meadow formerly known

Snow Pond/Frog Pond with Relay Peak, the TRT's highest point, in the background

as Incline Lake, Lake Tahoe, and Tahoe Meadows. Far below, the next section of the TRT can look like a brown snake wandering through the deep green of Tahoe Meadows.

The views remain panoramic and inspiring as the road continues gently downhill, passing plenty of early-summer wildflowers on its way to a junction with a singletrack trail at about 2.1 miles from the Snow Pond. Here the trail turns left and traverses gently uphill to the Mount Rose Summit Trailhead. (If you stay on the dirt road straight ahead, you will quickly reach NV 431, where you can turn left and go 0.3 mile to the Mount Rose Summit Trailhead, or turn right and go 0.4 mile to the Tahoe Meadows Trailhead.)

NEW TRT: The new TRT, or main TRT, turns left at the junction with the utility road and follows the ridgeline to the north of the Relay Tower. Here the trail is narrow and hugs the steep, north-facing slope. In addition to bikes, horses are not allowed, and those who have a fear of heights, like your fearless writer, will find this section not a lot of fun. I've been told you pass scattered whitebark pines and are treated to breathtaking views of the Mount Rose Wilderness, but I was too busy watching my footing and sweating profusely to look up and enjoy them. After a short, level traverse, the trail then climbs for a short distance before reaching a junction at about 0.5 mile from the junction at the Mount Rose Wilderness boundary. Here an out-and-back trail climbs to the top of Mount Houghton (see Side Trip "Mount Houghton," left).

From the junction with the Mount Houghton Trail, the TRT starts heading downhill on a long traverse across open ridgeline. Below the trail are terraces built more than a half century ago in an effort to control flooding and slow the melting of snow.

You pass scattered whitebark pines, aromatic pennyroyal, and ground lupine before reaching a switchback, which is just before a deep gully and a large black volcanic rock formation. Now the trail heads gently down to the west, with

SIDE TRIP
Mount Houghton

Although Mount Houghton is more of a high point on a ridge than a true mountain, the views and the interesting lichen-covered rocks on the way up are certainly worth the trip. After a moderate climb of about 0.75 mile, you reach the summit, where views of the Bronco Creek drainage and the whole of the Mount Rose Wilderness unfold before you to the north. From here you can wander east along the pleasantly gentle ridgetop until you reach a steep drop into a cirque. Far below is the saddle of the Mount Rose Trail and the trail to the Mount Rose Summit. Once you've enjoyed the view, retrace your steps back to the TRT.

Galena Falls

more open views all the way south to Freel Peak above Lake Tahoe's south shore. You reach an interesting jumble of volcanic boulders where a small spring feeds a charming garden of flowers, including rock fringe.

Past the spring, you roll in and out of little gullies before the trail turns east, the grade eases, and hemlocks start to appear. Look for a few flat potential tent sites before you hit a dirt road and a junction. From here, a right takes you 100 yards to the former TRT that comes down from Relay Peak. From there a left takes you past Snow Pond on the dirt road to the Mount Rose Summit Trailhead in about 3 miles. At the junction, instead of turning right and heading to the old TRT, you could turn left to follow an old road that descends 0.7 mile, past a stream and wildflowers, to meet the Mount Rose Summit Trail.

The main TRT is straight ahead, crossing the faint road and heading toward Galena Falls through forest. It starts out fairly level and then becomes a gentle descent through whitebark pines. There are several level campsites above the trail. To your left you see meadows and Mount Rose looming high above. At an open area with flat rocks, you can sit a spell and gaze up at the Relay Peak towers and see where you have been the last 2 miles. The trail soon reaches the top of Galena Falls, where flat rocks make an enticing spot to lie back and enjoy the views and the sound of cascading water. The water for these falls springs out of the ground a few hundred yards upstream. Until now, this section of trail has been lightly used, but expect crowds from here on. The Mount Rose Trailhead is one of the busiest in Nevada, and the bulk of the folks hike the easy 2.5 miles from the Mount Rose Highway to the falls.

From here the trail switchbacks down through thick hemlock forest to the bottom of the falls and another trail junction. If there is a shortcoming with the TRT, it is a lack of water, especially on the east side of the lake, so take a minute to relax by these glorious falls while deciding where to head next. For a special experience, come here in the autumn, when low temperatures create a border of ice on both sides of the falls.

If you turn left (north) at the falls, you are now on the Mount Rose Summit Trail, which quickly crosses Galena Creek and then skirts a meadow, before a gentle rise brings you across another creek and to a junction. Here a right turn takes you up to the top of Mount Rose (see Side Trip "Mount Rose," below). A left turn takes you over the creek you just crossed and then on a moderately steep ascent past a wonderful display of midsummer wildflowers. You reach the junction with the TRT that descends from Relay Peak in 0.7 mile. Going straight here would take you quickly to the Relay Peak dirt road and Snow Pond.

SIDE TRIP Mount Rose

From the junction of the TRT and Mount Rose Summit Trail, you can climb 2.6 miles and 1,700 feet to summit Mount Rose, the Tahoe area's third-highest peak. If you are up for a good climb, it is worth it, as the views along the way and at the top are extraordinary. Mount Rose is unique in several ways and has a superb "garden" of alpine plants, including the woody fruited evening primrose, found almost exclusively on this mountain's slopes. This low-lying plant produces one or more large yellow blossoms on short stalks close to the ground. The flowers, which are pollinated by nocturnal moths and then die shortly afterward, smell like coconuts.

Mount Rose also seems to have its own weather pattern. Often you can hike in shorts and a short-sleeve shirt until the last, treeless 0.5 mile, where you encounter fierce winds and chilling temperatures. During a major winter blizzard, the top of Mount Rose must be truly frightening. The easiest way to the top is to start at the Mount Rose Summit Trailhead, which makes for a 10-mile round-trip with a little less than 2,000 feet of climbing.

Back at the falls, note the first of several avalanche pathways you'll cross over the next 2 miles on your right as you begin your walk. The TRT goes straight ahead (southeast) and circles above a large meadow. It then continues on a gently rising traverse below the slopes of beautiful, volcanic Tamarack Peak. The well-laid-out trail passes some awesome views of both Mount Rose and Tamarack Lake.

At about 2 miles from Galena Falls, a wide panorama of Lake Tahoe and Tahoe Meadows opens up before a gentle downhill traverse to the Mount Rose Summit Trailhead. This trailhead facility is located at the very top of the Mount Rose Highway, across the street from the Mount Rose Campground. It has pit toilets and parking. Thru-hikers can cross the highway to the campground, walk along the paved road about a quarter mile, and then hike an almost level 0.8 mile on the Tahoe Meadows Interpretive Trail to the Tahoe Meadows Trailhead.

From near 10,000 feet looking toward Slide Mountain

Rim to Reno Trail

The Rim to Reno Trail (R2R Trail) connects the Tahoe Rim Trail and the outskirts of Reno at the Thomas Creek Trail. The 21-mile trail ranges in elevation from 5,900 feet to nearly 10,000 feet and travels through the heart of the Mount Rose Wilderness. Although the R2R Trail shares 4 miles with the Mount Rose Summit Trail, one of the busiest trails in Nevada, once you leave the Mount Rose Summit Trail, the R2R is lightly used; in fact, please go hike it to keep it from disappearing.

Would you prefer 4,000 feet of climbing or descent? Which is stronger, your lungs or your knees? If you are a climber, start at Thomas Creek and head up, but most will start at the TRT Mount Rose Summit Trailhead. After 4 miles of hiking on the Mount Rose Summit Trail, you reach a saddle. Here the R2R heads straight ahead, while the trail to the summit of Mount Rose takes a right.

From the saddle, the R2R meanders through a lovely bowl down to Bronco Creek. As the last source of water until Thomas Creek, this is the place to get your water and to camp. After the creek, a long ascent heads up to a 9,700-foot ridge. The slopes are open, and the views back to Mount Rose and Mount Houghton are sublime. You are now officially in the middle of nowhere, and it is here that the Mount Rose Wilderness really lives up to its "wild" name.

The trail then heads into a several-miles-long, level traverse through a thick forest before reaching a junction at 11 miles into the hike. Here you can take the North or South Loop, but the North one is 2 miles longer. On the South Loop, the trail switchbacks to the ridgecrest and then begins a 9-mile steady downhill to Thomas Creek. If you time it right, you will be treated to a plethora of wildflowers and some awesome rock formations, but it is still an interminable downhill to the trailhead, which is finally assuaged by the sound of running water at Thomas Creek. Sorry, your feet may be tired, but you still have quite a bit of walking through aspen groves along the creek before finally reaching the trailhead at the edge of the desert.

Trail Directions: The TRT–Mount Rose Summit Trailhead is located at the top of the Mount Rose Highway (NV 431), 17 miles west of US 395/I-580 and 8 miles northeast of Incline Village. The Thomas Creek Trailhead is located on Timberline Drive off NV 431, about 1 mile east of the Galena Creek Visitor Center and about 5 miles southwest of the intersection of I-580, US 395, and NV431 near the Summit shopping center south of Reno.

Tahoe Meadows to Spooner Summit

23.1 miles

DIFFICULTY This section is strenuous, mostly because of how long it is, but also because of the elevation gain. While the trail starts at 8,740 feet and ends at about 7,140 feet, there are two portions of the trail where you encounter climbs of more than 700 feet. In the opposite direction, the climb from Spooner Summit to just below Snow Valley Peak is about 1,800 feet.

BEST SEASONS It is best to hike this section of the trail between mid-June and late October. The segment between Spooner Summit and Snow Valley Peak may be open as early as mid-May in years with light snowfall. However, the section between Twin Lakes and Snow Valley Peak may hold snow well into July.

HIGHLIGHTS There are spectacular vistas of Lake Tahoe along much of this section of trail. Some of these are among the most stunning views to be found anywhere along the Tahoe Rim Trail. In particular, the Christopher Loop (Herlan Peak) spur trail offers especially remarkable vistas. The trail provides views on both sides of this north-to-south-oriented ridge, of Lake Tahoe to the west, and of the Great Basin to the east. While the thin decomposed-granite soils along the trail limit wildflower growth, several locations have flowers in abundance. This is especially the case if you take a side trip down to Marlette Lake, where the wildflower display is one of the best to be found anywhere. If you are looking for yellow and orange aspen leaves, it is hard to beat the bounty of leaves at Snow Valley, Marlette Lake, and Spooner Lake.

Much of this section of trail can be covered on a mountain bike and, for the expert rider, affords some of the best mountain biking at Lake Tahoe. This section of trail is home to the Tahoe Mountain Milers Running Club's Tahoe Rim Trail 50K, 50-mile, and 100-mile endurance runs that occur in July. As the event's slogan says, it truly is a glimpse of heaven and a taste of hell. For more information, go to tahoemtnmilers.org.

HEADS UP! There is very little water available on this section of trail. Bring some along for your dog. About 0.7 mile beyond the Tahoe Meadows Trailhead, you cross Ophir Creek, a beautiful little stream. At around mile 3 you pass two unreliable seasonal springs. At about 9.5 miles from the trailhead, you reach the Twin Lakes. These two small, very shallow lakes may dry up by late summer; as they shrink, the water becomes less attractive and takes on a

Tahoe Meadows to Spooner Summit

NOTE: BIKES ALLOWED ON
EVEN-NUMBERED DAYS
FROM TAHOE MEADOWS
TO TUNNEL CREEK RD

NOTE: NO BIKES ALLOWED
FROM SPOONER SUMMIT
TO NORTH CANYON ROAD

LAKE TAHOE

Competitors in the Tahoe Mountain Milers Running Club's Tahoe Rim Trail 100-mile endurance run near Snow Valley Peak

green hue. The hand-pump well at Marlette Campground, 13.8 miles from Tahoe Meadows, is the best source for water on this section. Another source is Spooner Lake, near Spooner Summit.

If you're thru-hiking, note that there are no trailside sources of water on the next 12 miles south of Spooner Summit. Obtain water at Spooner Lake unless you have made prior arrangements for water to be delivered to you. Although Spooner Lake's water itself looks marshy, you can also walk over to the Spooner Lake parking lot above the lake. Here you will find tap water and restrooms. You will see Marlette Lake from the trail. If you are thirsty or looking for a swim, it may be a worthwhile detour. From the intersection of the TRT and Hobart Road, it is 1.75 miles to the lake, mostly a steep downhill. About 0.75 mile down, where two gullies converge, there is a usually reliable stream.

Most of the trail is exposed to the sun and wind, so bring extra water, extra clothing, and lots of sunscreen. Camping is allowed only in two locations. One site, Marlette Peak Campground, is along the TRT near Marlette Peak, about 13 miles south of the Mount Rose Summit Trailhead; the second campsite is along North Canyon Road. At a minor saddle, just before you reach Snow Valley Peak, take a dirt road 1.2 miles steeply down to North Canyon Road. Turn left and go about 1 mile south down to North Canyon

Campground, just east above the road. All you will see is an outhouse, with campsites behind it, out of view from the road. Get water from the stream just west of the road. You can also continue on the TRT, past Snow Valley Peak an additional 1.7 miles, to a signed junction with a connector trail, which heads downhill 1.4 miles to the campground.

TIPS FOR MOUNTAIN BIKERS For the experienced mountain biker, this section of trail is perhaps the finest section on the entire Tahoe Rim Trail. It is best to ride from north to south. The U. S. Forest Service has ruled that mountain bikers should use the northernmost 9.2 miles of this section of trail (from Mount Rose Highway to Tunnel Creek Road) only on even-numbered days of the month so that hikers may experience the trail without bikers on the odd-numbered days. On an even-numbered weekend day in the middle of the summer, be prepared to see as many as 100 bikes.

Marlette Lake and Lake Tahoe from the saddle below Snow Valley Peak

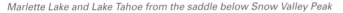

After an initial fun ride across the meadow and then along the old Ophir Creek Trail, you turn right and climb to a saddle. Then it is a wonderful, sometimes challenging ride, mostly downhill, for the next 8 miles to Tunnel Creek Road. The trail is sandy and soft in some sections, but in most places it is firm and a real pleasure to ride. Some will feel challenged by portions of the trail; for most, the trouble is well rewarded.

At Tunnel Creek Road you can turn right and ride downhill 3 miles to NV 28, where you can have a car shuttle awaiting you. You could also meet the Tahoe East Shore Trail at the lake. This 3-mile bike trail provides access to Sand Harbor State Park as well as some spectacular swimming beaches along the route.

Or you can cross Tunnel Creek Road and head a short distance to Twin Lakes. The next few miles after Twin Lakes are a challenging, steep uphill ride but worth the effort, as they eventually lead to spectacular views of Marlette Lake and Lake Tahoe. When you reach Hobart Road, turn right. Bikes are *not* allowed on the rest of this section of the TRT. Hobart Road takes you down to Marlette Lake, where you follow North Canyon Road out to the parking lot at Lake Tahoe Nevada State Park, where fees are required for parking or for riding through the park.

GETTING THERE, NV 431 (MOUNT ROSE HIGHWAY) TO SPOONER SUMMIT The trailhead is 7.3 miles north on NV 431 (toward Reno) from the junction of NV 28 and NV 431 in Incline Village. You will drive past Tahoe Meadows to a parking area and restroom facility on your right. The trail starts from the western edge of the lower parking lot. From Reno, this trailhead is found about 0.75 mile after the highway tops the Mount Rose Summit.

GETTING THERE, SPOONER SUMMIT TO NV 431 (MOUNT ROSE HIGHWAY) From Tahoe City you travel 27 miles east on CA/NV 28 to reach the junction with US 50. Turn left on US 50, and drive 0.7 mile to the trailhead on the north (left) side of the road (approximately 14 miles northeast of South Lake Tahoe on US 50). There is a small paved parking area on the north side of the highway, situated across from a larger paved parking lot, which provides access to the southbound TRT. It is important to realize that Spooner Summit is not the same as Spooner Lake. Spooner Lake is about 0.5 mile west of the junction of US 50 and NV 28 on NV 28. Entrance to the popular Spooner Lake area (with access to the Flume Trail) requires a fee; to reach it, drive 0.6 mile northwest from the junction.

Trail Description

FROM NV 431, known locally as the Mount Rose Highway, the southbound TRT runs parallel to the highway, descends past several streamlets, and then crosses through the middle of Tahoe Meadows, a large subalpine area that can be muddy in June or a wonderful wildflower tramp in July. Stay on the trail to avoid damaging the fragile meadow ecosystem. Near the south edge of the meadow, a bridge crosses Ophir Creek, a charming year-round stream bordered by elephant's heads, lupines, and other wildflowers. Except for the fact that you just left the trailhead 0.75 mile ago, it would be the best source for water on this section of trail. After crossing Ophir Creek on the wide bridge, the trail heads into a forest of lodgepole and whitebark pines and meets the Ophir Creek Trail, where you turn left (south). For the next 0.2 mile, you are walking past lodgepole pines on a smooth, wide trail. You soon see to the left Tahoe Meadows and the radio towers atop Slide Mountain before the trail meets a junction 1 mile from the trailhead. For information on the network of trails heading out from the Ophir Creek Bridge, refer to the side trip "Tahoe Meadows," right.

Straight ahead is the Ophir Creek Trail. It starts out level in the lodgepole forest and then heads downhill, sometimes steeply, past prolific groves of aspen trees and western white pines to the back side of Slide Mountain.

In 3 miles on the Ophir Creek Trail you reach what remains of Upper Price Lake, which was significantly reduced in size by a landslide in 1983. This is a great trail for fall colors and to see how Slide Mountain got its name. It also seems to be a very popular area for hang gliders. One beautiful fall day I sat mesmerized by the antics of eight gliders riding the thermals above Slide Mountain. Eventually, after a lot of descent, you reach Davis Creek County Park in 7 miles, although most will find the venture to Upper Price Lake and back a better way to spend their time.

> **SIDE TRIP**
> **Tahoe Meadows**
>
> Three interconnected loop trails let hikers access the beauty of Tahoe Meadows. These are popular, easy hikes for families and people with dogs. The longest of the trails is 3 miles, with about half in the trees using the Tahoe Rim Trail and Ophir Creek Trail, and the other half on the edge of the meadow, where you can hear and see the creek. A section of the trail near the TRT bridge is on boardwalk, which protects the fragile meadow from damage while also allowing walkers to get very close to the narrow but deep creek. A connector trail travels along the east side of the creek directly from the TRT to NV 431, providing a shorter route to the meadow trails. There is a map of the different routes adjacent to the bridge.

The TRT turns right and starts a gentle climb south up the sandy surface past more scattered lodgepole pines and occasional western white and whitebark pines. Exposed to high winds and heavy snows on this north-facing slope, the trees are smaller than those you will see later on the south-facing side of the ridge. To the north you can see the rose-colored top of Mount Rose.

At 1.7 miles from the trailhead, you reach a saddle, about 250 feet above the Ophir Creek Trail. This area is informally known as Chickadee Ridge because during the winter months chickadees enjoy begging for food right from the palms of the snowshoers and skiers who inundate the area. Here you get your first views of Lake Tahoe through the vegetation. The views keep getting better and better as the miles go by. Now your pathway is along a long, north–south-oriented ridge for the next 7.5 miles, going in and out of the tops of east–west-oriented gullies. Along the route you will experience numerous gentle ups and downs and from the saddle have an overall drop in altitude of about 900 feet to Tunnel Creek Road.

The first mile past the saddle is a gentle, sandy contour along the western slope of the ridge. You pass scattered white granite boulders, appearing as if they were tossed there haphazardly by a giant playing with rocks. Lodgepole pines are now fewer and larger, and there are some impressively large western white pines, with their long, narrow cones hanging from the top. Some may mistake the western white pines for sugar pines, but the sugar pine's cones are quite a bit larger, and sugar pines are usually found at lower elevations. At 2.5 miles from the trailhead, you cross the head of a gully; here the trail changes from its eastern direction to a southern direction. You see a wide view of the lake, looking toward Emerald Bay and Mount Tallac. Several large, flat granite boulders just below the trail make this a great spot to sit and enjoy the views.

Next you ascend gently and enjoy more views of the lake looking toward the Nevada–California border, which lies on a large peninsula jutting straight south into the lake. Soon, about 3 miles from the trailhead, you reach two spring-fed streamlets and colorful, lush vegetation, which provide a cool break from the dry, sandy terrain that surrounds the area. The trail next winds up and down past a few hemlock trees before reaching another saddle, 3.6 miles from the trailhead, with views of Mount Rose to the north. You then begin a short, moderately steep descent over a number of evenly spaced granite steps (a joy for the experienced mountain biker), followed by a short climb to another viewpoint.

Every half mile you walk provides an even wider and more beautiful view of the lake. On a clear, windy day, the wind ripples shimmer in the sun as the lake turns a deep blue. At a little more than 4 miles from the trailhead, your trail now crosses to the east-facing side of the ridge, passing a flat opening with stumps from ancient logging. Here you get your first glimpse of Washoe Lake and the Great Basin to the east. A gentle descent leads to a wider opening with a view of all of Washoe Lake.

At 4.6 miles from your Tahoe Meadows Trailhead, you go southwest, gently uphill, followed by a moderate descent, back to the west-facing slope. Here, where the trail takes a sharp left, you find another viewpoint just off the trail to your right. Again, several flat boulders provide a resting spot to appreciate the views. Southwest across Lake Tahoe you see Twin Peaks (8,878'), prominent above the northwest shore, and to the southwest, Emerald Bay and behind it, Maggies Peaks (8,699' and 8,499'). Incline Village lies directly below you to the west.

The top of Diamond Peak Ski Area from the TRT

Past this viewpoint you travel into a thicker forest of red firs and scattered western white pines as you cross to the east-facing side of the ridge once again. Soon you reach a trail hanging on the edge of the steep bank and pass just east of the top of a Diamond Peak Ski Area lift before reaching a saddle at 5.7 miles from the trailhead. Here you find wide-open, east-facing views toward Carson City and Washoe Lake. The trail next bends west and Lake Tahoe so dominates your senses that it appears as if you could walk right into it. Jeffrey pines now predominate, as you head down a short, steep rock staircase (many bikers will want to get off their bikes; others will wish they had halfway down). The long ridge that includes Mount Baldy, Rose Knob Peak, and Relay Peak can be seen to your north. Below you to the west are the ski runs and condominium developments of Diamond Peak Ski Area, the town of Incline Village, and the Incline-area golf courses.

About 1 mile past the Diamond Peak ski lift, the trail climbs through granite boulders to the eastern slope again. Here you pass from the land of Jeffrey pines to the land of red firs and meander up and down gently through the forest before reaching another viewpoint opening through the trees to the east. About 7 miles from the Tahoe Meadows trailhead, you start a moderate

View from Christopher Loop

Looking toward the TRT section from Brockway to Mount Rose

descent on a long switchback. If you are hiking, you will enjoy views to the east, of Little Valley and Washoe Lake. If you are on a bike, you will be hanging on, trying not to lose your balance on the deep, soft sand. From the bottom of the descent, you pass ground-hugging pinemat manzanita and chinquapin, briefly head through a fir forest, and then end up back out on a mostly treeless west-facing slope, about 8 miles into your hike.

The final stage of your journey to Tunnel Creek Road is a gentle up and down through a moderately dense forest of red and white firs on a trail cut out of the side of the ridge. Views of the lake are mostly filtered, with one last dramatic viewpoint to the west toward the beaches of Incline Village, Twin Peaks, Dollar Point, and the Lake Forest "island" (a peninsula during low-water periods, an island during high-water periods). CA 267 can be seen climbing over the top of Brockway Summit.

At Tunnel Creek Road, 9.2 miles from the Tahoe Meadows Trailhead, you meet a junction with the Red House Flume Trail. Now you are in an

SIDE TRIP **Flume Trail**

A left turn here soon takes you downhill steeply on the Red House Flume Trail, a popular bike loop in combination with the Flume Trail. A right turn takes you downhill steeply for 0.5 mile to a junction with the Flume Trail. From this junction, a left turn will take you on the Flume Trail (although it is recommended that you ride the Flume Trail in the opposite direction, starting from Spooner Lake), and a right turn goes down Tunnel Creek Road steeply for 2.6 miles to NV 28.

area that is very busy with mountain bikers much of the year. If you are hiking, keep your eyes open for riders; if you are riding, watch out for hikers (see Side Trip "Flume Trail," left).

To continue on the Tahoe Rim Trail, go straight through level terrain about 0.3 mile to the lower of the two Twin Lakes. These lakes have been the site of several backcountry camps sponsored by mountain biking groups and the Tahoe Rim Trail Association, who use the camps as they work to maintain and improve the trail. These shallow, grass-lined lakes may dry up by midsummer after most winters. If you're desperate for water, the higher of the Twin Lakes, not visible from the trail, dries up later than the lower lake.

From the east shore of Lower Twin Lake, you face a 1.5-mile-long, 750-foot climb, usually moderate but sometimes steep, through a mixed forest of pine and fir trees. With its soft sand surface, this trail feels steeper on a bike. There are

A rare view of Lower Twin Lake with water in it

occasional views of Mount Rose back to the north and Lake Tahoe to the west. After a series of switchbacks, you almost reach the top of Peak 8,706. Traverse west below it, then go south downhill into a level, open area before traversing briefly west and climbing again. This climb is shorter, a mere 0.25 mile, and just before leveling off, you reach a junction at about 2.4 miles past the trail intersection with Tunnel Creek Road. This is the Christopher Loop viewpoint trail on Herlan Peak. If you are on your bike, leave it here, as bikes are *not* allowed on this viewpoint loop (see Side Trip "Christopher Loop Trail," below).

You are now about halfway through Section 3. Heading southeast on the TRT, you find that the route has leveled off before it enters an area thick with hemlock trees, which can hold the snow until early summer. A short distance farther, you pass through a flat area of scattered pine trees before reaching a wide-open treeless ridgetop. Here you meet a vista trail that provides views of both Marlette Lake directly below in the foreground and the wide expanse of Lake Tahoe in the background. Or you can save a few steps and get pretty much the same view by contouring below the vista on a new section of the TRT built in 2020.

This new trail segment allows you to walk gently downhill through the open sagebrush, marveling every step of the way at the awesome views not only of the lakes but also of Marlette and Snow Valley Peaks to the south. After a view-filled half-mile stroll, you meet a trail junction, at about 1.7 miles from the Christopher Loop junction.

From here you have two alternative TRT routes to choose from. The trail to the right is for hikers only; in 1 mile it traverses the west and south slopes of Marlette

SIDE TRIP
Christopher Loop Trail

This 1.2-mile loop is well worth the climb. The trail switchbacks steeply up to the top of a sandy ridge. Now you are at the top, but the best viewpoint is still a bit of a walk west toward the lake. Your trail goes across an open plateau and in a fairly short distance reaches Christopher Loop. Turn left—the right side doesn't receive much use and is less maintained.

Once there, you are standing on a granite cliff looking down on Sand Harbor while the entire lake unfolds before you. It is the best view of Lake Tahoe I have seen anywhere. The first time you see it, your jaw will drop in amazement. The view to the south of Marlette Lake and Snow Valley Peak is also spectacular. This is a great spot to stop for lunch, although because it is about 12 miles from the Tahoe Meadows Trailhead, you must get a very early start or bike instead of hike to get here by lunchtime. Backpackers hiking the trail counterclockwise can spend the night at Marlette Campground and then be at the viewpoint for an excellent photo opportunity within an hour of leaving camp in the morning.

Marlette Lake and Lake Tahoe from north of Snow Valley Peak

Peak, providing panoramic views of Marlette Lake, Snow Valley Peak, and Lake Tahoe. A left turn at the junction keeps you on the Tahoe Rim Trail, which continues to be multiuse here. You head through more rolling, forested terrain and in 0.5 mile meet the Marlette Peak campground, which has a pit toilet, food-storage lockers, a few picnic tables, and water via a hand-cranked well. The campground sits in a thick forest and gets pretty dusty by midsummer. The well has had mechanical issues in the past. Check the Trail Conditions section of the Tahoe Rim Trail Association's website before depending on it. Just 0.2 mile farther, the TRT meets the trail that circled Marlette Peak, and the trails rejoin. Which route should you take? If you are riding your bike, please stick to the east section. If you are a hiker and would enjoy more sensational views, take the slightly longer (by 0.3 mile) Marlette Peak Trail.

From where your trails meet, you head 0.3 mile mostly downhill through open, sandy terrain to a junction with Hobart Road. At this junction, if you would like to head to Marlette Lake, see the Side Trip on page 100.

Back at the Hobart Road junction, which is about 14.3 miles from the Tahoe Meadows Trailhead and about 8.8 miles from the Spooner Summit Trailhead, the TRT crosses the road and begins the 2.9-mile, 700-foot climb to the saddle below Snow Valley Peak. Head initially east into the trees and soon begin a moderate ascent south. After about 0.7 mile, the TRT reaches a jeep road and follows it about 140 yards west before turning south again. If you are low on water, take this road 0.2 mile southwest down a gully to where the road starts to climb northwest. Continue about 200 yards down the gully to a spring.

Beyond the jeep road, your ascent gets steep as you journey through a forest of red firs and western white pines. You see occasional glimpses of Snow Valley Peak to the south and of Marlette Lake to your west. As you near the top of the ridge and Snow Valley Peak, there are fewer trees (a few windblown whitebark pines) and the views are more spectacular. You pass through expansive fields of lupine and sagebrush bordered by piles of granite boulders. To the north, you can see downtown Reno and its surrounding desert as well as Mount Rose.

Just before reaching the saddle below Snow Valley Peak, the trail crosses to the west-facing side of the ridge, providing unobstructed views of Marlette Lake and Lake Tahoe. This viewpoint makes for a wonderful spot for lunch or rest before beginning the long descent to Spooner Summit. At a shallow notch by the northwest base of Snow Valley Peak, the TRT crosses a dirt road coming up from North Canyon below, the large valley and meadow area to the southwest (see Side Trip "Spooner Lake," page 101).

The TRT snakes through waves of lupine

SIDE TRIP Marlette Lake

If you need water or would enjoy a swim in a wonderful lake or if you are on a mountain bike, leave the Tahoe Rim Trail, turn right on Hobart Road, and head 2.1 miles down to a junction by the southeast shore of Marlette Lake, named after Seneca Hope Marlette, the first surveyor general of California and one of Tahoe's first map makers. Mountain bikes are not allowed on the remaining portion of this section of the TRT, so you must turn right if you are biking. Hobart Road is level for about 0.5 mile and then heads downhill steeply over some very soft decomposed granite to a flatter section of great riding past springtime wildflowers and aspen trees to the junction next to Marlette Lake. In the spring or early summer the east shore of Marlette Lake has one of the most prolific exhibits of wildflowers anywhere. More than 50 species of flowers, such as lupine, paintbrush, monkshood, horsemint, columbine, tiger lily, and elephant's heads, are reported to be in this area.

From the junction, a short road descends to the southeast shore of Marlette Lake, where you can stop to swim and then continue south on the main road on your left, which heads moderately steeply 0.7 mile up to the top of the saddle. From the saddle, follow North Canyon Road 3.9 miles on hard-packed sand down to the Spooner Lake parking lot. On a bike this is a fun downhill, but watch out for hikers and obey the speed limits—yes, speed limits (5 miles per hour on turns or when passing someone and 20 miles per hour anywhere else).

If you are walking, bound for Spooner Lake via North Canyon, and wish to avoid bikers, take the Marlette Lake Trail, where bikes are not allowed. It starts on the south end of the lake, near the main creek that drains into the lake, and heads 4.5 miles to the Spooner Lake parking lot. Along the trail you enjoy beautiful views of Snow Valley and Snow Valley Peak, lots of aspens, several streams, and the remnants of a logger's cabin. Next to the beginning of the Marlette Trail is a fish-spawning station. To see the fish in action, visit this spot in June or early July.

From the junction of the TRT and this dirt road near Snow Valley Peak, you can also climb in 0.3 mile to the top of Snow Valley Peak, which at 9,214 feet is the highest peak on the eastern slope of the Tahoe Basin. To get there, follow the road east as it climbs up the mountain. The walk to the top of Snow Valley Peak requires an additional 270 feet of climbing for a view that to my mind is not as good as the one of Marlette Lake and Lake Tahoe you just passed, but peak baggers will have bagged a peak.

If you stay on the Rim Trail heading south, you will hike 5.9 miles from the junction with the dirt road to the trailhead at Spooner Summit. The first mile is a rambling, gentle downhill across an exposed ridge with sagebrush, tobacco brush, lots of granite boulders, and a few stunted whitebark pines. You get expansive views of Lake Tahoe, as well as views of the North Canyon Road and a vast forest of aspen trees. The view is especially spectacular in the fall with a sea of yellow aspen leaves. Enjoy the open view because soon you will be in a dense forest. If you have a pair of binoculars, you can count the numerous bikers grunting their way up the steep North Canyon Road toward Marlette Lake, where the popular Flume Trail begins.

In this area, several charming log cabins close to the Tahoe Rim Trail are available for rental year-round, as is a shuttle service for mountain bikers and hikers who are using the Flume Trail or the Tahoe Rim Trail. For more information about the cabins, contact Nevada State Parks at 775-831-0494. For information about shuttle services, contact Flume Trail Bikes at 775-749-5349 or visit theflumetrail.com; they operate shuttle services from Tunnel Creek Cafe, at the end of the Flume Trail in Incline, where they also provide food and rental bikes.

After an abundance of Lake Tahoe views, the trail ventures to the east-facing side of the ridge for views of Eagle Valley, with its sprawling Carson City. Then you head into a thick forest of red fir and Jeffrey pine as the trail continues down the ridge. Along this ridgeline section, as you may have seen earlier on the trail, are old weathered stumps cut as high as 5–6 feet off the ground. These trees were cut in the 1870s during the winter to provide wood for the Marlette Flume below Marlette Lake, from which the wood traveled by water to Carson City, and eventually Virginia City, to support the silver mines. The dry climate of the east shore has kept the stumps from decomposing over all these years. At 1.7 miles from the junction with the trail to the top of Snow Valley Peak, you meet a junction on a minor saddle. From here, a trail descends northwest, losing more than 700 feet in elevation as it switchbacks in 1.4 miles to primitive North Canyon Campground and adjacent North Canyon Road. Near this campground, there is water at a small creek that flows through a grove of aspens just west of the road.

SIDE TRIP Spooner Lake

To go to Spooner Lake, turn right and in 1.2 miles of steep downhill you will reach a spring and then immediately meet North Canyon Road, where you turn left. From here, an additional 3.8 miles on a moderate then gentle downhill path takes you to Spooner Lake at the parking area for Lake Tahoe Nevada State Park. Remember, this is Spooner Lake, not the Spooner *Summit* Trailhead parking lot for the TRT.

When you arrive at North Canyon Road after coming down from Snow Valley Peak, you could also take the Marlette Lake Trail to Spooner Lake or Marlette Lake. Cross the road and hike about 50 yards cross-country west to the Marlette Lake Trail. For Marlette Lake, turn right and go downhill about 0.5 mile to the lake. For Spooner Lake, turn left and go about 3 miles moderately steeply downhill to a junction with North Canyon Road. Cross the road and follow the pathway another 0.5 mile to the Spooner Lake parking lot and nearby lake.

On the TRT, with a little more than 4 miles to go, your trail now winds gently downhill along a heavily forested ridgeline of pine and fir trees. The trail is soft dirt and an easy walk (although if you are doing this whole route in one day, it may not seem easy at this point). Occasional filtered views open up, but this is primarily a walk through a shady forest. At 1.4 miles south of the campground trail junction, a vista trail leads to the right. After a 100-yard jaunt up this trail, you will find views of Lake Tahoe and the mountains above its west shore. If you started hiking from the Spooner Summit Trailhead, this vista point is 2.8 miles from the trailhead and 1,000 feet above it.

Your gentle-to-moderate walk winds through the forest pathway for another 2.25 miles before ending with a short, steep descent to a dirt road. On it, the TRT turns left and you walk 0.5 mile, passing a large grove of aspen trees with filtered views of Spooner Lake to the end of the section.

Alternative Routes

Do you like beautiful views but do not feel ready for a 23-mile jaunt? These alternative routes are shorter but still reach some great viewpoints.

- Start at the Tahoe Meadows Trailhead, hike as far as you want, and then turn around. You will find an abundance of great viewpoints and numerous lunch spots on the flat granite rocks. This relatively easy trip is an excellent route for families hiking with children.

- Start at Tahoe Meadows, and hike 9.2 miles south to where the TRT meets Tunnel Creek Road. Turn right (west), and walk or bike steeply downhill for 3.1 miles to NV 28. Be careful going downhill, as the sand can be quite deep, especially later in the summer and fall. If you time it correctly, the fall colors in Tunnel Creek Canyon can be spectacular. Shuttle service may be available through Flume Trail Bikes (775-749-5349), and food and drink await you at the Tunnel Creek Cafe.

- Start at the Spooner Summit north Trailhead, and hike 5.9 miles to the saddle below Snow Valley Peak, where you meet a dirt road. Turn left and follow this road 1.2 miles to where it intersects the North Canyon Road. Turn left again and walk 3.8 miles to the Spooner Lake parking lot. You can then walk around Spooner Lake and find the trail to the Spooner Summit parking area.

Spooner Summit to Kingsbury Grade

19.4 miles

DIFFICULTY Moderate. There is a steady climb of about 1,600 feet in the first 5 miles and a wonderful almost-level mile in the middle, filled with views. Then the trail is generally downhill. The starting elevation is 7,150 feet, and the ending elevation is 7,780 feet, with the high point just a little below the top of South Camp Peak (8,866').

BEST SEASONS Early June–late October. The east shore gets less snow, and it melts faster here than on the west shore, so this is a good choice for early-season hiking. There are several heavily forested, north-facing sections that may retain snow until late June, but in most areas the snow melts by late May.

HIGHLIGHTS The biggest highlight of this section is the spectacular view of most of Lake Tahoe and the west shore from South Camp Peak. This unobstructed view looks directly up the entrance of Emerald Bay to the mountains of Desolation Wilderness. At South Camp Peak you will find lots of rocks to sit on and even a wood bench that some kind trail builder provided. This could be the perfect TRT lunch spot. Making South Camp Peak your turn-around point for an out-and-back hike or ride makes good sense whether you are starting from the Spooner Summit Trailhead or from Kingsbury Grade. The enormous granite boulders through which the trail meanders between Kingsbury Grade North Trailhead and Kingsbury Grade (NV 207) are quite spectacular.

HEADS UP! Water is not available between Spooner Summit and the Kingsbury Grade North Trailhead. Several streams provide water between Kingsbury Grade North and Kingsbury Grade South. Be sure to bring plenty of water for yourself and your pets. If you are thru-hiking, be sure to fill your water containers at Spooner Lake before you reach the trailhead because the trailhead has only pit toilets, no water. (There is water at a restroom facility at the Kingsbury Grade North Trailhead).

About a mile south of Kingsbury Grade is a steady 700-foot climb.

While South Camp Peak itself might make a good camping spot, the lack of water makes this hike best for a day trip. The segment from Spooner to Kingsbury Grade North is the shortest segment you can hike on the TRT.

Much of the trail is open and exposed to the sun, so be sure to bring plenty of sunscreen.

Spooner Summit to Kingsbury Grade

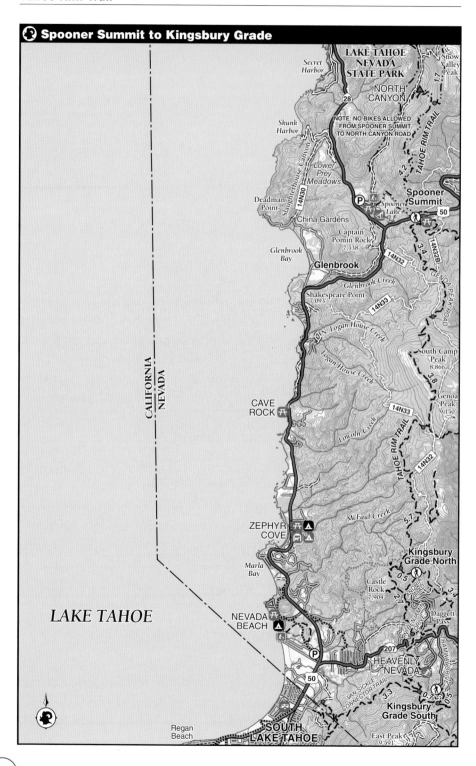

LAKE TAHOE
NEVADA
STATE PARK

Secret Harbor

Snow Valley Peak

1.7

NORTH CANYON

28

NOTE: NO BIKES ALLOWED FROM SPOONER SUMMIT TO NORTH CANYON ROAD

Skunk Harbor

4.2

TAHOE RIM TRAIL

Lower Prey Meadows

14N30

Slaughterhouse Canyon

Deadman Point

Spooner Lake

Spooner Summit

50

China Gardens

Captain Pomin Rock 7,538'

14N32

3.4

14N32B

GENOA PEAK ROAD

Glenbrook Bay

Glenbrook

Glenbrook Creek

Shakespeare Point 7,093'

14N33

N. Logan House Creek

South Camp Peak 8,866'

3.8

Logan House Creek

CAVE ROCK

14N33

Genoa Peak 9,150'

CALIFORNIA
NEVADA

Lincoln Creek

TAHOE RIM TRAIL

14N32

McFaul Creek

5.7

ZEPHYR COVE

Kingsbury Grade North

Marla Bay

0.5

Castle Rock 7,904'

2.1

NORTH DECK

3.4

NEVADA BEACH

Daggett Pass

207

TRAMWAY DRIVE

LAKE TAHOE

50

HEAVENLY NEVADA

0.7

0.5

VAN SICKLE CONNECTOR TRAIL

3.3

Kingsbury Grade South

Regan Beach

SOUTH LAKE TAHOE

East Peak 9,591'

If you are hiking, watch out for mountain bikers because this is a popular biking trail. If you are biking, watch out for hikers because it's popular with hikers too. Both groups should watch out for horses.

Note: In the past, this was the shortest of the eight sections of the TRT. Not anymore. The addition of more than 12 new miles of trails in the Kingsbury Grade area and the lack of an official trailhead right on NV 207 make the official TRT section now 19.4 miles from Spooner Summit to Kingsbury Grade South. It is still possible, however, to hike the 12.2 miles between Spooner Summit and the Kingsbury Grade North Trailhead.

TIPS FOR MOUNTAIN BIKERS Mountain bikes are allowed on this entire section. The ride can be completed from either direction, with the impressive views of South Camp Peak in the middle making a good location for a break. The section from Spooner to South Camp Peak is a great ride. It is an easy to moderate climb most of the way on smooth and sandy trails. If you get to the top and turn around, the downhill is a thrill—fun but not too difficult. The section from South Camp Peak to Kingsbury is more technical because of rocky steps and challenging terrain.

GETTING THERE, SPOONER SUMMIT TO KINGSBURY GRADE From the Y intersection at CA 28 and CA 89 in Tahoe City, drive 27 miles east on NV 28 past Incline Village to the top of Spooner Summit, where NV 28 meets US 50. Turn left on US 50, and drive 0.7 mile to the south trailhead parking lot on the right, which has room for 20 cars. (Directly across US 50 is the Spooner-to-Tahoe Meadows [Mount Rose Summit] Trailhead.) The Spooner-to-Kingsbury Trailhead has a pit toilet and several picnic tables in a nice setting under a grove of aspen trees. The trailhead is about 14 miles northeast of South Lake Tahoe on US 50.

GETTING THERE, KINGSBURY GRADE NORTH TO SPOONER SUMMIT From US 50 at Stateline, Nevada, drive 2.9 miles up (east) NV 207 (Kingsbury Grade), and turn left on North Benjamin Drive. (This is 0.3 mile before the top of Daggett Pass.) North Benjamin becomes Andria Drive, and you go a total of 1.9 miles from the highway to the end of the pavement and a trailhead with the Tahoe Rim Trail sign on your left. There is a restroom and water at the trailhead.

GETTING THERE, KINGSBURY GRADE SOUTH TO SPOONER SUMMIT Follow the directions above, but continue east on NV 207 past North Benjamin Drive and turn right on Tramway Drive when you reach the top of Kingsbury Grade.

Follow Tramway Drive 1.5 miles to the Kingsbury Grade South Trailhead at the Stagecoach parking lot. The trail heads west from here 0.5 mile to the Tahoe Rim Trail.

Trail Description

FROM SPOONER SUMMIT, the mostly sandy trail climbs moderately up a somewhat open slope where manzanita, chinquapin, tobacco brush, and sagebrush grow. In a fairly short time, the grade eases, and you begin a steady, but less steep, climb through open forest, meadows, and thicker stands of Jeffrey pines and red firs. Here the trail is smooth, hard-packed sand, which is wonderful for mountain bikers. This open forest is a popular area for both deer and bears, and mountain lions have also been spotted in the area. During the drought of the early 1990s, a high percentage of trees in the area died because they lacked the necessary moisture to fight off invading bark beetles. The area was logged heavily, resulting in a more open forest and dramatic views of the surrounding mountains.

Along the way south toward South Camp Peak, you intermittently glimpse Lake Tahoe and Desolation Wilderness to the west, and Snow Valley Peak to the north. Mule-ears, paintbrush, lupine, and several aspen groves grow along the trail. After about 550 feet of ascent and 1.5 miles, you reach a little knoll with a short spur trail to the top, providing views into the Carson Valley and to the north toward Snow Valley Peak (9,214') and Mount Rose (10,776'), two mountains of the Carson Range.

While enjoying the view, contemplate the Carson Range, which is the transition zone between two very different environments. To the west, along the slopes above the western edge of Lake Tahoe, is the heart of the Sierra Nevada, where copious amounts of snow fall every winter. That area is lush with a thick forest, green meadows, and countless lakes. The snow lasts well into summer. The area where you are standing in the Carson Range, on the other hand, receives about half as much snow as the western slope does. Trees are more scattered, and lakes are rare. The drier area that you see to the east is the edge of the basin and range high desert zone, which dominates most of Nevada and Utah. This area receives considerably less annual precipitation than the Carson Range does. Although many factors determine what the natural surroundings look like, in the western United States the biggest determining factor is how much winter precipitation an area receives.

View from South Camp Peak

About 0.6 mile past the spur trail, your route turns from south to east, and after a nearly level 0.4-mile traverse, it crosses a minor road about 250 yards north of where it ends at Genoa Peak Road, a major U.S. Forest Service road. You've climbed only about 100 feet in the last mile, but now you turn southward and climb gently 0.8 mile through open forest with lupine lining the trail to a short spur trail. Now you descend 0.3 mile west to a crossing of the major Genoa Peak Road, about 3.5 miles from the Spooner Summit Trailhead, adjacent to a large, open staging area for logging operations.

The trail then becomes increasingly steeper as you begin an unrelenting 800-foot climb to the crest of South Camp Peak through heavily forested terrain. You may see signs of logging, including numerous blackened stumps. The trees were cut down, and the brush and debris from them was burned. Just before reaching the northwest edge of South Camp Peak, the trail passes through a thickly forested, north-facing section where you may see snow in early summer.

South Camp Peak is a large, nearly level, open area with great picnic sites. You walk along the broad summit's west rim, and its low-lying shrubs do not obstruct the spectacular views, which you have for 1 mile. The summit is so broad and level, in fact, that *peak* is a misnomer. The highest rock outcropping is about 0.75 mile along your rim traverse, and looking southeast from it, you see Genoa Peak, the nearby pointy peak with a radio tower on top. Scanning clockwise, next you see Heavenly Mountain Resort and beyond it to the south, brown, rounded Freel Peak; the South Lake Tahoe area including Stateline and its casinos; a treeless swath, evidence of the 2007 Angora Fire; Fallen Leaf Lake;

South Lake Tahoe and Desolation Wilderness

Desolation Wilderness, including the pointy spire of Pyramid Peak; Mount Tallac, which seems to rise up right from the lake; another treeless swath, evidence of the 2017 Emerald Fire that burned across CA 89 near Cascade Lake; Emerald Bay and evidence of the landslide that occurred in 1955, just after the construction of CA 89 along the bay. Next comes Stony Ridge, with Jacks Peak and nipple-topped Rubicon Peak, and then to the west, the deep westshore canyons: Blackwood and Ward (with Twin Peaks on the ridge between the two). Increasingly northwest, you see Alpine Meadows, Squaw Valley, and, to their north, Castle Peak above Donner Summit. While the views are spectacular, sometimes the winds are ferocious as you gaze from this exposed lookout straight into prevailing westerly winds. From this angle you can see right into Emerald Bay and may get the mistaken impression that Lake Tahoe is 100 miles long and 5 miles wide. Hopefully you brought your binoculars.

Unless you take a steep side trip up to Genoa Peak (see Side Trip "Genoa Peak," opposite), South Camp Peak, at around 8,800 feet, is the highest point along this section of trail. If you would like to hike an out-and-back on this section of the TRT, turn around here. It makes for a wonderful 10- to 12-mile round-trip (the mileage depends on where you turn around). If you complete the entire point-to-point route from Spooner Summit to Kingsbury Grade, you will probably drag yourself away from the views and start heading gently downhill and away from the sometimes stiff winds in the direction of Genoa Peak. In 0.5 mile you reach a saddle with a dirt road that climbs southeast to Genoa Peak.

On the TRT, from the junction with the Genoa Peak jeep road, you begin a 5-mile-long, usually gentle descent toward the Kingsbury Grade North Trailhead.

SIDE TRIP Genoa Peak

In 0.8 mile of steep climbing you will be at the top of Genoa Peak (9,150'). The views of Lake Tahoe from the top are similar to those from South Camp Peak, but you get the bonus of views of Carson Valley to the east. On the negative side, you will be standing next to a radio tower. The area around Genoa Peak is popular with glider planes. Once, I saw one fly so close to the peak that the pilot and I could wave at each other.

The forest here is composed primarily of small young Jeffrey pines, red firs, and western white pines, and you may continue to see the blackened stumps left behind by past logging. Pinemat manzanita, a lush green ground cover, is especially prolific in this section and adds a nice verdant feel to the hike. About 0.7 mile past the road that led up to Genoa Peak, you cross a small dirt road, and here the trail turns northwest and then south as it rounds a peak. Just before passing this small dirt road, you meet a junction with the Sierra Canyon Trail (see Side Trip "Sierra Canyon Trail," next page).

View of the Mount Tallac cross, the Emerald Bay Fire scar, and Emerald Bay

The Sierra Canyon Trail (SCT) drops 3,500 feet in 9.6 miles to Genoa, Nevada's oldest town, and connects the Carson Valley with the Tahoe Rim Trail. In case you missed that, I said 3,500 feet, which is a lot of elevation gain or loss. This is not a Sunday stroll. The good news is that they built in a lot of switchbacks to ease the burden, and the views of the Carson Valley are excellent.

The TRT traverses the mountainside on a trail that has become more challenging and technical for mountain bikers. Your path is now bordered by granite boulders, and you have many rock steps to climb over. The forest has become thicker, and so you get only occasional glimpses of the lake. One of these views, however, is a dramatic look at Emerald Bay and Mount Tallac, which feels much closer to this section of trail. As you continue on a narrower, rocky trail, you see Heavenly Mountain Resort and its accompanying development.

The trail continues to roll up and down along short stretches until you meet a junction with the Kingsbury Stinger Trail, a popular mountain biking trail. In about another 0.5 mile, a left turn takes you on the Kingsbury Grade North access trail east 0.5 mile to the Kingsbury Grade North Trailhead on Andria Drive. The main TRT heads straight ahead. After a short, gentle climb, the trail winds through white firs and Jeffrey pines in a gentle descent. The TRT soon reaches an open area with sage and chinquapin before rolling up and down to an intersection with the Castle Rock Vista Trail (see Side Trip "Castle Rock Vista," left), on your right, about 0.5 mile past the junction with the Kingsbury Grade North Trailhead access trail.

SIDE TRIP
Castle Rock Vista

The trail climbs up 0.4 mile moderately steeply through lupine and pinemat manzanita to the top of this interesting rock formation. Primarily built by the Boy Scouts, the trail winds through a rock chasm to reach the narrow top, where the views of much of the lake and South Lake Tahoe make this side jaunt well worth the effort.

The TRT heads downhill for 0.1 mile where it meets the Castle Rock Road Trail, upon which a half-mile walk brings you to Andria Drive near the Kingsbury Grade North Trailhead. If you start at the Castle Rock Road Trail, you can reach the top of the Castle Rock Trail in a mile of walking.

As the TRT descends again, you pass huge granite boulders and walk into the cleavage between two rounded mounds. After passing a view of Castle Rock, the trail meets another junction, where a short use trail takes you to Maryanne Drive, whose houses you can see clearly through the woods. Just past it is a huge boulder next to the trail that might entice climbers. Now walking through these Kingsbury neighborhoods, prime

In the Sierra, it's all about the granite.

dog-walking terrain, you gently climb through fabulous rock formations between the two knobs. A path through the rocks leads to the Grubb viewpoint, where you find nice flat rocks and panoramic views of the lake. Just past the viewpoint is a 100-foot-long section; it took a crew of trail builders five weeks to move all the car-size boulders to provide a smooth surface for this little section of trail. We are talking world-class trail building here, folks.

Your trail crosses a minor dirt road under electric lines, then descends through the rocks to a grove of aspens and a dirt road that the trail follows for a short distance to a usually dry creek crossing. In the spring, if you do find water here it will be the first source since Marlette Campground, but there is a better source only about a mile farther. You head away from the aspens uphill to a junction 2.7 miles from the junction with the Kingsbury Grade North access trail and 1.3 miles from Maryanne Drive. Turn left if you would like to hike the 6.7-mile North Daggett Loop (see Side Trip "North Daggett Loop Trail," next page).

The TRT goes just another 0.2 mile to the Kingsbury Grade crossing by traversing a slope and topping a small ridge before a short, steep descent brings you to the highway. Carefully and swiftly cross this busy, windy road with little sight distance, and parallel Buchanan Road, which has an alternative access point behind a U.S. Forest Service gate, with just a few parking spots. On the TRT, an easy descent from the initial climb brings you through open forest to Edgewood Drive. You follow this lightly used dirt road 0.4 mile uphill along

SIDE TRIP North Daggett Loop Trail

From the junction with the TRT, the North Daggett Loop Trail climbs up 0.25 mile to North Benjamin Drive. The trail then climbs across a manzanita-covered slope to views of the lake. Just 0.4 mile from North Benjamin Drive, you will meet the North Daggett Summit Connector Trail. Here a right turn takes you 0.2 mile to the top of Kingsbury Grade, where you can cross the busy road to Tramway Drive and then follow Tramway past the Tramway Market 1.5 miles to the Stagecoach parking lot and the Kingsbury Grade South TRT Trailhead.

On the loop trail, veer left, go gently downhill, and cross over to the Carson Valley side of the ridge, where a steady climb up a warm, dry slope awaits. Then,

back on the Tahoe side of the ridge, your trail follows an old dirt road. At 1.8 miles from the North Benjamin Drive crossing, you reach a junction near a saddle, where a left turn takes you to a pleasant lake-view vista in 0.2 mile.

Past the junction for the vista, the North Daggett Loop Trail descends for 0.4 mile to Donna Way/Kimberly Brooke Lane, where you traverse up through manzanita, pass through a dry meadow, and top out on a ridge with views of houses below and the lake in the distance. At 3.5 miles from the southbound TRT, you reach Andria Drive, across the street from the Kingsbury Grade North Trailhead. Congratulations, you have completed the 6.7-mile combined TRT and North Daggett Loop Trail.

the riparian zone of unseen Edgewood Creek, until at a sharp right turn you leave the road and cross year-round Edgewood Creek. This is the first reliable source of water for southbound TRT hikers since Marlette Campground, 26 miles north. Need a place to camp? There are a few sites just several hundred yards past the creek.

Next, with views of nearby homes and Mount Tallac, the trail crests a ridge and then starts downhill through a boulder field. Stop to enjoy the best lake views since crossing Kingsbury Grade and to get ready for an uphill that is coming soon.

A sharp downhill takes you under power lines and a crossing of another branch of Edgewood Creek before the beginning of a steady climb through thick forest up a north-facing slope, which holds the snow longer than the rest of this section of trail. Although you are climbing in earnest, there are regular breaks and well-placed switchbacks to ease the burden. You'll see deer frequently, along with bike riders and neighborhood dog walkers. You pass some ancient western white pines before meeting a junction at 2.3 miles from Kingsbury Grade, at the top of a series of long switchbacks. You've just climbed about 500 feet, so perhaps a view break is in order (and you have 200 more feet to go on this climb). A left turn takes you in 0.1 mile to the Brisack Viewpoint, where you find a view of a good swath of big blue from atop a boulder pile.

Heavenly Resort and the bare patch from the Gondola Fire

Back on the TRT, just 0.3 mile past the vista junction, you reach the Van Sickle Trail junction at the top of the saddle immediately before entering Heavenly Ski Resort lands (see Side Trip "Van Sickle Trail," below).

From this junction, a long gentle traverse takes you to the top of a swale, with a ski run on your left and a chairlift below it. You cross over the ski run to the forested slope and pass underneath the North Bowl chairlift. You soon meet a major ski run (dirt road) right at a hairpin turn in the road. The

SIDE TRIP Van Sickle Trail

Completed in 2012, the combination TRT and Van Sickle Bi-State Park Trail is a wonderful addition to the TRT trail network. In 3 miles, TRT hikers can walk to the heart of the casino area in South Lake Tahoe.

The trail starts out as a mile-long, westerly traverse on a steep north-facing slope, with occasional glimpses of the lake and the mountains to the north. Then the trail comes around the slope of the ridge, and voilà, the whole world unfolds before you. Over the next mile, you pass spectacular lake views and creek crossings before walking right through the middle of the burn zone of the 2002 Gondola Fire to a waterfall 2.2 miles from the TRT junction. The incredible views continue, and the crowds increase during the last mile down through open slopes to the Van Sickle Bi-State Park.

Located on the California–Nevada line, the entrance to the park is only 100 yards from Heavenly Village, where you'll find supermarkets, restaurants, cinemas, and casinos. Thru-hikers looking for a quick return to civilization or a reminder of why they went into the woods in the first place would enjoy this trail halfway through their two-week adventure. In addition, bus service is available from the visitor center in Stateline to the Kingsbury Grade South Trailhead.

junction can be confusing; look for the TRT to the right and slightly uphill from the turn of the road. Do *not* follow the road as it goes off to the left and downhill.

Another third of a mile on the trail takes you under the Stagecoach chairlift and then to the Stagecoach ski run, which you cross to meet the original TRT route and the end of this section. Thru-hikers continue straight ahead. The TRT Kingsbury Grade South Trailhead is now accessed with a left turn, which takes you downhill moderately steeply, through thick brush and trees and around a condo development, to the trailhead in the Stagecoach parking lot in about 0.5 mile. Just before reaching the parking lot, you pass a monorail-looking contraption, which is Ridge Tahoe's Hilltrac Skier Express, a gondola that brings guests from the Ridge Tahoe development to the base of the Stagecoach Chair.

Rocks near Kingsbury Grade

SECTION 5

Kingsbury Grade to Big Meadow

23.7 miles

DIFFICULTY This long and relatively strenuous section has a lot of elevation changes and a 9,730-foot high point. Although this trail is too long for many to hike in one day, for the truly strong hiker it is a wonderful day hike.

BEST SEASONS Each end of the trail can be hiked as early as mid-June. The highest part of the trail, near Freel Peak, is usually not open until early July or later, depending on the amount of snow that fell the previous winter. The first major snows at Freel Peak may come as early as mid-October.

HIGHLIGHTS This trail section provides tremendous views of Lake Tahoe, Carson Valley, Desolation Wilderness, and the Carson Range. In addition, it has a wonderful high-elevation lake, Star Lake, and access to the summit of the two highest peaks in the Tahoe Basin: Freel Peak (10,881') and Jobs Sister (10,823').

HEADS UP! Some sections of the trail are above 9,000 feet, and much of the trail is open and exposed to the sun and wind—*bring your sunscreen.*

As with all sections of the trail along the east shore of Lake Tahoe, water is in short supply. In the first few miles out from the Stagecoach parking lot, there are several seasonal streams, with the South Fork of Daggett Creek lasting the longest. Mott Canyon Creek usually flows through the summer. Star Lake, which you will reach 8.8 miles from the Kingsbury Grade South Trailhead, is a delightful swimming spot, but its high silt content may clog your filter. Better drinking water is available about 1 mile past Star Lake, where you find the lovely, swift-moving Cold Creek, fresh from the slopes of Freel Peak. On slopes west of Freel Peak, several small streams cascade across the trail into late summer. From Armstrong Pass you may find water by heading southeast from the TRT on the steep Armstrong Pass connector trail. It is 0.4 mile long, and near its bottom you cross a small stream. From its trailhead a dirt road descends almost 0.5 mile to cross larger Willow Creek. You can find reliable water just below the west edge of the western Freel Meadow. Finally, east of the Big Meadow Trailhead, you will find Grass Lake Creek, a major stream, at approximately 0.5 mile, and another stream 2 miles from the trailhead at the Grass Lake Trail junction. As with the entire East Shore, the amount of water in creeks varies tremendously from year to year. I have seen Mott Canyon Creek roar in September and be dry as a bone in August. Always take into account how much it snowed in the area the previous winter when making

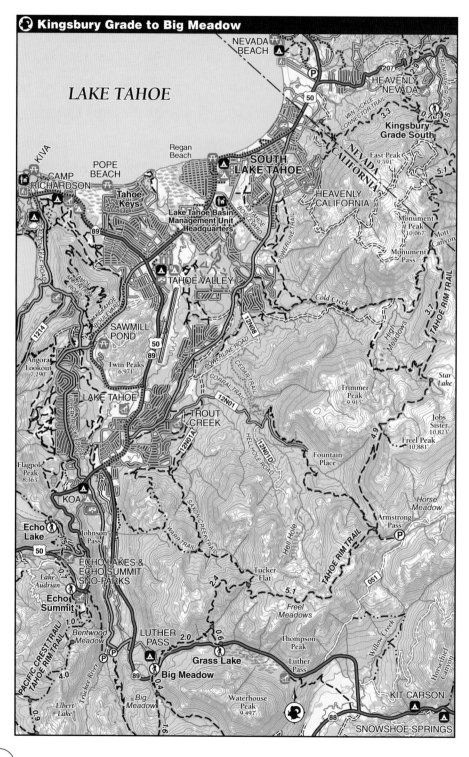

Kingsbury Grade to Big Meadow

NEVADA
BEACH

LAKE TAHOE

HEAVENLY
NEVADA

207

50

3.3

Kingsbury
Grade South

East Peak
9,591'

5.1

Regan
Beach

SOUTH
LAKE TAHOE

NEVADA
CALIFORNIA

HEAVENLY
CALIFORNIA

KIVA

CAMP
RICHARDSON

POPE
BEACH

Tahoe
Keys

Lake Tahoe Basin
Management Unit
Headquarters

Monument
Peak
10,067'

Mott
Canyon

89

Monument
Pass

POWERLINE TRAIL

Cold Creek

3.7

TAHOE RIM TRAIL

1214

SAWMILL
POND

12N08

High
Meadows

Star
Lake

Angora
Lookout
7,290'

50

89

Twin Peaks
6,971'

POWERLINE ROAD

CEDAR TRAIL

CORRAL TRAIL

Trimmer
Peak
9,915'

LAKE TAHOE

12N01

Jobs
Sister
10,823'

Freel Peak
10,881'

TROUT
CREEK

12N01A

12N07D

HELLHOLE ROAD

Fountain
Place

4.9

Flagpole
Peak
8,363'

KOA

SAXON CREEK TRAIL

WTR TRAIL

Hell Hole

Horse
Meadow

Armstrong
Pass

Echo
Lake

Johnson
Pass

051

50

ECHO LAKES &
ECHO SUMMIT
SNO-PARKS

2.4

Tucker
Flat

5.1

TAHOE RIM TRAIL

Lake
Audrian

Echo
Summit

Freel
Meadows

1.0

PACIFIC CREST TRAIL

TAHOE RIM TRAIL

Bentwood
Meadow

LUTHER
PASS

2.0

0.6

Thompson
Peak

Willow Creek

Horsethief Canyon

4.0

Truckee River

89

Grass Lake

Big Meadow

Luther
Pass

KIT CARSON

0.4

Elbert
Lake

0.9

Big
Meadow

1.6

Waterhouse
Peak
9,497'

88

SNOWSHOE SPRINGS

water plans. If you don't know what sort of winter it was, ask any Tahoe local, but be prepared for an animated and detailed explanation.

Those with a fear of heights may be challenged by several exposed sections of trail south of Mott Canyon.

TIPS FOR MOUNTAIN BIKERS This section is challenging, loved by some and hated by others. It has lots of technical areas with hundreds of rock benches that will require almost all riders to dismount. Portions of the trail are along steep drops that may unnerve some riders. The first 5 miles are primarily a long, steady climb. Once you get to the top of Monument Pass, just about when you are wondering why you are doing this, the trail levels off a bit before climbing again for several miles to Star Lake. After Star Lake it is a major, difficult climb again up to 9,700 feet. Almost all the mountain bikers will be walking near the top. From the saddle of Freel Peak, it is time for a big downhill with a few tight switchbacks that may scare some riders.

Eventually you reach Armstrong Pass, a great place to escape if you have had enough. A short trail descends to a dirt road, Forest Route 051F, that you can follow 0.5 mile down to FR 051; take it 3.5 miles to CA 89. If you do this, you will reach CA 89 about 0.8 mile east of signed Luther Pass and 1.8 miles west of the CA 88–CA 89 junction in Hope Valley. If you continue toward Big Meadow, you will confront another long uphill with lots of granite steps, followed by another long downhill. Among the rocky sections, there are some long, smooth, fun parts as well.

Along the downhill section, you pass the junction to the Saxon Creek Trail. This very popular mountain biking trail, usually accessed via the Big Meadow Trailhead, is known as Mr. Toad's Wild Ride (see sidebar, page 128). While some may find it a wild ride, I found it to be very chewed up, steep, and impossible to navigate in many sections. If you go, be prepared for difficulty. Past Toad's is a brief steep uphill, followed by a steady downhill to the end of the trail, which is fun but still has several technically challenging sections. I've talked to a lot of people while they were riding this section of the TRT. Some loved it, but many others wondered what in the heck they were doing on this trail. It all comes back to being honest about your riding ability. It's also a good idea to know the riding ability of those you ask about the trail. For those skilled at riding rocky sections, a trail may not seem technical, but to another rider those sections would be a very challenging and frustrating ride.

GETTING THERE, KINGSBURY GRADE SOUTH TRAILHEAD TO BIG MEADOW TRAILHEAD From Stateline in the South Lake Tahoe area, drive east up NV 207 (Kingsbury Grade) 3.2 miles to Tramway Drive at Daggett Pass, the summit of Kingsbury Grade. Follow the signs 1.5 miles to the Heavenly Valley Resort Stagecoach parking lot. Park near the bottom of the chairlift, and follow the metal stairs to the TRT, which begins at your left.

GETTING THERE, BIG MEADOW TRAILHEAD TO KINGSBURY GRADE SOUTH TRAILHEAD From the intersection of CA 89 and US 50 in Meyers, drive 5.3 miles south on CA 89 to the Big Meadow Trailhead and parking area on your left. Luther Pass is 3.3 miles farther. This trail can also be accessed from the Grass Lake Trailhead, which is located 1.5 miles east of the Big Meadow Trailhead on CA 89. Park in a pullout on the right side of the road, and cross the highway to the trail. If you pass Grass Lake, the lake that looks like a meadow on the right, you have gone too far.

Trail Description

AMID HIGH-RISE CONDOMINIUMS and a huge parking lot, the trailhead is located near a ski lift. Are we talking a wilderness experience here or what? Don't worry—it gets better. You start by passing under Ridge Tahoe's Hilltrac Skier Express, a gondola that brings guests from the Ridge Tahoe development to the base of the Stagecoach Chair. The trail then climbs steeply 0.4 mile through thick brush and forest on this TRT access trail to a junction with the main TRT. Here, a right turn takes you across a ski run and toward the Van Sickle Trail and Kingsbury Grade North. Your route is to the left, where the trail switchbacks moderately up through a forest of red firs and Jeffrey pines and provides views of the condos below and later brief glimpses of Lake Tahoe and Washoe Valley. You walk over numerous granite boulders and steps, which are challenging to those on bikes.

After climbing for close to 1 mile, you reach a saddle and then descend gently for 0.5 mile, passing under another Heavenly Ski Resort ski lift. In another 130 yards you cross the South Fork of Daggett Creek, which is a fickle water provider. Sometimes it runs most of the year, and other times it is dry by July. It provides a patch of greenery and wildflowers in this land of ski runs. As you ascend again, western white and lodgepole pines replace the red firs and Jeffrey pines.

Freel Peak

Next the trail gently climbs through alternating areas of dense forest and a more open combination of brush and forest, with manzanita, chinquapin, and tobacco brush dominating the scene. The open vegetation allows views east to Carson Valley and the desert ranges beyond it. About 0.75 mile past the creek, you reach the north rim of Mott Canyon, where you see Freel Peak. You follow the rim for a moderate 0.5-mile ascent west, then climb gently 0.25 mile south to a trail junction about 3.2 miles from the Kingsbury Trailhead. From here, the old trail continues straight, reaches a saddle and ski-area maintenance road, and drops very steeply over soft, sandy soil to a crossing of Mott Canyon Creek. The new trail goes left, gently downhill along a ridge through some impressive western white pines. Soon it reaches the end of the east-heading ridge and you get dramatic panoramic views of the Carson Valley far below. The trail then traverses around the edge and heads west again, soon reaching the old trail at the bottom of the road, just before the creek. The new trail is just a bit longer, and much easier to hike. The new trail is especially an improvement if you were going the opposite direction and will no longer have to climb that sandy road.

The largest western white pine in the Tahoe region (notice the author at the bottom)

Beautiful little Mott Canyon Creek sits just underneath the Mott Canyon chairlift. In the early summer, its banks are covered with Lewis's monkeyflower, yellow monkeyflower, delphinium, and columbine. The lovely stream runs most of the season but may dry up by fall.

After a short distance with a moderate climb along a narrow precipice, you come out of Mott Canyon and round the corner to an open traverse. Your route is now mostly treeless and facing east with stunning views of Carson Valley far below to the east and Jobs Sister, with its huge drop in elevation from mountaintop to valley floor, in the distance to the south. Here you will see mountain mahogany and a jaw-droppingly big western white pine just to the left of the trail. With a circumference of 24 feet, the pine provides shade in this hot, exposed section of trail. The U.S. Forest Service has designated this tree as the largest western white pine in the Tahoe region. While this cliff-edge section is beautiful to hike, anyone afraid of heights will find it unnerving and a challenging bike ride, which becomes steeper toward Monument Pass.

Approximately 5 miles from the trailhead, you trudge up several switchbacks on the final climb to Monument Pass, which is crossed by power lines and is about 0.4 mile beyond the Nevada–California boundary. At the pass, you cross from the Carson side (eastern slope) to the Tahoe side on the western slope. Monument Peak, at higher than 10,000 feet, is a towering presence to the west. Dramatic views of Jobs Sister and Freel Peak immediately open up. Here you reach a junction with the Monument Pass to High Meadows Trail (see Side Trip "Monument Pass to High Meadows," below).

On the TRT it is 3.7 miles from Monument Pass to Star Lake. The first 2 miles are on a gentle, sandy path through mostly open terrain and provide a wonderful opportunity to marvel at the views of Desolation Wilderness, including Pyramid Peak, the Crystal Range, and Lake Tahoe to the west. The results of the Angora Fire can be seen as a wave of green brush where once was a mass of blackened trees. This fire in the summer of 2007 burned more than 3,000 acres and 250 homes near South Lake Tahoe.

As you get closer to Star Lake, the immense size of the Freel Peak massif becomes more and more impressive. A little over 1 mile before Star Lake, the trail, which has been traversing south, heads briefly east, passing ancient junipers and a small creeklet, and begins to ascend again south. The tree cover of western white pine, lodgepole, and hemlock gets thicker as you climb.

Finally, the trail heads east again, climbing above the lake's outlet creek, before you reach Star Lake, located at the base of Jobs Sister, which rises dramatically from its shores. This alluring lake will take your breath away, especially if you venture into its cold waters (although after an extended warm period the water temperatures can become quite bearable). As the only large lake on the

SIDE TRIP Monument Pass to High Meadows

This beautiful trail drops more than 1,000 feet in 3 miles through unique rock formations and aspen groves to High Meadows, where you can join Cold Creek Trail and in an additional 3 miles reach the High Meadows Trailhead. You can also hike a loop by taking High Meadows to Star Lake Trail, which heads uphill 1,500 feet in 4.5 miles to the shores of Star Lake. If you're spending a layover day at Star Lake, then perhaps this 11-mile loop will make an afternoon swim in Star's chilly waters especially attractive.

Star Lake and Jobs Sister

Tahoe Rim Trail between Mount Rose and Luther Pass, it may be the best place for those who are doing an overnight trip to set up camp. There are several overused camping spots close to the lake and lots of wonderful camping spots farther above the lake. The Star Lake to High Meadows Trail, completed in 2012, descends 1,500 feet in 4.5 miles, to High Meadows, where an additional 3 miles on the Cold Creek Trail will bring you to the High Meadows Trailhead.

I find the first 2 miles after Star Lake to be the most interesting part of this section of the TRT. You begin with a moderate climb from Star Lake, with views of Lake Tahoe getting better as you rise. You are now in the wide open at a high altitude where western white pines, whitebark pines, and hemlocks are scattered about the sandy soil. Many of the trees have been tortured by high-altitude winds and are stunted and bent. You also see numerous large pieces of white quartz along this section, as well as patches of snow that hang on late into the summer. You head steadily toward 10,000 feet, passing an early-summer waterfall and then viewing the imposing hulk of Freel Peak.

You arrive at a swiftly moving, clear mountain stream, a tributary of Cold Creek. It's only a foot or two wide but bustling with happy energy. Bordered

Freel Peak saddle

by wildflowers, it creates a green, grassy path through the desolate sand and rock and is an excellent water source.

A bit more climbing on the TRT brings you to the saddle below Freel Peak, the high point of this trail section at 9,730 feet. Don't be surprised to find a patch of snow even in late July. This often wind-swept spot is about 1.9 miles south of Star Lake and 3 miles north of Armstrong Pass (see Side Trip "Freel Peak," right).

Those who find more than 23 miles just about enough to hike can skip Freel Peak and continue on the TRT. Here you are almost midway through Section 5, about 11 miles south of the Kingsbury Grade South Trailhead and about 12.5 miles north of the Big Meadow Trailhead. Your trail begins with a long, steady, thinly

SIDE TRIP Freel Peak

At this saddle, you can begin a steep climb to the top of Freel Peak, at 10,881 feet the tallest peak on the Tahoe Basin rim. The trail begins with a ton of switchbacks up the steep slope, getting quite close at times to the rocky cliffs. Later it crosses the wide slope among the beaten-down whitebark pines. All told, it is 1,150 feet in elevation in just a mile to the top of the peak. It's a worker! But the views from the top and the feeling of climbing the region's tallest peak are worth it. From Freel Peak you can hike cross-country over to the top of Jobs Sister (10,823'). Climbing these peaks makes for challenging but beautiful jaunts if you are camping in the Star Lake area.

A Tale of Two Fountains

The Fountain Place you see on the map is a meadow area below to the west. Fountain Face and Fountain Place were both named for a man named Garret Fountain, who built a way station at Fountain Place in 1860 in an effort to supply miners on their way from California to the Comstock Lode in Nevada. Fountain had hoped they would go over Armstrong Pass, but they chose Daggett Pass, and his dream failed.

forested descent along the slope of Freel Peak 0.7 mile south to a switchback, which turns you back to the north. You continue downhill an additional 0.3 mile before switching back again to the south. Once again, you will enjoy excellent views of the Crystal Range, the massive granite ridge on the western edge of Desolation Wilderness. You soon cross three spring-fed creeks that are usually flowing and provide much-needed water and beautiful wildflower displays; especially prominent are giant delphiniums. These little ribbons of color in this dry, brown landscape are a welcome relief. Less than 0.5 mile past the last streamlet is a huge mass of granite with a steep cliff face and lots of fascinating rock formations, known as Fountain Face, about 1 mile north of Armstrong Pass.

Your gentle up-and-down traverse continues, and on the final 0.3 mile before Armstrong Pass you are treated to many large juniper trees, with their light-blue berries and gnarled trunks and branches.

At the deep crest notch of Armstrong Pass, you can leave the TRT to shorten your hike. (Or, if you come in from Armstrong Pass, it makes for a relatively short way to access Freel Peak.) The short, steep Armstrong Pass Trail takes you 0.4 mile to an old abandoned road. Follow this road 0.5 mile to trailhead parking just across a small bridge. From here it is 3.4 miles south to CA 89 and about 5 miles to Hope Valley. Follow the Armstrong Pass Trailhead directions below in reverse (see Side Trip

Giant junipers

"Armstrong Pass," right). Follow FS 25 right (southwest) on a steady descent. In about 0.75 mile stay straight. In another 0.25 mile cross a cattle guard and bear right. Continue to descend until reaching pavement just before CA 89.

The Armstrong Pass three-way junction is located at the top of the U-shaped valley at the end of the long southward traverse. Here the TRT rounds a corner of the ridge and heads west. From Armstrong Pass the journey to Big Meadow is 9.5 miles. In addition to the Armstrong Pass Connector Trail on your left, which heads down to the alternative trailhead described above, the Armstrong Pass trail on your right is a popular route, mostly for mountain bikes, that heads toward South Lake Tahoe and a series of other mountain biking trails. It is also another access to the TRT from South Lake Tahoe.

The TRT quickly begins a steady, sometimes moderate uphill climb on sandy soils through a forest of scattered western white pines, lodgepole pines, and red firs. Your distant views are now fewer and less dramatic, with occasional glimpses of the Freel massif to the northeast as you switchback up the ridgeline. But you get to look at humongous western white pines, lupine, and waves of pinemat manzanita and smell the pennyroyal as you climb.

The area between Big Meadow and Armstrong Pass is popular for mountain biking. If you are on your bike, enjoy, but watch out for hikers. Be a little more vigilant if you are hiking. While portions of this section are a fun, sandy ride, there are a lot of short rocky sections that will force many riders to get off their bikes; other sections are composed of deep granitic sand that will make it tough, whether you are going up or down.

SIDE TRIP Armstrong Pass

To access Armstrong Pass from CA 89 (a section of road recommended only for four-wheel-drive vehicles with high clearance), take CA 89 south from its junction with US 50 in Meyers 8.5 miles up to signed Luther Pass, just beyond a large grassy meadow containing Grass Lake. Start on a long downhill to Hope Valley, going 0.8 mile to a junction with Forest Service Road 051 on your left. Slow down and watch closely; it is easy to miss. (This junction is 1.8 miles up from the CA 88 junction down in Hope Valley.) Take FS 051 steeply uphill. In 1.1 miles the road divides. There is a gate on the right fork, but stay to the left. At 1.6 miles bear left. At 1.8 miles cross a cattle guard and then continue to bear left.

At 2.4 miles you reach the first bridge as you follow a stream. At 2.7 miles, at a fork in the road, go straight. At 3.4 miles, you will reach a second bridge; cross the bridge, and then immediately make a 180-degree left turn into a small parking area. Park here, and then walk across a trail bridge and go 0.5 mile uphill on the now abandoned road to the Armstrong Pass connector trail. Take this trail 0.4 mile steeply uphill to the junction with the TRT.

Corn lilies in Freel Meadows

Midway up the climb, you pass fascinating granite boulders and then cross to a different slope, this one nearly void of ground cover, that is dotted with occasional ancient western white pines, whitebark pines, and lodgepoles. After 2 miles of switchbacking uphill, you reach an open, broad ridge with large boulders and views to the south of numerous peaks above 10,000 feet, including Round Top (10,381') near Carson Pass.

The trail soon leaves the ridge, proceeds through a rocky area with stone steps, and then continues through an open forest until, at a little less than 3 miles from Armstrong Pass, you traverse the largest of three meadows known as Freel Meadows. United States Geological Survey maps show this area as Freel Meadows, but they are not specific about how many meadows are included. When I scouted the area, I found three meadowlike areas within 1.5 miles. The first meadow is a mostly treeless slope covered with mule-ears, lupine, sage, and paintbrush (the actual meadow lies at the base of the slopes, which is a long way down). Visible to the south are beautiful Sierra peaks, as well as Hope Valley. Just past the open slopes, you reach an excellent viewpoint to the north. Here you see deep, boggy Hell Hole Canyon directly below you to the north, and farther in the distance, Lake Tahoe. To the northeast, Freel Peak stands out in full relief. I dry-camped here once and found that it was the perfect spot to enjoy a sunset.

Sunset over Freel Peak

Next you pass through an open forest before reaching a large grassy meadow just to your left (the second meadow). Then shortly you reach a third meadow, this one loaded with wildflowers, including corn lily, lupine, and delphinium. You can get water from the west end of this meadow at the headwaters of Saxon Creek. To do so, you will have to bushwhack to where the meadow ends just before the trail heads away from the meadow. If you can't see where the water is, stop for a moment and listen. It can be clearly heard. The Freel Meadows area is a wonderful green divide between the more barren sandy slopes of the higher elevations to the east and the thick forest that appears as you travel west.

After leaving this meadow, you descend at a moderate pace through denser forest. About 1 mile later and 5.1 miles from Armstrong Pass, you reach the Saxon Creek Trail (aka Mr. Toad's Wild Ride, page 128) on a broad saddle just above Tucker Flat.

With 4.4 miles left, you continue on the TRT over a short uphill section northwest, followed by a short traverse west, and then you meander downhill 2 miles through primarily dense forest of red and white firs and western white and Jeffrey pines to the Grass Lake Trail. Along the way you see several small meadows with many wildflowers, especially mule-ears. There are also two viewing spots. The first is near the top on a very short use trail to a rock

SIDE TRIP
Mr. Toad's Wild Ride

The popular mountain biking trail known as Mr. Toad's Wild Ride is usually accessed by way of the Big Meadow Trailhead. If you start at Big Meadow, the trail starts with a long uphill followed by a big, challenging downhill. Before you ride it, read the mountain biking tips at the beginning of this section; this trail is recommended only for expert riders who enjoy technical terrain.

outcropping with views to the northwest of Lake Tahoe. The second viewpoint is after the trail switchbacks down through the forest to another rock outcropping on the east side of the ridge. Here you have views of the mountains to the east and southeast. A small creek that you cross, shaded by lush aspen trees, pops out of a jumble of huge granite boulders and is a special visual treat.

At 2 miles from the Big Meadow Trailhead, you meet the Grass Lake Trail, an alternative TRT route to CA 89. On the Grass Lake Trail, you can hike only 0.6 mile to meet CA 89, which is 1.4 miles shorter if you are walking or riding (and 400 feet less climbing and descending) than the trail to the Big Meadows Trailhead. If you are heading to the Grass Lake Trailhead,

Star Lake and hemlocks

you will find a moderately steep downhill through the trees to the trailhead located next to CA 89. You have now had the pleasure of being on the first section of the Tahoe Rim Trail, which was built by the Tahoe Rim Trail Association in 1984.

There is a small but reliable stream near the junction of the Grass Lake connector and the Tahoe Rim Trail. There is only one more water source, Grass Lake Creek, in the next 1.6 miles, about 0.4 mile from the Big Meadow Trailhead. It is a larger stream, crossed by a bridge, and is a good water source.

If you continue to the Big Meadow Trailhead, you will journey through more of the same terrain, a gentle downhill on many switchbacks through a mostly thick forest of predominantly Jeffrey pine and red fir. While you cannot see CA 89 from the trail, you can often hear it. At the finish, you arrive at a paved road, on which you turn left and go 100 yards to the entrance to a large parking lot and restroom facility (which has no water). At this junction you can also turn right and find an overflow campground with a toilet, trash receptacles, food storage lockers, and tent sites only 0.25 mile down the paved road. The next section of the TRT heads up to Big Meadow, Round Lake, and eventually the Pacific Crest Trail; it is past the trailhead restrooms at the southwest corner of the parking lot.

SECTION 6

Big Meadow to Echo Summit

15.7 miles

DIFFICULTY This section is moderately strenuous. Most of the trail is gentle up-and-down terrain or almost level through meadows or open fields. While there are several sustained climbs, they are not too steep, and most people will not find this section of the TRT exceptionally difficult. The most difficult portion of the trail, especially with a backpack, is between Bryan Meadow and Benwood Meadow, where you will experience an almost continuous, steep descent (or a steep climb if you are coming from Echo Summit).

BEST SEASONS This section of trail is best hiked from late June to early October. While you may see a few snow patches well into July, the trail is mostly snow-free by late June. The wildflowers come into full bloom in late July or early August, which makes that the best time to hike this section. When those flowers are in bloom, you are in for an incredible treat.

HIGHLIGHTS There are three beautiful lakes on this trip: Round Lake is only a 5.2-mile round-trip from the Big Meadow Trailhead. Dardanelles is 1.4 miles off the TRT and provides a 6.8-mile round-trip. Showers Lake is a good half-way stop 7 miles into the 15-mile hike. You will find impressive volcanic rock formations jutting high above the shores of Round Lake and on the ridges above Meiss Meadows. There are two large meadows, Big Meadow and Meiss Meadows, which, if you come at the right time of year, will provide you with some of the most stunning displays of wildflowers you will see on the Rim Trail. In addition, the trail has other interesting flora, including some spectacular juniper trees and enormous hemlocks. In a wonderful large bowl just past Showers Lake, you will encounter waterfalls and numerous wildflower-bordered streams caused by springtime snowmelt, as well as spectacular castle-like volcanic-rock formations. This section may have the greatest variety of views and habitats of any section of the TRT.

HEADS UP! While the trail has several good water sources and places to swim, the second half of the trail, between Showers Lake and Echo Summit, has more-limited water supplies, especially in the fall. Water can be found at the following locations: About 0.7 mile south of the Big Meadow Trailhead you will find Big Meadow Creek, which may dry up in the fall, at the edge of Big Meadow. The Upper Truckee River in Meiss Meadows is a major, swift-flowing stream. About halfway through the hike is Showers Lake, an excellent water source. Less than

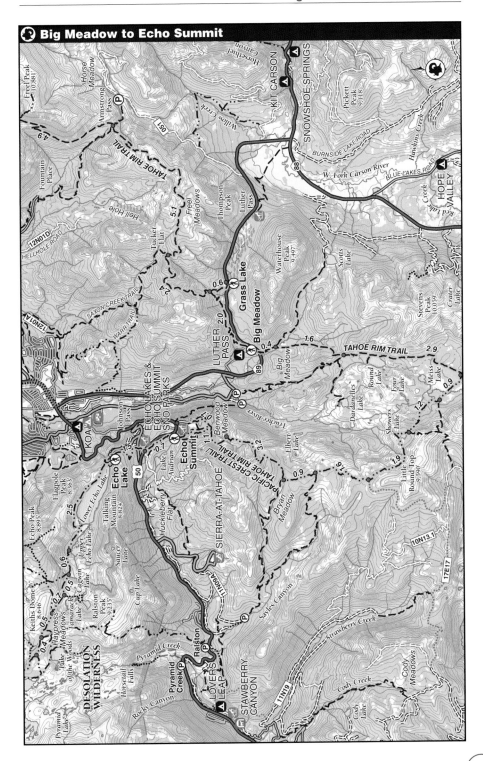

Big Meadow to Echo Summit

a mile past Showers Lake you will find several streams cascading down from the lava flows above. Just before reaching Benwood Meadow you will cross a small stream that is usually flowing.

The 2 miles of the trail descending to Benwood Meadow are quite steep, which can be very hard on the knees and every other body part. From the Echo Summit end, this is a major uphill starting just 1 mile into your hike.

TIPS FOR MOUNTAIN BIKERS From the Big Meadow Trailhead, bikes are allowed on the first 5 miles to the junction of the Tahoe Rim Trail and the Pacific Crest Trail. Bikes are *not* allowed on the PCT, so this ride is a 10-mile out-and-back. Much of this ride is technically challenging, with lots of rocks.

GETTING THERE, BIG MEADOW TO ECHO SUMMIT From the junction of CA 89 and US 50 in Meyers (south of South Lake Tahoe), drive 5.3 miles south on CA 89 to the Big Meadow Trailhead on your left (about 3.3 miles before signed Luther Pass). The previous segment, from the Kingsbury Grade South Trailhead to the Big Meadow Trailhead, ends here, and you start across the road and head uphill toward Big Meadow. The trailhead has a restroom facility and information kiosks.

An ancient juniper

GETTING THERE, ECHO SUMMIT TO BIG MEADOW From the intersection of CA 89 and US 50 in Meyers, drive 4 miles west on US 50 to the top of Echo Summit. Just 0.3 mile past Echo Summit, make a left turn, which is marked with an Echo Summit Sno-Park sign. Park on the southern end of the parking lot, and find the trail just to the west.

The author swimming in Showers Lake

Trail Description

THE TRAIL STARTS OUT at the lowest point in the Big Meadow Trailhead parking lot (southwest end). You walk about 250 yards through a forest of white fir, Jeffrey pine, and juniper before crossing CA 89. Once you cross the road the trail starts south. It is moderately steep, taking you uphill over rocky terrain through a thicker forest of Jeffrey pine, western white pine, and fir. After a little more than 0.2 mile you pass to the left of Big Meadow Creek, whose bed is filled with huge granite boulders and lined with aspen trees. At 0.3 mile from the trailhead the grade moderates, becoming almost level as you walk close to a stream on the right that is surrounded in the fall by the yellow leaves of aspen trees. Stop and close your eyes, and listen to the quaking sound that gives the aspen its name.

Soon you reach a junction. A left turn here would take you to Scotts Lake. Your trail, however, continues straight ahead to a large flat meadow with the new and original name Big Meadow. Just as you enter the meadow, the trail crosses a stream, which is good-sized in the spring but may dry up in late summer. This is, of course, Big Meadow Creek. As you head south across the

Hiking across Big Meadow

meadow, you are treated to views of the surrounding mountains to the south-west. As the meadow is only 0.7 mile from the trailhead, you can reach it in half an hour and enjoy a wonderful setting.

After you cross the meadow, the trail heads uphill again through the fairly dense forest of lodgepole, western white pine, and red fir. The tree cover thins now and then as you pass through more-open and sunny areas with sage-brush and a variety of wildflowers, including lupine, mule-ears, prettyface, and pennyroyal. You now occasionally pass through small meadows and groves of aspen trees, although for the most part this is a climb through a conifer forest. About 1 mile past the meadow, you reach a saddle and head 0.25 mile down-hill on steep trail that affords you great mountain views to the south and west. At 2 miles from the trailhead you reach a junction. To your right, the Meiss Meadows Trail (signed CHRISTMAS VALLEY) will take you to Dardanelles Lake in 1.4 miles (see Side Trip "Dardanelles Lake," opposite).

On the TRT you continue straight ahead and begin a gentle ascent through some very interesting volcanic rock formations, including lots of huge boul-ders of conglomerate that look like they were tossed haphazardly by a giant. At 2.6 miles from the trailhead (and 0.6 mile from the last junction), you reach the northeast corner of Round Lake. This lake is the largest you will encounter on this section of trail, and it offers great swimming and camping. The best camp-site is at the lake's northwest corner by the outlet, but the lake can get crowded on a sunny summer weekend. Thanks to an influx of volcanic sediments, Round Lake's color varies from a brownish green to an unusual aqua blue that is more reminiscent of the lakes and streams of western Canada than it is of most of the lakes in the Sierra. As you walk past Round Lake, a spectacular steep cliff of volcanic rock reaches skyward on your left. You will have the pleasure of gazing at this fascinating rock formation, known as the Dardanelles, from several locations as you complete your hike.

Paintbrush, lupine, and volcanic columns

SIDE TRIP
Dardanelles Lake

To reach Dardanelles Lake, you descend northwest on the Meiss Meadows Trail 0.2 mile through a mixed forest of pine, fir, and a few junipers to another trail that takes you an additional 1.2 miles to Dardanelles Lake. This trail first crosses a creek and then levels off in a grassy meadow before climbing again up a rocky tread. You reach Dardanelles Lake on a big granite flat overlooking the lake.

Above the lake's south shore is a massive rock cliff reaching right down to the water. There are great camping spots at Dardanelles Lake above a large, flat expanse of granite that reaches down to the northeast shore of the lake. The midsummer water can be warm in this beautiful lake, so enjoy a swim and then bask on the granite slab. Ahh . . . now you know why you put that backpack on. Be warned, however; because the lake is only 3.4 miles from the trailhead, you are not likely to be swimming alone.

Just after Round Lake you pass a small seasonal stream and lush meadow area rife with willows and wildflowers, including lupine, monkshood, Lewis's monkeyflower, paintbrush, ranger's buttons, and groundsel. You then ascend for about 0.5 mile through fine volcanic rock and sparse forest to an open area with aspen and sagebrush that provides views of the volcanic ridgeline to your west. The next 0.5 mile or so is a pleasant, mostly level walk through

The Dardanelles

wildflowers and scattered aspen groves quaking in the wind. Beautiful mountain views are available in every direction. You begin a gentle ascent into a forest of scattered conifers and then head downhill again past a luscious meadow with more mountain views to the east before you reach the Pacific Crest Trail (PCT) 4.9 miles from the Big Meadow Trailhead. Across the large open meadow, you will see two charming cowboy cabins built around 1880 by the Meiss family, for whom the meadows were named. They lived here while grazing their cattle through the 1930s, when they sold the land to the Schneider Family (the Schneider Cow Camp is a few miles southwest). The land was acquired for the U.S. Forest Service in 1965, but cattle grazing continued until around 2000. You cannot enter the cabins, but a use trail leads to an information plaque next to them.

You have now reached the PCT, which extends from Canada to Mexico. If Mexico is your goal, turn left, and in a few months you will be there. If you would prefer heading up to Canada, turn right. Either way, it's a long trip. This junction is located at the southernmost point of the Tahoe Rim Trail, and as you turn right at the junction, you begin heading north. For about the next 50 miles, the PCT and TRT are one trail. In addition to the Pacific Crest Trail

Meiss Meadows

and the Tahoe Rim Trail, your footpath was once a part of the little-used, unofficial Tahoe-Yosemite Trail (TYT), which traveled from Tuolumne Meadows in Yosemite to Meeks Bay on the west shore of Lake Tahoe, a distance of a little more than 185 miles. Now more of an idea than a trail, the TYT leaves the TRT north of Middle Velma Lake and heads over Phipps Pass, past a chain of lakes known as the Tallant Lakes, down to Meeks Bay.

Turning right at this junction, you begin your journey northwest with a lovely walk up the long valley of the Upper Truckee River. With high volcanic ridges to the east and west and a beautiful, almost level valley floor seasonally filled with wildflowers to walk across, Meiss Meadows can be the delight of your day. The flowers will vary from year to year, but you can expect to see low-lying lupine and elephant's heads in prolific display. As you walk northwest for about 0.5 mile on the PCT, you can see Meiss Lake across 0.5 mile of swampy meadow to the north. This shallow, warm lake makes a pleasant swimming hole in late summer. During early summer, the walk to the lake is swampy, and you may lose blood to mosquitoes.

Mostly through the meadow you meet the Upper Truckee River, a good source for water but a potentially wet ford in early summer. It's a lovely spot

Looking toward the ridge above Showers Lake

to sit in the grass and cool your feet while watching the brook trout frolic. After crossing the river, the trail heads uphill gently before rolling past a small pond and then beginning a fairly steep 0.5-mile climb up to Showers Lake. This steady uphill push through a mixture of deep forest and open fields gives you prolific displays of tall lupine, fireweed, and paintbrush. As you rise, you are rewarded with glorious views to the south and east of Meiss Meadows and the Dardanelles.

Just before you reach the shores of Showers Lake, a trail on your left heads steeply up to the ridge above the lake. It leads to Schneider Cow Camp and provides access to awe-inspiring views of the whole of Meiss Meadows and, if you follow the flat ridgetop away from the trail, views of Showers Lake far below.

Showers Lake itself is beautiful. The southern side is marshy, but the northern side provides great swimming opportunities enhanced by flat granite rocks that reach down to the water. There are several camping spots surrounded by hemlock, lodgepole pines, and—before late summer—mosquitoes, above the north and east sides of the lake. Unfortunately all that goodness comes with a price. This might be the most popular place to camp on the Tahoe Rim Trail. If you seek solitude, or wish to give this overused lake a break, stop for a swim and keep hiking to camp in a more remote setting farther north.

To continue past Showers Lake, your trail first heads steeply down below the lake's outlet and then climbs back up on the other side of the outlet's gully. For the next 0.5 mile you head through a pleasant forest with scattered trees (a few campsites are to your right) and wildflower-dotted meadows until you reach the edge of an enormous bowl. This 0.7-mile-wide bowl is a beautiful mixture of castle-shaped volcanic-rock formations; little streams plunging down steep, rocky gullies; thick fields of lupine, paintbrush, and mountain bluebells; and sometimes even late-season snowfields. Several swiftly moving cascades and stunning views to the east of Lake Tahoe, Dardanelles Lake, and Freel Peak complete this idyllic picture. It is a gentle climb across the bowl, and during midsummer the streams cascading down from the slopes above provide water for you and support an abundance of wildflowers. Near the end of the bowl, the path becomes steeper and the terrain drier, until you reach a minor saddle on a crest, where the surroundings change. Now you enter an area with sandy soils and scattered trees, mostly western white pine, lodgepole pine, and hemlock.

A distant Freel Peak from the bowl near Showers Lake

First you climb slowly; then the trail levels off and soon reaches the Schneider Cow Camp Trail, which turns left and heads first west and then southwest. Now at 1.9 miles north of Showers Lake, you continue north and make a 0.2-mile moderate descent to a saddle. Then your broad crest trail continues through the open hemlock forest, making several minor ascents and descents before leveling off and passing several more small meadows. At 3.5 miles from Showers Lake (and 1.6 miles north of the Schneider Cow Camp Trail junction), you meet a saddle junction, where a faded marked trail (that appears to be in danger of disappearing altogether) leads to Sayles Canyon.

The TRT continues along the sandy crest, mostly devoid of views, until a nice view opens up to the northwest of Pyramid Peak, the tallest peak of the huge granite ridgeline known as the Crystal Range, which lies in the heart of Desolation Wilderness. If you are thru-hiking, you will get much closer views of the Crystal Range as you walk along Lake Aloha about 15 miles north of here, but first you must finish this section. At 4.4 miles from Showers Lake, you reach Bryan Meadow and the trail that leads to it, which is about 3.9 miles from the Echo Summit Trailhead (see Side Trip "Bryan Meadow Trail," left).

SIDE TRIP
Bryan Meadow Trail

The Bryan Meadow Trail joins the Sayles Canyon Trail, and the combined trail descends an additional 0.6 mile to trailhead parking near the Sierra-at-Tahoe ski area, about 4 miles from Bryan Meadow. These trails provide another way to access Showers Lake for those in the upper US 50 area. Bryan Meadow is a large, gently sloping meadow of grass and seasonal mud. There is no apparent drinking water near the trail, but you can find water about 0.5 mile down the Sayles Canyon Trail, at or just below the west end of the meadow.

Just past the meadow, you climb, sometimes steeply, through a thick forest almost 0.5 mile to a ridge. After a steep uphill, what do you do next? Go downhill steeply, of course, passing a rock outcropping just off the trail to the right. From here you can enjoy views of the Upper Truckee River Canyon, South Lake Tahoe Airport, and Lake Tahoe in the distance. Your trail quickly levels off briefly, and you pass a pleasant little camping spot next to a small, usually reliable stream in a flat area in the trees. This is one of the last good campsites before you reach Echo Summit.

Beyond the campsite you begin a descent that starts out steep and becomes very steep as the trail heads down along the side of a granite ridge. The last time I walked this trail I found this downhill bone-jarring, toe-jamming, and knee-breaking—and those are just the words I can repeat! Since the first edition of this book, the TRTA has added several switchbacks to ease the grade, but

Upper Truckee River

the rocky descent is still very steep, so steep at times that it becomes slippery, so watch your step. The trail follows the east ridge of a big granite canyon that ends at Benwood Meadow. While for those descending this is a knee crusher, heading up from Echo with a backpack on is a challenge as well, especially for those of us with short legs trying to climb over the rocks.

Take a few rest breaks to enjoy the beautiful granite rock formations and the especially large hemlocks you pass. Keep your eyes open for marmots, as you are in their prime territory. Gazing across this deep canyon, you can see a higher ridge of granite on the west side. You'll pass a massive juniper at a crest saddle, which provides a viewpoint to the south. Views are highlighted by the Dardanelles and Round Top, which holds its north-facing snowfields well into late summer. After a grueling 2-mile descent, the downhill largely abates, and you cross the canyon's stream on a wooden bridge and head into a lush shady area loaded with tiger lilies, thimbleberries, and ferns. Over the next 0.75 mile you continue on a gentle downhill, with Benwood Meadow visible through the trees on your right.

By the meadow's northeast edge, you reach a junction with an older trail coming from a little-used alternate trailhead. With only 0.75 mile remaining to Echo Summit, turn left at the junction, and ascend gently north through a more open, drier forest of large Jeffrey pines and manzanita. Less than a third of a mile before reaching the Echo Summit Trailhead, you'll reach a junction.

Turn left to stay on the PCT/TRT, which contours above the Echo Summit Trailhead. Adventure Mountain Lodge, which provides sledding in the winter, can be seen below. The trail crosses a saddle amid some large boulders and then provides views down the American River Canyon along with filtered views of Lake Audrain as you proceed downhill toward the crossing of

The author crossing the Upper Truckee River

US 50 at Scout Peak Road, about 1.4 miles from the junction. This section was still under construction as of this writing but was set to be completed prior to publication.

Those headed to Echo Summit turn right on the TRT/Echo Summit Access Trail. This trail winds through boulders on sandy trail a third of a mile to the summit parking lot. There is a fee to park in this lot. The current Echo Summit parking lot was the location of the 1968 Olympic Trials for track and field. American athletes who competed here went on to Mexico City to win more Olympic medals in track and field than any other team in history. A plaque commemorating their accomplishments can be found in the parking lot.

SECTION 7

Echo Summit and Echo Lake to Barker Pass

32.7 miles from Echo Lake, 34.9 miles from Echo Summit

DIFFICULTY This strenuous section has many ascents and descents. While other segments of the Rim Trail can be hiked or biked in a day, this trip requires at least two days (for most people), and I recommend three. It can also be completed in sections by hiking out to Fallen Leaf Lake on the Glen Alpine Trail or to Emerald Bay from either Dicks Lake or Middle Velma Lake via the Bay View Trail.

BEST SEASONS In a typical year, most of this section is snow-free from mid-July to late October. Sections of this trail, especially the area on the north side of Dicks Pass, may have patches of snow into August following heavy snow years.

HIGHLIGHTS A wonderful wilderness experience awaits you as you travel through the heart of Desolation Wilderness. You will pass or see many beautiful lakes, including Lower Echo, Upper Echo, Cagwin, Ralston, Tamarack, Aloha, Heather, Susie, Grass, Gilmore, Half Moon, Alta Morris, Dicks, Fontanillis, Upper Velma, Middle Velma, and Richardson. If you like to swim in mountain lakes, this is the trail for you. You will also cross a high mountain pass with incredible views into two enormous watersheds.

HEADS UP! The starting elevation is about 7,400 feet at Echo Lake, and you will rise to nearly 9,400 feet at Dicks Pass. Water is plentiful for most of the trail, until you get north of Middle Velma Lake, where the water sources between it and Richardson Lake can quickly decline. Beyond the latter, there are several streams and springs. Miller Lake Creek is located about 1.75 miles north of Richardson Lake. A few miles farther gets you to Bear Creek. Neither are especially robust. There is another stream that should be big enough to filter water from a few miles south of Barker Pass. If you are thru-hiking, consider that you will not reach water again until another 2 miles north of Barker Pass.

You can cut off 2.5 miles of hiking by taking the Echo Lakes water taxi from the Echo Lake Trailhead to Upper Echo Lake. The taxi runs only during the summer and when water is high enough for safe passage between Lower and Upper Echo Lakes. For information about the water taxi, call the Echo Chalet at 530-659-7207.

This section, which overlaps the Pacific Crest Trail (PCT), is one of the more popular trails into Desolation Wilderness. It's beautiful, accessible, and

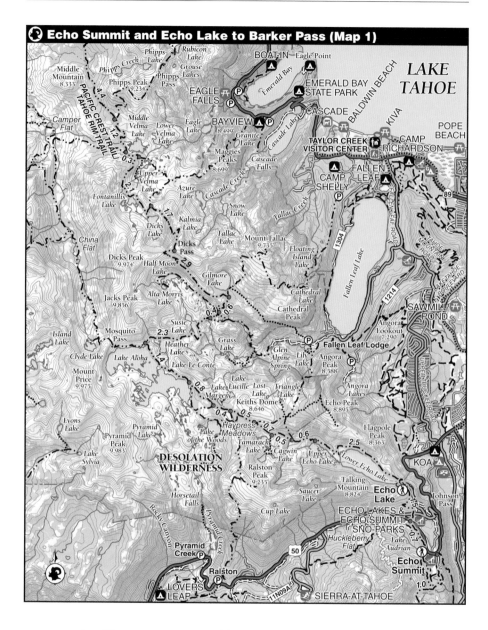

Echo Summit and Echo Lake to Barker Pass (Map 1)

very popular. If you want a true wilderness experience, Middle Velma Lake on a weekend in July is not the place to find it.

Wilderness permits are required to enter Desolation Wilderness. Day-use permits are available at the trailhead. If you are camping, you must obtain a permit through the U. S. Forest Service (USFS). (Permit information can be found in Chapter 1, page 4.) The biggest concern with this section of trail,

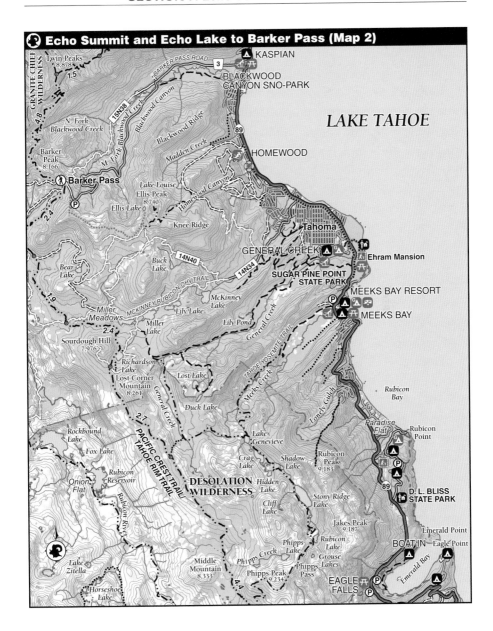

Echo Summit and Echo Lake to Barker Pass (Map 2)

KASPIAN

BLACKWOOD CANYON SNO-PARK

Twin Peaks
8,878'
1.5

GRANITE CHIEF WILDERNESS

4.8

BARKER PASS ROAD

15N38

N. Fork
Blackwood Creek

Blackwood Canyon

M. Fork Blackwood Creek

Blackwood Ridge

Madden Creek

89

HOMEWOOD

LAKE TAHOE

Barker
Peak
8,166'

Barker Pass

P

Lake Louise
Ellis Peak
8,740'

Ellis Lake

2.4

Homewood Canyon

Knee Ridge

Tahoma

GENERAL CREEK

Ehram Mansion

Buck
Lake

14N40

14N34

SUGAR PINE POINT
STATE PARK

Bear
Lake

MCKINNEY RUBICON OHV TRAIL

McKinney
Lake

MEEKS BAY RESORT

1.9

Miller
Meadows

MCKINNEY RUBICON

Lily Lake

Lily Pond

General Creek

MEEKS BAY

2.4

Miller
Lake

Sourdough Hill
7,976'

Richardson
Lake

Lost Lake

TAHOE YOSEMITE TRAIL

General Creek

Lost Corner
Mountain
8,261'

Meeks Creek

Lonely Gulch

Rubicon
Bay

Duck Lake

2.7

PACIFIC CREST TRAIL
TAHOE RIM TRAIL

Paradise
Flat

Rubicon
Point

Rockbound
Lake

Lake
Genevieve

P

Fox Lake

Rubicon
Reservoir

Crag
Lake

Shadow
Lake

Rubicon
Peak
9,183'

89

D. L. BLISS
STATE PARK

Onion
Flat

Rubicon River

DESOLATION
WILDERNESS

Hidden
Lake

Stony Ridge
Lake

Cliff
Lake

Jakes Peak
9,187'

Emerald Point

BOAT-IN

Eagle Point

Lake
Zitella

Phipps
Creek

Phipps
Lake

Rubicon
Lake

Grouse
Lakes

Emerald Bay

Middle
Mountain
8,333'

Phipps Creek

Phipps
Pass

EAGLE
FALLS

P

Horseshoe
Lake

4.4

Phipps Peak
9,234'

P

however, is that it is so magnificent you may want to stay forever, so be sure to bring along enough food.

GETTING THERE, ECHO SUMMIT TO LOWER ECHO LAKE This trail begins at either Echo Summit or Lower Echo Lake. Most people prefer to start at Lower Echo Lake (see "Getting There, Lower Echo Lake to Barker Pass," next page), where you can avoid 2.2 miles of mostly viewless hiking, much of it close to US 50 or among summer cabins. If you do start at Echo Summit, there are two hiking routes to Echo Lake, which are described here.

From Meyers take US 50 westbound about 4.5 miles to Echo Summit. From the summit, drive about 0.1 mile to a left turn. You will see a sign for Adventure Mountain Tahoe. Park in the parking lot, which requires a fee. The first hiking route to Echo Lake, the all-TRT route, is about 0.75 mile longer than the second route but provides more views and less road noise: Take a left in the parking lot on the TRT access trail, and in about 0.7 mile of gentle ascent you meet the TRT. A right turn then leads to a crossing of US 50 in about 1.4 miles. The TRT/PCT contours to a saddle and provides views down the American River Canyon and filtered views of Lake Audrain as you proceed downhill. At US 50, cross this very busy highway to where the trail resumes on the other side. The second route to the US 50 crossing is to use the Pony Express Trail, which is a right turn from the parking lot. It climbs slightly then follows US 50 down to a junction with the TRT just a short distance from the road crossing.

From the US 50 crossing, the trail heads uphill through a thicker forest 0.2 mile to Johnson Pass Road, the access road you would take if you were starting at Echo Lake. You cross the road, head up a steep embankment, and then see a swiftly moving stream to the left. With 1.1 miles to go to Lower Echo Lake, the trail crosses the stream, which could be challenging when the stream is filled with midsummer snowmelt. Walk through a lush and moist forest that will hold the snow until midsummer and then provide late-summer wildflowers. Soon afterward, you pass several summer cabins and head downhill to the parking area for Lower Echo Lake. Cross this large paved parking lot and another smaller dirt parking lot to a short trail. You will find restrooms and the Echo Chalet Store here before you cross the lake's dam and reach the main trailhead.

GETTING THERE, LOWER ECHO LAKE TO BARKER PASS From South Lake Tahoe drive west about 11.3 miles on US 50 to Echo Summit. From Echo Summit, drive 1 mile and turn right on Johnson Pass Road. Take this road 0.6 mile to a junction, where you will turn left on Echo Lakes Road (Forest Route 11N05). Go an additional 0.9 mile to a large parking lot on the left above the lake. Echo Chalet requests that people using the trail not park in the lower parking lot near the lake. You reach the trail by walking from the Echo Chalet Store and the lower parking lot over the dam to a TRT sign.

From Dicks Pass: Susie Lake, Half Moon Lake, Alta Morris Lake, Lake Aloha, and Pyramid Peak

GETTING THERE, BARKER PASS TO ECHO LAKE AND ECHO SUMMIT From Tahoe City, take CA 89 (West Lake Boulevard) about 4.25 miles south, and turn right onto Blackwood Canyon Road, starting opposite Kaspian Beach. Drive 7 miles to the crest above Blackwood Canyon, bearing left where the road splits at 4.3 miles, to where the paved road turns to dirt, and then continue another 0.4 mile to the PCT Trailhead's dirt parking lot on your right. To access the trail, walk south across the dirt road and uphill about 50 yards.

Barker Pass Road is closed during the winter months. The road has a gate at the entrance and another one 2.5 miles farther, just above where it crosses Blackwood Creek. The road is not usually plowed, and these gates stay closed until the snow is melted to the top of Barker Pass. If you are planning to use the Barker Pass Trailhead before mid-July, check the Trail Conditions section of the TRTA website at tahoerimtrail.org to make sure the road is open. Drive carefully on this narrow road, as it is popular for bike riding.

Trail Description

FROM LOWER ECHO LAKE'S DAM, the trail heads initially east and uphill, and near a switchback west you have a view toward South Lake Tahoe and Meyers. You walk west above the northern shore of long, narrow Lower Echo Lake. Your route is mostly minor ups and downs, bordered by spectacular granite formations, the deep-blue lake, and mountains. The most dramatic granite cliff towering above you to the north is topped with a flagpole, which explains its name, Flagpole Peak (8,363').

The trail rambles for about 1 mile and passes a few gnarled junipers and Jeffrey pines that are hanging on through cracks in the granite. Then it ascends above lakeshore cabins. Your footing becomes more challenging as the terrain becomes rockier. You pass the west end of Lower Echo Lake. Magnificent views of the entire lake open up, and you will see some charming rustic cabins along its granite shore. If you yell at Echo Lakes on a nice calm day, you will supposedly hear an echo, but please enjoy the tranquility and don't test the theory.

After a traverse, you then curve south over the rocky peninsula between Lower and Upper Echo Lakes. At 2.5 miles you come to a junction. A left turn takes you on a short trail down to a pier, which provides access to Upper Echo Lake and the Echo Lakes water taxi. The taxi pier is also a great location for an afternoon swim.

Continue west on the TRT from the junction, and climb steadily on more rocky terrain. You can enjoy breathtaking views of both Upper and Lower Echo Lakes from this section of trail. Upper Echo Lake is especially striking with its multiple granite islands topped with windblown trees. At 0.6 mile from the boat taxi, your trail levels off briefly, and you arrive at the boundary of Desolation Wilderness. Hiking beyond this point requires a permit, which you can get at the trailhead or through the USFS (permit information is found in Chapter 1, page 4). You will be hiking in Desolation Wilderness for more than 20 miles on the Tahoe Rim Trail. Just past the wilderness boundary, you reach a junction. To your right is a trail that leads steeply uphill to Triangle Lake, with access to Echo Peak (8,895') (see Side Trip "Triangle Lake," left).

You continue on the TRT/PCT, climbing 0.5 mile to a junction on your left that leads to nearby Tamarack Lake. The trail to this charming lake is located 3.6 miles from the Echo Lake Trailhead (and just 1.1 miles from the taxi), just inside the wilderness boundary. While it is a great place to stop, its proximity

SIDE TRIP Triangle Lake

The side trail near the Desolation Wilderness boundary leads first to Triangle Lake, then over a steep ridge down to just east of Lily Lake, and then by road down to Fallen Leaf Lake. The steep downhill trip is pretty, with many lush stream crossings loaded with early summer wildflowers. The trail faces north, however, so snow lasts well into the summer. If you hike this section before July, you may find several dangerous icy spots.

Lake Aloha and Crystal Range

to the trailhead means it is usually very busy. Your views are glorious, with imposing Ralston Peak (9,235') to the south and Echo Peak to the northeast.

After another 0.7 mile of rocky climbing, you reach another junction on your right, leading toward Fallen Leaf Lake. I've hiked this section dozens of times, and each time I stumble along in frustration over the rocky and tricky footing. Am I the only one who fantasizes about several hundred sledgehammers pounding these rocks into submission? The climb west finally abates in 0.4 mile at a junction in Haypress Meadows. Here you encounter a mixed forest of red firs, mountain hemlocks, and western white pines scattered around small grassy meadows that bloom with wildflowers throughout the spring and summer. Perhaps most important, though, you encounter a smooth walking tread. The trail southwest heads over to Lake of the Woods, as does a southbound one 300 yards later. About 150 yards past it you meet a trail descending north to lovely Lake Lucille and Lake Margery.

About 0.3 mile later, at 5.2 miles from the Echo Lake Trailhead, you meet another junction. The left turn takes you 0.5 mile west down to the southeast corner of Lake Aloha (from which you can wind 0.75 mile west over to the lake's 20-foot-high dam above granite-lined America Lake). The TRT/PCT goes straight ahead, through an area thick with midsummer wildflowers, to the east shore of Lake Aloha in 0.8 mile. This heavily forested trail section may be covered in snow through early summer.

Lake Aloha (8,116') provides an incredible, unique landscape. There are only a few wind-beaten trees surrounding the lake, but hundreds of small, flat rock islands are scattered across its surface. The Crystal Range, a huge ridge of granite topped by pointy Pyramid Peak (9,983') in the south and Mount Price (9,976') in the north, rises right up from the western shores of the lake. The trail meanders between granite boulders hugging the shore of Lake Aloha. Above the lake to the east is Cracked Crag, a big pile of rocks that families of marmots call home.

Along the entire length of the barren landscape above Lake Aloha, you will find great swimming and scattered camping spots. Aloha is one of my favorite places to take children camping. The little islands are fun to swim to, and the expanses of flat granite are perfect to stretch out on as you gaze at Pyramid Peak. A dam controls the waters of Lake Aloha, however, and the lake shrinks dramatically in the fall. That great waterside spot you visited in June may be a long distance from the shore after Labor Day. In fact, the watermasters can let the water out of the lake very quickly. I have seen the lake full, and then two weeks later and 5 feet lower, you could hardly recognize the place.

Heather Lake

Susie Lake

When you reach the northeast corner of the lake, you meet a junction, 1.4 miles from the last one. Straight ahead a trail goes over Mosquito Pass. (Sounds enticing, doesn't it? It's actually quite nice and leads to Clyde Lake, China Flat, Camper Flat, and a host of other remote lakes.) The TRT turns right. With Freel Peak (10,881') visible in the distance, the trail begins a descent that in 0.5 mile brings you to the north shore of Heather Lake. Along the way, you will pass stunning multicolored, rocky panoramas; lots of flowing water; early-summer wildflowers; hemlock; and mountain heather with its small red flowers. In early summer much of this area may be under snow. Heather Lake is a picturesque, large mountain lake with several tree-topped islands. There are limited campsites above the lake. Your 0.3-mile traverse along the north side of the lake on rocky tread leads toward its outlet and provides a special photo opportunity looking west: Heather Lake's biggest island is in the foreground, and the Crystal Range looms above the lake in the background.

Just past Heather Lake, a unique phenomenon is often visible in spring or early summer. Where the outlet creek melts under the snow, it forms a snow tunnel. I have seen it when the entrance to the snow cave was 10 feet high and at least 30 feet deep. Stepping into the cave provides you with a shower

Susie Lake

as well as the sight of the sun filtering through the blue geodesic shapes of the suncups above.

You now walk over a low, rocky saddle and begin a short descent to Susie Lake, another beautiful Sierra lake, this one bordered by red rock and dotted with islands. Susie Lake is loaded with campsites near its shore, many of which are illegal. Camps are required to be at least 100 feet from the shores of any lake, and you may be cited if you camp any closer to the water. Unfortunately, Susie Lake can be quite busy because it is only about 4 miles from the popular Glen Alpine Trailhead above Fallen Leaf Lake. The trail circles about half of the lake and offers views of imposing Dicks Peak (9,974') to the northwest; Jacks Peak (9,856') to the west; and the saddle of Dicks Pass to the north, 1,600 feet above you. This awesome view may lose some of its appeal when you realize that Dicks Pass is your next major goal.

Consider stopping at Susie Lake to relax and swim (Susie can be quite warm by midsummer) before making the big jaunt up the hill. About halfway along your trip around the lake, just before you reach the outlet for Susie Lake, about 1 mile past Heather Lake's outlet and a little more than 9 miles from the Echo Lake Trailhead, go around the bend to the right, and traverse the side of the hill

Dicks Lake, Dicks Pass, and Dicks Peak

about 50 yards to a tremendous viewpoint of Grass Lake and Keiths Dome to the southeast. Then return to the trail and cross the outlet creek. In the spring this crossing can be quite a challenge. If the main crossing is too deep, try going slightly upstream to cross on the logs. Be careful, whatever you choose.

Across the creek (hopefully you are still dry), continue around Susie Lake on the rocky terrain. After 0.25 mile, the trail veers east away from the lake and heads downhill (yes downhill, all of which and more must be made up a little farther on). In about 0.5 mile you reach a junction and the climbing begins. A right turn heads 3.8 miles to the Glen Alpine Trailhead above Fallen Leaf Lake. You, however, continue straight ahead on the TRT. After 0.4 mile you meet another junction on the right that also provides access to the Glen Alpine Trailhead in 3.6 miles, and just a bit farther on the left, a trailhead for Half Moon Lake (see Side Trip "Half Moon Lake," page 154).

From here, the TRT continues a climb of 3.5 miles to Dicks Pass, (9,380'). After a steady uphill grind, climbing dozens of wide steps, you reach a junction 0.6 mile from the Half Moon Lake trail junction. To visit Gilmore Lake, you can go an additional 0.2 mile straight ahead. Gilmore Lake is a large round lake bordered by big red firs and lodgepole pines that makes a pleasant spot for a

Half Moon Lake, Alta Morris Lake, Jacks Peak, and Dicks Peak

visit or an overnight stay, especially if you want to hike up nearby Mount Tallac (9,735'), which is about 1.75 miles farther and about 1,450 feet higher. Tallac's panoramic views of Lake Tahoe are considered to be among the best. At a little less than 11 miles from the Echo Lake Trailhead, Gilmore makes an excellent camping choice.

Ahead, the TRT climbs gently then becomes a more moderate climb traversing a ridge toward a conspicuous saddle. Along the way, the views of Susie Lake, Half Moon Lake, and Alta Morris Lake are magnificent. As you get closer to the top you conquer a few switchbacks. In summer and sometimes as late as early fall, the trail passes wildflowers in abundance, especially paintbrush, lupine, and fireweed. In the fall you may also see more explorer's gentians than I've seen anywhere else on the TRT. These deep-purple flowers are one of my

SIDE TRIP
Half Moon Lake

A left at the junction just beyond the Glen Alpine Trailhead junction takes you toward Half Moon Lake, which you will reach in 1.2 miles. Alta Morris Lake is another 0.7 mile. Both of these lakes are worthwhile goals for another trip. They lie at the foot of Dicks Peak and Jacks Peak, at the edge of a massive cirque, and may be less crowded than the lakes along the TRT/PCT.

favorites. While much of the journey is treeless, you will pass several gnarled junipers that have been battered by the wind, as well as hemlocks and western white pines, and then near the top, you'll pass the highest-elevation tree in the Sierra, the whitebark pine.

The trail finally reaches the saddle between Dicks Pass and Dicks Peak. From this location, your north view includes all of Dicks Lake directly below, as well as Fontanillis Lake, Middle Velma Lake, and a wide panorama of mountains in the distance, including Twin Peaks (8,878'), about 20 miles away, and on a clear day, Lassen Peak (10,457'), more than 130 miles away. Because the trail is covered in snow much of the year, it is important to understand the distinction between the saddle and the pass. While from the saddle it is another 200 feet of climbing to the pass, don't try to avoid the climb by starting toward Dicks Lake from

Dicks Lake

the saddle. It is a very steep, north-facing slope that is covered in ice much of the year. To reach the pass, continue on the trail east past a few particularly twisted whitebark pines to a level, treeless pass at 9,380 feet. Since the junction near Gilmore Lake, you have now climbed 1,100 feet over 2.9 miles.

Once you reach the top of the pass, you may be ready to collapse—I mean relax and enjoy the view. And what a view! To the south, you can see Lake Aloha; Pyramid Peak and the tip of Mount Price; Susie Lake; Half Moon Lake; Alta Morris Lake; and all the way south-southeast to Round Top (10,381'), about 20 miles away. Towering above you to the west is the imposing Dicks Peak and, to the southeast, Jacks Peak, both bearing patches of snow throughout most of the year. The best viewpoint is actually just before the top of the pass on a flat rock south of the trail.

You've had your fun. Now, 13.6 miles into your route, it is time for

SIDE TRIP Emerald Bay and Tim's Knob

A right turn at the junction east and above Dicks Lake will take you to Emerald Bay in 4.9 miles via the Bay View Trail. Straight ahead, a short distance northwest, is a rock knob once christened Tim's Knob by a hiking group that I was leading. With a quick scramble, you will discover tremendous views here of Fontanillis Lake, Dicks Lake, and Dicks Peak.

the long downhill to Dicks Lake. In the next 1.7 miles you drop about 900 feet via 18 switchbacks to a saddle above Dicks Lake. While the south-facing side of Dicks Pass is loaded with grasses and wildflowers growing in the volcanic soil and between the rocks, the north-facing side of fractured granite is dominated by thick stands of mountain hemlock with just a few grasses here and there. A north-facing slope, near 9,000 feet elevation on the western side of the Sierra, holds a tremendous amount of snow for much of the year. Thus the growing season is too short for most trees except the hardy hemlock. In addition, the hemlock is so prolific that it shades out the competition. But fortunately there are enough gaps in the trees to catch some awesome views of Dicks Lake and Peak. At the saddle east of and above Dicks Lake, you meet a junction (see Side Trip "Emerald Bay and Tim's Knob," above).

Fontanillis Lake

A left at the saddle continues your TRT/PCT journey. After a 0.2-mile descent southeast, you reach a short spur trail south to Dicks Lake, a large lake with plenty of space along its shore to roam or camp. Tucked away on the shady north side of Dicks Peak, this lake may still be frozen over in July after a big winter. At about 15.5 miles from the Echo Lake Trailhead, with about 17 easier miles to go, this locale may be a good one to spend the night. From the spur trail, your trail veers northwest and continues another 0.3 mile to Fontanillis Lake, one of my favorites. Exposed granite and plenty of hardy western white pines, hemlocks, and lodgepoles surrounding this lake make for a lovely visage. The trail approaches the granite-lined lakeshore in about 0.3 mile, but it takes another 0.3 mile to reach the shore. You hike in and out of numerous little bays, all with glorious views of Dicks Peak hulking above. You pass some lunch and swimming spots along the way (perhaps a bit cold for a swim, but how about a quick jump in?), but camping sites are in short supply. At the end of the lake, at 0.3 mile farther, the trail crosses its outlet creek (another tough early-season crossing) and descends toward Middle Velma Lake (see Side Trip "Upper Velma Lake," above).

> ### SIDE TRIP
> ## Upper Velma Lake
>
> For another interesting side trip, follow the creek you crossed as it falls down a steep granite slab almost 0.5 mile to Upper Velma Lake. The granite slab is steep enough that the water, which is usually quite shallow, cascades down the slope, but it is not steep enough to prevent you from walking right next to the water. A trail runs from Upper Velma Lake to Middle Velma Lake, where you can rejoin the Tahoe Rim Trail or head out to Emerald Bay. Or you can hike cross-country south from the bottom of the falls above Upper Velma Lake and up a drainage to a small unnamed lake tucked against the granite face (one of my favorite swimming holes). Here you meet the trail to Dicks Lake. A left turn here takes you out to Emerald Bay.

After crossing Fontanillis Lake's outlet creek, you begin a descent through a deep forest of mostly red firs. In 0.8 mile of walking and about 400 feet of descent, you reach a junction where the TRT heads left (west). A right turn would lead you out to Emerald Bay, about 5 miles away. On the TRT in a short distance you see Middle Velma Lake, a large lake with many islands that makes a great camping or swimming spot, although like much of Desolation Wilderness, it can be quite popular in the summer. In fact, of all the lakes you pass on the TRT, this is probably the busiest. If you are continuing north, be aware that the next lake, Richardson Lake, is smaller and marshier. Its accessibility by four-wheel-drive vehicles makes it less attractive to those backpackers hoping to enjoy a motor-free experience.

Fontanillis Lake's outlet creek roars out to Upper Velma Lake.

Once you have relaxed or camped at Middle Velma Lake, 17.5 miles from the Echo Lake Trailhead, you continue your journey north along the TRT/PCT. This second half of the hike from the Velma Lakes to Barker Pass is dramatically different from the first half. While the first half goes through the heart of Desolation Wilderness, with more rocks than trees and beautiful rock-lined lakes (and lots of people), you are now embarking on a 15-mile journey through forest with only one lake (and fewer people). Before you leave Middle Velma Lake, be sure to filter water: the next reliable source is Richardson Lake, 8.3 miles north.

Shortly after you leave Middle Velma Lake, you meet a junction, 0.3 mile past the previous one. Here a trail heads west down to Camper Flat and provides access to a host of Desolation Wilderness lakes and the Rubicon River. From this intersection, the TRT/PCT turns north and in 0.3 mile crosses boggy lands bordering Middle Velma Lake's outlet creek. It then goes 0.9 mile gently uphill to a junction with the Phipps Pass Trail, which turns off to the right (see Side Trip "Meeks Bay," opposite).

The TRT/PCT continues for the next 4.4 miles after the junction with the Phipps Pass Trail to a junction with a faint trail that heads over to Lake

Genevieve. (This little-used trail is over-grown in many spots and is not recommended.) Much of the trail now is smooth dirt, allowing swift passage through a forest dominated by ancient western white pines. There are two important features along this stretch. The first is seasonal Phipps Creek, reached after a 1.5-mile, mostly gentle descent. You could camp near it (if you must, as it is unlikely to have much water). The second is after a 2-mile, erratic ascent to a high point with

> ### SIDE TRIP Meeks Bay
>
> The Phipps Pass Trail heads about 12 miles to Meeks Bay. Along the way, you pass Phipps Pass and Peak (9,234') as well as Rubicon Lake, Stony Ridge Lake, Shadow Lake, Crag Lake, and Lake Genevieve. A wonderful point-to-point hike starts at Emerald Bay and ends at Meeks Bay via the Velma Lakes and Phipps Pass. This 18-mile route takes you by a string of lakes as well as exceptional viewpoints.

a short spur trail west, from which you can survey the Rubicon River lands. Along the way you pass several small meadows blooming with asters, Queen Anne's lace, groundsel, corn lilies, and elephant's heads. Eventually you roll up and down before climbing to the top of a ridge, where a short jaunt over fascinating granite rock formations leads to a viewpoint. Here Crag Peak and the deep, densely forested cirque containing the beginnings of General Creek can be seen. Thru-hikers are the primary users of this lightly traveled section of trail. If you meet someone who is hiking all the way from Mexico to Canada, be sure to take advantage of the opportunity and talk to them about their experiences. They have already walked more than 1,100 miles and surely have some fascinating stories to tell. One thing is certain: if they have made it this far, they are persistent. After the viewpoint to the east, another half mile of nearly level walking brings you to the junction with the General Creek Trail, leading to Lake Genevieve.

Beyond this junction, the combined TRT/PCT starts going downhill and then rolls gently up and down. You can enjoy the views of Mount Tallac and Dicks Peak in the distance to the south and contemplate the ancient junipers basking in the sunlight. As the trail moves into a more densely forested area, you will be leaving Desolation Wilderness at its north boundary, about 1.5 miles past the junction. Then, 0.75 mile north of the wilderness, traversing the base of Lost Corner Mountain, you reach a minor saddle. Next you head 0.7 mile down to the northwest corner of tree-lined Richardson Lake. This pleasant little lake has several campsites set among the trees, but look out for mosquitoes in the spring. Richardson Lake, about 6.7 miles from the Barker Pass Trailhead, is accessible via a four-wheel-drive dirt road, so be prepared for outdoor recreational vehicles approaching from Tahoe's west shore. The main users of the north-shore campsites, however, are long-distance TRT/PCT hikers who realize this is the only lake for a long way in either direction.

From Richardson Lake, the trail heads north, first descending the lower east slopes of Sourdough Hill and then proceeding west above Miller Meadows, beyond which it crosses an abandoned road. Shortly after, the TRT crosses Miller Creek, a seasonally good source of water that can dry up by late summer yet be potentially difficult to cross in the spring. About 200 yards farther is the popular McKinney Rubicon OHV Trail, which heads east down to the McKinney Estates subdivision on the west shore of Lake Tahoe or west on a famously difficult stretch of four-wheel-drive terrain to the Rubicon River.

Onward, your journey is pleasant as you pass through thick fir forest and occasional small meadows teeming with wildflowers. The gently rolling terrain heads northwest 1.5 miles to Bear Lake's sparkling outlet creek (which may last longer than Miller Creek) and then 0.4 mile farther up to the Bear Lake Road.

Turn left on the road, walk about 50 yards to the trail, and stay just above the road. You now have a 2-mile, 420-foot ascent to Forest Route 3. On it you will first pass one good-size stream that may be big enough to provide water, and then five smaller ones that will most likely only provide opulent flower displays. The trail climbs through Barker Meadows, with several open slopes dotted with mule-ears and views of Barker Peak. Eventually you reach Barker Pass, where the trail ends on a major dirt road that provides access through Blackwood Canyon to Lake Tahoe. (It starts out as dirt, but traveling toward Lake Tahoe it becomes paved in about 0.5 mile.) The TRT/PCT from Barker Pass to Tahoe City begins across the road and slightly to the west.

Barker Pass to Tahoe City

16.7 miles

DIFFICULTY This moderate to strenuous section has several hefty climbs, but more of the trail runs downhill than uphill. The starting elevation at Barker Pass is 7,650 feet, and the hike ends near the Truckee River at about 6,300 feet. If you are starting from the Tahoe City end, it is more strenuous.

BEST SEASONS This section can usually be hiked from late July to mid-October (or until the first major snowfall). Most of the first 7 miles is at high elevations that receive a lot of snow. Much of the trail faces north or east—a combination that leads to a late snowmelt.

HIGHLIGHTS This section has beautiful ridgeline views of Lake Tahoe, Granite Chief Wilderness, both Blackwood and Ward Canyons, and lush areas loaded with wildflowers in both canyons. Twin Peaks (8,878 feet), a Sierra Crest landmark, is accessible from the trail. In addition, there are numerous small stream crossings, several good camping spots, and a pretty series of meadows known as Page Meadows. A lovely little waterfall cascades near one part of the trail in upper Ward Canyon. Dense forest areas with huge pines, firs, and hemlocks grow in both the Blackwood and Ward Creek watersheds. Wildlife is abundant, including bears, coyotes, raccoons, blue grouse, and perhaps goshawks and spotted owls.

This lakeless stretch between Barker Pass and Twin Peaks tends to get less use than the trails in the Desolation Wilderness area, which has mountain lakes. However, in the Page Meadows vicinity, bikers, hikers, and joggers abound. At the end of your trip you may find that the Truckee River is a perfect place to swim or to complete your day with a rafting trip.

HEADS UP! In the fall, as streams dry up, the water supply can be limited. You reach the North Fork of Blackwood Creek, about 2.5 miles north of Barker Pass, at the bottom of a meadow. In the next mile, you may find one or more springs before late summer. However, the most dependable water source is Ward Creek, about 8.5 miles north of Barker Pass. You parallel the creek, sometimes at a distance, for more than 3 miles, and by the time you start north from the canyon's main road, you have only 5 miles to the Tahoe City Trailhead.

There are several short sections of trail that are challenging for those who experience a fear of heights: just before reaching two large volcanic plugs, and near the North Fork of Blackwood Creek.

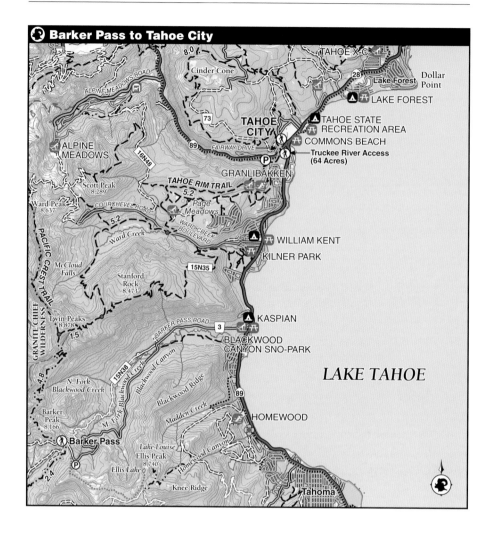

Barker Pass to Tahoe City

The only places to swim are the Truckee River at your destination and at adjacent Lake Tahoe. The Commons public beach is about 0.25 mile east of the TRT on CA 28 in the center of Tahoe City. There are lots of junctions and turnoffs on this section of trail, so follow the TRT trail markers, and pay attention to where you are going.

Barker Pass Road is not plowed and remains closed to cars until the snow melts in late spring or early summer. Often the road is not open until late June or possibly even later, given a really big winter. The road is narrow in spots and is a favorite for bike riding. If you're a cyclist, observe the 20 mph speed limit and watch out for in-line skaters, rollerskiers, wayward dogs, and parents with strollers.

TIPS FOR MOUNTAIN BIKERS The first 5 miles of the TRT overlap with the PCT, and bikes are *not* allowed on the PCT. From Twin Peaks to Tahoe City, however, bikes are allowed: Start at 64 Acres in Tahoe City (also known as the Truckee River Access parking lot; see directions on page 165), follow the TRT along the Truckee River, and then head uphill rather steeply. In some places there are lots of loose rocks. After 1.7 miles, you reach the east edge of the Page Meadows area and a whole network of great biking trails. Here the TRT turns right (to the left, a trail crosses a small meadow and heads uphill into the trees) and provides a great gentle uphill ride through the forest above the perimeter of the meadows. In another 1.3 miles, you reach another junction, where you have two riding options.

Your first option: Turn left and follow the TRT as it skirts the edge of a meadow and crosses another one. The section of trail is built up on bricks above the meadow to protect the fragile ecosystem. After passing Page Meadows, the trail heads into the woods. At first the TRT follows a moderate downhill course, and then it descends more steeply on an old dirt road. Just 0.1 mile before reaching Ward Creek Boulevard, the TRT turns right, becomes a single-track trail, and heads southwest. From here you go more gently downhill to

Camas lilies in Page Meadows

Ward Creek Boulevard, a paved road that leads west to the Alpine Peaks subdivision. The TRT continues directly across the road.

Your second option: The alternative route to Ward Creek Boulevard and the TRT is to go straight for about 1 mile to the next major junction. Turn left and enjoy a fun downhill to paved Chamonix Road in Alpine Peaks. Just before reaching Chamonix a singletrack heads off the dirt road to the paved road. Take Chamonix downhill to Courchevel, turn left, and head downhill. In a little more than 1 mile, you will see the TRT on your right. (Along the way, the road name changes from Courchevel to Ward Creek Boulevard.)

From Ward Creek Boulevard, the TRT follows an old dirt road about 2 miles to a washed-out bridge. After the bridge, the trail starts uphill in earnest through a beautiful area of small meadows where aspens are interspersed with forests of tall old-growth trees. As the trail gets steeper, most bikers will walk their bikes or stop and turn around. Eventually, about 5.2 miles beyond Ward Creek Boulevard, you reach a saddle between Twin Peaks on your right and Stanford Rock on the left. The trail to the right leads steeply uphill to Twin Peaks, where bikes are not allowed. The trail to the left leads uphill very steeply to a great lookout point and then a 4-mile fun downhill on a former dirt road converted to a flow trail in 2019 to Ward Creek Boulevard. Just before reaching the road, you cross Ward Creek in an area that can be deep and difficult to ford until late summer. An alternative route is to take a right turn just before reaching Ward Creek and follow singletrack through Ward Creek State Park to CA 89 near Sunnyside.

The 4-mile section between Stanford Rock and Ward Creek is also challenging going the opposite direction as an uphill ride. The start is about 0.5 mile east of the TRT on Ward Creek Boulevard. You will see a gated trail leading off from the road next to a large open, flat area on the south side of the highway. Immediately after passing the gate you cross Ward Creek. The climb varies between moderately steep to very steep and provides tremendous views of the lake and Blackwood Canyon. Eventually you reach the Stanford Rock viewpoint and a spectacular view of Ward Canyon, Twin Peaks, and the Sierra Crest. After enjoying the view, turn left (south) and follow the trail downhill to a junction with the TRT. Or you can turn around and ride back the way you came. If you choose to ride from here on the TRT, be prepared for a challenging and steep ride on loose soil, with several technical, rocky sections.

GETTING THERE, BARKER PASS TO TAHOE CITY From Tahoe City, take CA 89 (West Lake Boulevard) south about 4.25 miles, and turn right onto Blackwood

Canyon Road, starting opposite Kaspian Beach. Drive 7 miles to the crest above Blackwood Canyon, bearing left where the road splits at 4.3 miles, to where the paved road turns to dirt, and then another 0.4 mile to the dirt PCT Trailhead parking lot on your right.

GETTING THERE, TAHOE CITY TO BARKER PASS From the junction of CA 89 and CA 28 at the stoplight in Tahoe City, head south on CA 89 (West Lake Boulevard) about 0.25 mile to the Truckee River Access parking area (64 Acres). Park in the lot. The trail starts along the south side of the Truckee River. As you follow the Truckee River west and downstream, the trail begins as a bike trail. Walk on the trail as it passes underneath CA 89 and leads to a junction where the bike trail heads left and the TRT goes straight ahead. The trail quickly becomes a wide dirt path with the Truckee River just to your right. It climbs gently, then descends past good swimming holes in the river to meet a seasonal stream crossing next to the river before crossing a gravel road to the start of the singletrack section of the Tahoe Rim Trail.

The Sierra Crest

Trail Description

AT BARKER PASS (7,650') the trail begins by traversing through thick forest west around the south side of Barker Peak (8,166'), to a more open slope where you get excellent views of Desolation Wilderness to the south. In 0.9 mile your moderately steep walk through a field of mule-ears reaches the Sierra Crest, where you have views east down the expanse of Blackwood Canyon to Lake Tahoe. Beyond the crest, your route continues with a gentle ascent northeast across the canyon's upper slopes. In 0.25 mile you pass a beautiful stream bordered with aster, delphinium, tiger lily, columbine, and paintbrush, among other wildflowers.

After a pleasant walk gently up through mostly open volcanic terrain that is interrupted by a red fir forest, you cross a steep face to the base of two lofty volcanic plugs, about 0.5 mile past the stream. (This is the section that might be of concern for those afraid of heights). From here you have wide-open views of Lake Tahoe and Blackwood Canyon to the east. From these lofty twin rock formations, the trail descends into a large bowl lush with wildflowers and greenery late into the summer. Mountain hemlock is now the dominant tree.

Blackwood Canyon

Granite Chief Wilderness boundary

These fascinating trees are laden with cones on their thick green foliage. The hemlock can be most easily identified by its drooping top, which gives it a fairy-tale appearance. The U.S. Forest Service (USFS) has identified one tree in this grove as the largest hemlock in the Tahoe region, but there are so many big trees, you might have trouble figuring out which one it is.

As you descend farther into this lovely bowl, you pass several areas graced by Sierra wildflowers, including explorer's gentian, which blooms into the fall. At the bottom of the bowl, about 2.5 miles from the trailhead, you find several nice camping sites. There is a running stream (North Fork of Blackwood Creek), a nice flat place to rest your head, and views of Lake Tahoe and Blackwood Canyon. Just beyond this camping spot, the trail rounds a corner, descends along the steep canyon wall, and then passes several spring-fed creeks. It's a wild-flower haven with late-season water and a continuing series of views.

After about a 1-mile traversing descent from the camping spot, your trail starts a series of long switchbacks up almost to the crest of the ridge. The climb begins in a dark, viewless forest of large red fir trees. As you climb, you will see Ellis Peak to the southeast, Desolation Wilderness to the south, and almost all of Blackwood Canyon to the east. Just below the top of the crest, you climb out of the trees and then round the ridge to find new views of the south side of Twin Peaks (8,878').

Soon you ascend to the Granite Chief Wilderness boundary sign and quickly reach the Sierra Crest, where there are views in all directions. To the north and west, you can see the full expanse of Granite Chief Wilderness; to the northeast, you see nearby Twin Peaks; and to the east, Lake Tahoe. To the south, Desolation Wilderness lies in the distance. In the foreground you can review the knife-edge ridge whose back side you just climbed. If you are looking for a great place to sit a spell and have lunch, you might have found it.

Just 0.25 mile beyond this viewpoint you meet a junction, at 4.8 miles from Barker Pass. This is where the TRT and PCT part ways after running together for a total of about 50 miles. Straight ahead are the PCT and Canada. A right turn takes you along the southern slope of Twin Peaks on the TRT. Those of you without the time or inclination to hike to Canada should turn right.

In 0.5 mile you meet a spur trail to the top of the eastern Twin Peak. (For those hiking south, this junction is about 6.2 miles from the Ward Canyon Trailhead.) If you plan to take this trail, be forewarned that it can be treacherous, but the views are spectacular.

Hemlocks and Twin Peaks

The best rock to lie on

From the summit trail junction, descend along a ridgeline on the TRT for 1 mile through a mixed forest of red fir, hemlock, and western white pine to a saddle. Along the route you have scenic views of Squaw Valley and Alpine Meadows to the north. The saddle has nice dry campsites with views just before reaching a junction. At 1.5 miles from the PCT junction, the TRT turns left (north), while the trail straight ahead continues east to Stanford Rock, as described above in the mountain biking tips.

You are now heading north down a rather steep hill through a deep forest of fir and hemlock trees into Ward Canyon. This portion of the trail is quite steep, but the views, especially of Twin Peaks to your left, are glorious. After about 1.1 miles of downhill, you encounter a large meadow at the base of Twin Peaks. This beautiful meadow, surrounded by imposing peaks high above, is a splendid resting spot. Next, the descent is less steep and takes you into a more thinly forested section. You pass another meadow and then see 30-foot McCloud Falls, just off the trail on your left. Switchback down toward Ward Creek for 0.9 mile, and then pass several lush meadows that are surrounded by aspen trees, as well as large red firs and Jeffrey pines.

Cross Ward Creek on a wide bridge. The usually swiftly moving creek is a great place to take a break and soak your feet in the water before a few more dusty miles. Across the bridge you walk on a former road that first traverses 0.5 mile and then heads gently downhill. After passing a tributary of Ward Creek (a potentially challenging ford early in the season), the trail joins an old dirt road. You can camp immediately past the bridge site, north of the road, in an opening in the trees, which the USFS used as a camp when they were building the TRT between here and Twin Peaks. You can usually find water in the creek or in a spring on the northeast edge of the camp.

The TRT heads gently downslope for 1.75 miles through meadows and forest on old roadbed to a trailhead on Ward Creek Boulevard, a paved road leading west to Alpine Peaks, a development on the back (south) side of Alpine Meadows Ski Area. Along this stretch of trail, there are several nice views, including one of Grouse Rock, which you can see from a particularly pretty meadow that borders Ward Creek on your right. (Grouse Rock is the large volcanic rock on the ridgeline to the west between Twin Peaks and Ward Peak that sits right above the Pacific Crest Trail. It is a popular destination for backcountry skiers.) You are following Ward Creek, but it is mostly unseen until you approach Ward Creek Boulevard. Your trail, blocked at the trailhead by a gate, was once used regularly as an off-highway-vehicle route. In the New Year's floods of 1997, the road was washed out in several locations. Where it was once smooth dirt, the trail in many places became a jumble of rocks after the soil washed away.

At Ward Creek Boulevard you see a TRT kiosk. With 5 miles to go to Tahoe City, cross the road and begin climbing through a forest of white fir and Jeffrey pine. After about 0.25 mile the trail turns left onto a dirt road and heads uphill more steeply. Near the top of the hill, Ward Canyon, Ward Peak, and the Sherwood chairlift at Alpine Meadows Ski Area are visible through an opening in the trees.

After a steep 0.6 mile, the trail levels at a junction with another dirt road. A right turn here would take you to eastern Page Meadows and the Talmont Estates development in about 1 mile. The TRT angles left and winds up through a young forest for 0.4 mile to the road's end, where posts were installed to block vehicles. Here a lateral trail heads left to the lowest of the Page Meadows and provides access to the Alpine Peaks neighborhood about 0.25 mile away (see Side Trip "Basque Sheepherders' Oven," left).

You are now in the Page Meadows area, a series of five interconnected meadows that serve as a popular retreat for hiking, mountain biking, and cross-country

SIDE TRIP Basque Sheepherders' Oven

Just off this lateral trail is an oven built by Basque sheepherders. Built in the 1950s, the oven provides evidence of a unique lifestyle once present in Page Meadows. Sit next to the oven and imagine sheepherders enjoying freshly baked bread while watching sheep graze in the meadow under the beautiful aspen trees. If you continue on the lateral trail through the meadow leading to Alpine Peaks, you will find lots of flowers, aspens, and a clear stream.

skiing. For residents who live in nearby developments, the meadows provide an easily accessible outdoor haven and are especially popular as a place to go cross-country skiing on full-moon nights.

From the trail that headed to the oven, the TRT goes straight ahead through the road gate and climbs gently past a grove of aspens on your left for a short distance before entering a large meadow. The trail is built above the meadow to prevent damage to this fragile ecosystem. About a third of the way across this beautiful meadow, you meet a trail starting east. It provides access to three other large meadows, as well as a route to Tahoe City. The TRT continues straight. At the end of the meadow, turn around to enjoy a tree-framed view of Twin Peaks. Are you a yogi? This is a great place for a headstand. Your trail now heads north out of the meadow into a grove of aspens before entering a forest of fir trees. About 0.2 mile from the meadow you meet another junction with a spur trail heading left (see Side Trip "Alpine Meadows," above).

The TRT turns right (east), however, and parallels the mostly unseen meadows on your right. The next 1.3 miles are primarily downhill, with several short uphills. This is a popular mountain biking section for a good reason. It rolls along with lots of fun little twists and turns on a fairly smooth surface. The trail levels out near the edge of a small meadow, and you meet another junction (see Side Trip "Rawhide Drive," right).

The TRT turns left (east) and begins a 0.6-mile steep descent down a narrow canyon, with rocky and challenging (for bikes) terrain, to a junction. The TRT veers left. If you are on your bike and would like to avoid this difficult section, refer to the side trip "Rawhide Drive" for an easier route to Tahoe City. From the TRT marker, you

SIDE TRIP
Alpine Meadows

At the junction north of the meadow with that good Twin Peaks view, a spur trail leads left (west). In about 3 miles you would reach the Alpine Meadows residential area. In addition, spurs from this trail lead to the top of Scott Peak, the Alpine Meadows Ski Area, or Tahoe City via the bike trail along the Truckee River. These trails are fun mountain biking routes or pleasant hikes through the forest.

SIDE TRIP Rawhide Drive

A right turn at the junction in the small meadow leads across a snippet of meadow and then, after a short uphill, runs into a major trail. A right turn at this trail junction will take you to the biggest meadow in the Page Meadows area in 0.5 mile. Turning left at the junction takes you 1.5 miles downhill to Rawhide Drive, near Tahoe City. To head to Tahoe City from this point, proceed north on Rawhide Drive to Granlibakken Road, turn right, and then follow Granlibakken Road to West Lake Boulevard (CA 89). Turn left on the bike trail, and in 0.5 mile you will be in Tahoe City.

Page Meadows

travel almost 1 mile, generally downhill, winding through the shade of fir, cedar, and sugar pine trees. Along the way you pass close to the Granlibakken Resort and the Tree Top Adventure Park at its edge. You might hear the sound of a zip-liner zipping through the air just off the trail. Soon after Granlibakken you descend to a trail junction on the Truckee River. Turn right and follow the trail 0.1 mile east to a gravel road where the trail tread ends. You now walk across the road slightly left and across a small seasonal stream. Stop here to swim in the Truckee River or to watch summer rafters. Your trail is now a dirt road heading along the river upstream 0.3 mile to a paved road. This road becomes a bike trail that travels under CA 89 and then leads to the 64 Acres (Truckee River Access) parking lot.

From the parking lot, a 0.3-mile walk along bike paths and roads reaches the beginning of the next section of the TRT, from Tahoe City to Brockway Summit (Section 1, page 60). Follow the bike trail to the pedestrian bridge across the Truckee River, which leads to CA 89. Turn right, and follow the bike trail 50 yards to its end. Cross CA 89 to Fairway Drive, which is directly across the highway. Go 0.2 mile up Fairway Drive to the Fairway Community Center parking lot on your right. The TRT continues across the street.

7

Other Tahoe-Area Hiking and Biking Trails

ONCE YOU HAVE exhausted all of the recreation possibilities on the Tahoe Rim Trail, you may want to check out some other Tahoe-area trails. Here are brief summaries of a few of my favorites.

Hiking

Emerald Bay

DIFFICULTY Easy. Depending on where you go, the distance is anywhere from 2 to 9 miles.

MAP *Tahoe Rim Trail Section 7: Echo Summit and Echo Lake to Barker Pass (Map 2), page 145*

BEST SEASONS Do this hike in early spring or later in the fall. After a mild winter, you can hike it from April through December.

HIGHLIGHTS Emerald Bay provides many great hiking opportunities. On the edge of a beautiful sandy beach at the western edge of the bay is the Vikingsholm castle with its granite touches, carved wood spikes and gargoyles, roof covered with wildflowers, and gorgeous stained glass windows. The castle was constructed from 1928 to 1929 by Lora Knight, after she had purchased 239 acres at the end of Emerald Bay for $250,000. Trails lead from the Vikingsholm to a beautiful waterfall and along both sides of Emerald Bay. The Emerald Bay area is loaded with osprey nests, so here is your chance to experience this magnificent bird.

HEADS UP! During the summer, these trails (especially the 1-mile portion from the parking lot to the Vikingsholm) can be very busy! The best time to

Vikingsholm at Emerald Bay

go is on a weekday in early spring or late fall, when you will be more likely to have the place to yourself.

GETTING THERE From Tahoe City, drive 18 miles south on CA 89 to the Vikingsholm parking lot located on the left (10 miles north of the intersection of CA 50 and CA 89 in South Lake Tahoe). During the summer, this lot can be full early in the day. An alternative parking area is located a quarter mile south on CA 89 at the Eagle Falls Trailhead. There is a fee to use either lot.

BRIEF TRAIL DESCRIPTION The trail from the parking lot to the Vikingsholm is a gentle descent for a mile. Two trails lead out from the Vikingsholm. The first takes you 1.5 miles along the north side of Emerald Bay, in and out of sandy inlets, past the Emerald Bay Boat Campground, and to Emerald Point. This south-facing section of trail is the first area to emerge from the winter snows. From Emerald Point, the trail continues across a small peninsula and heads north 3 miles along the lakeshore to Bliss State Park (along the way, keep your eyes open for ospreys and eagles).

A second trail leaves the Vikingsholm and heads southwest a short distance to a junction at a bridge across Eagle Creek. A right turn leads you up to

Sunset near the Emerald Bay Boat Campground

Eagle Falls in a third of a mile. The falls are quite dramatic when they are filled with springtime runoff. If you turn left, you will cross Eagle Creek, travel past the Emerald Bay landslide of 1955, then continue along the southern side of the bay to Emerald Bay Campground, 1.5 miles from Vikingsholm.

Loch Leven Lakes

DIFFICULTY It is a moderately difficult but well-graded climb to the first of the three Loch Leven Lakes. The journey between the lakes is an easy ascent. If you visit all the lakes and return, it is a total distance of a little less than 8 miles.

MAP USGS *Cisco Grove* and *Soda Springs*

BEST SEASONS Late June–late October. The trail is at a relatively low elevation (5,880'), but it faces north in an area that receives much snow.

HIGHLIGHTS This hike is 30 miles closer to the Bay Area and Sacramento than are most other Sierra hikes. It is also easily accessible via I-80. In just a few miles you can reach three wonderful lakes lying on granite benches. The two farthest lakes provide good camping opportunities and excellent swimming in relatively warm water. These lakes make especially attractive locations for

Upper Loch Leven Lake

family camping trips, as they are great to explore and easy enough for many families to reach.

HEADS UP! This trail's easy accessibility keeps Loch Leven Lakes busy throughout the summer. You will almost certainly not have the lakes to yourself. Over the years, the trail has been severely eroded, making some parts of it a challenging traverse of a rock pile.

GETTING THERE Take I-80 eastbound to Exit 168 (Big Bend), which is about 2.5 miles east of Cisco Grove and 6 miles west of Soda Springs. Drive about 1 mile southwest on Hampshire Rocks Road (Old CA 40), past the Rainbow Lodge, and park on the right at the trailhead parking lot, which has a pit toilet and parking for about 15 vehicles.

BRIEF TRAIL DESCRIPTION The trail is a pleasant, woodsy walk up past several streams bordered by wildflowers before it crosses a railroad track. At that point, it begins a moderate, well-graded climb through a thick forest of firs and pines. A little less than 3 miles from the trailhead, you reach Upper Loch Leven Lake, followed in 0.3 mile by Middle Loch Leven Lake, and then at 3.9 miles from the trailhead, my favorite of the three, High Loch Leven Lake.

Also nearby is Salmon Lake, accessed via a trail near the lowest lake. It is also shallow and warm and is unique for the Tahoe Sierra in that it has catfish.

Winnemucca Lake and Round Top Lake

DIFFICULTY Easy–moderate. This is a fairly short hike—only 2.5 miles to Winnemucca Lake and 3.4 miles to Round Top Lake—with a round-trip distance of 6.8 miles. The high elevation of this trail may make it moderately difficult for hikers unaccustomed to high altitudes. The trail starts at 8,590 feet, with Round Top Lake sitting at 9,350 feet. A faint trail also leads from Round Top Lake up a very steep mile to the summit of Round Top (10,381'). If you add Round Top to your itinerary, this hike is strenuous.

MAP USGS *Caples Lake* and *Carson Pass*

BEST SEASONS Late July–October. This hike is in a high-elevation area that receives a tremendous amount of snow, which can last until midsummer.

HIGHLIGHTS If you are looking for relatively easy access to some tremendous high mountain scenery, this is a great choice. The area between Carson Pass and Winnemucca Lake has an incredible variety of wildflowers from late July through August. The prolific flower display may include lupine, elephant's-head, gentian, delphinium, monkeyflower, tiger lily, columbine, rein orchis, and a full palette of paintbrushes. The area around Round Top Lake and the accompanying peak has a rugged appeal and is a popular destination for summertime skiers and snowboarders, who are trying to find that last patch of snow. This hike is a good choice for those in the South Lake Tahoe area, which is only about 25 miles away.

HEADS UP! Permits are required to camp in the Mokelumne Wilderness Area, where much of this hike takes place. During the summer, permits are available at the trailhead at Carson Pass. During the rest of the year, you need to contact the Eldorado National Forest's Amador Ranger District in Pioneer, California, at 209-295-4251. Given the short distance to the lakes and the fragility of this high-altitude location, it is best to day hike this trail.

GETTING THERE The trail starts from Carson Pass near Kirkwood Ski Area south of Lake Tahoe. From Meyers, take CA 89 south about 11 miles to the intersection of CA 88 and CA 89 (Picketts Junction). Be sure to come to a complete stop at this remote intersection; the California Highway Patrol watches it closely. Turn right on CA 88, and go approximately 9 miles through

Hope Valley and up to Carson Pass. There is a parking area on your left just as the road reaches the summit. The trailhead also has an information center (summer only). There is a fee to park.

BRIEF TRAIL DESCRIPTION From the Carson Pass parking lot, your route is a gentle to moderate ascent for 2.5 miles to Winnemucca Lake. You pass incredible summertime wildflower displays in the open areas below Winnemucca Lake. A mile more of moderate climbing brings you to Round Top Lake, which sits in a basin just below huge rocky crags and Round Top (10,381'). From here you can follow a faint, very steep trail to the top of Round Top, where you will find awe-inspiring 360-degree views. Your views to the north include Lake Tahoe and a number of high peaks surrounding it, including Freel Peak (10,881'), Mount Tallac (9,735'), Pyramid Peak (9,983'), and on a clear day Mount Rose (10,776'), some 46 miles away. The last few hundred feet at the top of the mountain is steep, crumbly volcanic rock. Stop where the ridgetop trail meets the steep rock for equally spectacular views without the added danger.

Crag Lake

DIFFICULTY Easy–moderate (about 4.6 miles)

MAP *Tahoe Rim Trail Section 7: Echo Summit and Echo Lake to Barker Pass (Map 2),* page 145

BEST SEASONS Mid-June–mid-October. This trail provides late-spring access to eastern Desolation Wilderness.

HIGHLIGHTS With the high granite slab of Crag Peak looming over it, Crag Lake is an especially magnificent spot. This hike is the easiest route into Desolation Wilderness from the Tahoe Basin, and it is usually snow-free a month earlier than Eagle Falls, Bay View, and Echo Lake (the other Tahoe area trailheads used to access Desolation Wilderness). Both lakes are great locations for swimming or camping.

HEADS UP! This trail is quite popular for both day hiking and camping, so parking can be limited in the summer. A permit is required to enter Desolation Wilderness. Day-hiking permits are available at the trailhead. For backpacking permits, contact the U.S. Forest Service (USFS) office in South Lake Tahoe at 530-573-2694.

GETTING THERE From Tahoe City, drive 10 miles south on CA 89 to Meeks Bay (this is about 17 miles north of the intersection of CA 50 and CA 89 in South Lake Tahoe). The trailhead is on the west side of CA 89 at the bend in the road. Since parking is limited, you can turn this into a duathlon by riding the West Shore Bike Trail to the trailhead and then parking your bike there.

BRIEF TRAIL DESCRIPTION This trail starts out as a level walk through widely scattered forest and a wildflower-dotted meadow and then heads up into the trees, following the path of Meeks Creek. In 4.6 miles you reach Lake Genevieve, and Crag Lake shortly thereafter. If you would like to hike farther, you can continue past Stony Ridge Lake and Rubicon Lake before heading over Phipps Pass to the Tahoe Rim Trail and Middle Velma Lake. From Middle Velma Lake, Emerald Bay is only 5 miles away, making for a spectacular 18-mile point-to-point hike.

Fontanillis and Velma Lakes Loop

DIFFICULTY A strenuous 12-mile loop with 2,000 feet of elevation gain

MAP *Tahoe Rim Trail Section 7: Echo Summit and Echo Lake to Barker Pass (Map 2), page 145*

BEST SEASONS Mid-July–early October

HIGHLIGHTS Here is Desolation Wilderness in all its splendor, with spectacular views of granite peaks, mountain lakes, and a variety of plant life. Eagle, Granite, Fontanillis, and Dicks Lakes, as well as all three Velma Lakes, are excellent for swimming or camping.

HEADS UP! These trails, especially on the first mile to Eagle Lake, can be crowded in the summer. Day-use and backpacking permits are required. Day-use permits are available at the trailhead. To get a backpacking permit, contact the USFS office at 530-573-2694.

GETTING THERE You can start from either of two trailheads, both of which are located at the western end of Emerald Bay on CA 89. The Eagle Lake and Eagle Falls Trailhead is about 200 yards south of the Vikingsholm parking lot, which is about 17 miles south of Tahoe City and 10 miles north of South Lake Tahoe. There is a fee for parking. The Bay View Campground and Trailhead is 1 mile south of the Eagle Falls Trailhead on CA 89, across from the vista parking area. Drive through the campground to its western edge, where you will find trailhead parking.

BRIEF TRAIL DESCRIPTION The Eagle Lake Trail ascends about 1 mile to often crowded Eagle Lake. Then you stay left and climb steadily and sometimes steeply along the slope of south Maggies Peak to a junction 2.6 miles from the trailhead. If you are starting from the Bay View Trailhead, you hike about half a mile to a stunning view of Emerald Bay and then another half mile to Granite Lake. Next is a steep set of switchbacks into the cleavage between Maggies Peaks. These breast-shaped mountains, also known as Round Buttons, were named after Maggie. Who was she? Legend has it that she was a buxom barmaid at the Tahoe Tavern Resort.

The Bay View Trail reaches the saddle between the two peaks and then descends to a junction and a meeting with the Eagle Lake Trail. From here, with both trails as one, you hike along rolling, rocky terrain for a little less than a mile to a junction, where you take a left onto the trail leading to Dicks Lake. Now in the heart of the stark Desolation Wilderness, land of granite boulders, sandy soils, and scattered trees, you go about 0.5 mile to a beautiful pond. This shallow body of water is a good swimming spot and is especially pretty in the fall when the mountain heather surrounding the lake turns bright red. Your journey ascends across a granite slab to a saddle and junction. A left turn climbs up to Dicks Pass, but your right turn takes you to Dicks and Fontanillis Lakes. You are now on the combined Tahoe Rim Trail and Pacific Crest Trail. (For more detailed information on the next 2 miles of trail, refer to the TRT description in Chapter 6, Section 7, page 143). In 0.2 mile you meet another junction, with a left turn going to Dicks Lake in 100 yards, and a right turn heading to Fontanillis, your next destination. At Dicks Lake, look for osprey diving for fish in the evening. The trail follows along Fontanillis Lake and finally reaches its outlet creek.

The trail crosses the creek and heads downhill for about a mile along a ridge to a junction. If you turn left, you will be heading to Middle Velma Lake on the TRT/PCT. However, you should turn right, leave the TRT/PCT, and head uphill for a little more than a mile back to the Dicks Lake junction. Then retrace your steps back to the Bay View and Eagle Falls Trails junction. If you leave a car at both trailheads, you can hike a loop back to Emerald Bay via a different trail.

Donner to Squaw Valley

DIFFICULTY Strenuous (about 15 miles)

MAP USGS *Norden*

BEST SEASONS Mid-July–mid-October. Patches of snow can last until August on the north-facing slope of Anderson Peak.

HIGHLIGHTS This section of the Pacific Crest Trail provides miles of stunning 360-degree views from atop a windswept ridge. Ridgecrest views reach all the way from Mount Rose in the northeast to Lake Tahoe in the southeast, with the Granite Chief Wilderness to the south and west. You will see a wide variety of terrain and wildflower species, including large fields of mule-ears. This well-constructed trail has firmly packed, sandy soils good for fast-moving, long-distance hikers or runners. Everyone will enjoy its high-altitude remoteness. When Desolation Wilderness is packed with people, you may encounter only a few people on this trail. The trail goes by Roller Pass, a portion of the original Emigrant Trail used by pioneers when they came to California.

HEADS UP! Very little water is available on the trail, and if you are hiking in late summer or fall, assume that there will be no water.

Early in the summer, a northeast-facing 100-foot-long section about 3 miles into the trail may be treacherous if it is still covered with snow.

Most of the trail is treeless and exposed to the sun and wind; be sure to bring plenty of sunscreen and a windbreaker.

Your trail intersects with a variety of use paths descending from Shirley Canyon along the last mile of your route. Take care to avoid getting lost.

GETTING THERE Take I-80 to Exit 174 (Soda Springs), and drive 4 miles east on US 40 to Donner Summit. Take a right at the summit, just before the road starts to go downhill, and go 0.2 mile to the trailhead on your left. This point-to-point hike requires a shuttle; be sure to leave a vehicle behind in Squaw Valley.

BRIEF TRAIL DESCRIPTION Climb south on the Pacific Crest Trail, where in 1 mile you reach a junction with the Mount Judah Loop trail. This alternate route heads up to Mount Judah, which has excellent views, and then circles back and meets the PCT, adding 0.4 mile to your hike's length. About 2 miles into the hike, you reach a saddle, Roller Pass. Just off the trail to the southeast, the Donner Party of 1846 winched their wagons up the steep slope below. Another 0.3 mile of gentle climbing brings you to another saddle below Mount Lincoln. From here, the trail traverses a steep slope and then follows the ridgecrest, with views in all directions, for several miles to Anderson Peak. Your trail circles Anderson Peak and then climbs another ridge for a 1-mile journey to Tinker Knob, where a short use trail takes you to its summit.

At 8 miles into your hike, the trail descends from Tinker Knob into a deep, wide bowl (North Fork of American River Canyon) with wildflowers and sparse tree cover. You cross this bowl and then begin a steady climb, and at 4 miles from Tinker Knob, you reach a junction. Head east (left) on a steady downhill for 3 miles into Squaw Valley.

Aloha Lake Loop via Tamarack Trail

DIFFICULTY This 12-mile loop is strenuous overall, and the first 2.5 miles are very strenuous.

MAP *Tahoe Rim Trail Section 7: Echo Summit and Echo Lake to Barker Pass (Map 1),* page 144

BEST SEASONS Mid-July–mid-October

HIGHLIGHTS This is a classic hike into the heart of Desolation Wilderness, with views of more than a dozen lakes, numerous high granite and volcanic peaks, and a tremendous variety of mountain terrain.

HEADS UP! The first few miles up a canyon to a saddle are very steep, with almost 2,000 feet of elevation gain. Although it's not mountain climbing, it is certainly one of the steepest sections of trail I have ever hiked and is especially difficult if you are carrying a heavy backpack. In the early summer this steep section can be icy and requires extra caution.

GETTING THERE Go about 0.5 mile west of Camp Richardson on CA 89, and turn south on Fallen Leaf Lake Road (about 3 miles northwest of the intersection of CA 50 and CA 89 in South Lake Tahoe). Follow this road 5.3 miles along the edge of Fallen Leaf Lake to the Glen Alpine Trailhead. The first 4.5 miles of the route are one-and-a-half lanes wide, and the last 0.8 mile is only one lane wide. From the Glen Alpine parking area, walk on Fallen Leaf Lake Road back toward the lake about 0.25 mile to the Tamarack Trail on the right (south) side.

BRIEF TRAIL DESCRIPTION Hike 2.5 steep miles to a level junction with the Triangle Lake Trail. These first few miles are extremely beautiful. You will hike through lush, almost junglelike stream crossings with tiger lilies and columbines and then climb through open areas of granite boulders from which you can enjoy great views. From the Triangle Lake junction, go straight and climb more gently now to an open, almost treeless viewpoint that faces Echo Lakes and Ralston Peak. Then proceed downhill to a junction where the TRT/PCT climbs up from Echo Lakes. Turn right on the TRT/PCT, and follow the signs to Lake Aloha. For a more detailed description of the next 6 miles of trail along the TRT, refer to Section 7 (page 143).

When you reach Lake Aloha, turn right and head north along Aloha's eastern shore to a junction at its northern edge, where you turn right. In the next 2 miles you descend past two beautiful lakes, Heather and Susie. From Susie Lake you hike about 0.5 mile to a junction where you turn right. Now leaving the TRT/PCT, you hike 0.5 mile to another junction, turn right, and follow the TRT/PCT 3.3 miles, mostly downhill, to the Glen Alpine Trailhead.

Fall colors at Page Meadows

Mountain Biking

Page Meadows and Ward Canyon

DIFFICULTY This area has a whole system of interconnected trails, which vary from easy to strenuous.

MAP *Tahoe Rim Trail Section 8: Barker Pass to Tahoe City,* page 162

BEST SEASONS Late June–late October

HIGHLIGHTS These trails have it all: rolling forested terrain, lush green meadows in the summer, and glorious yellow and red leaves in the fall. It is a fun, smooth singletrack trail with good climbs and thrilling descents. The variety of trails encourages you to visit again and again.

HEADS UP! The meadow areas are fragile. *Do not ride through them when they are wet.* Sometimes the elaborate trail network can be confusing. You may end up coming out somewhere different than you think you will, but that's part of the fun.

GETTING THERE Five locations provide access to this great network of dirt roads and singletrack trails.

View while mountain biking from Tahoe Cross-Country Ski Area

1. **GRANLIBAKKEN ROAD** Go 0.5 mile south of Tahoe City on CA 89, turn right on Granlibakken Road, and then turn left on Rawhide, which you take to its end. The trail starts behind a gate.

2. **END OF SILVERTIP DRIVE IN TALMONT ESTATES** Take CA 89 about 2 miles south of Tahoe City, and turn right on Pine Avenue. Then turn right on Tahoe Park Heights Drive, right on Big Pine Drive, and left on Silvertip Drive, which you follow to its end.

3. **WARD CREEK BOULEVARD** Go south from Tahoe City about 2.5 miles on CA 89. Turn right on Pineland Drive. At the end of the straightaway, veer left and follow the Ward Canyon sign. Go about 1.5 miles on Ward Creek Boulevard to the TRT on your right, and start climbing.

4. **CHAMONIX ROAD** Follow the directions to #3 above, and go an additional 0.75 mile on Ward Canyon Boulevard, which becomes Courchevel. Turn right on Chamonix Road, and proceed to the end of the road, where a trail heads west.

5. **SNOWCREST ROAD, ALPINE MEADOWS** Take CA 89 about 3.5 miles north from Tahoe City to Alpine Meadows Road, where you turn left. Go about 1 mile, and turn left on Snowcrest Road. Follow this road to a gated dirt road on your left.

BRIEF TRAIL DESCRIPTION Because there are so many different entrances and a complicated network of trails, I do not give exact directions for this trip. A number of loop trails go around Page Meadows, up to the top of Scott Peak at Alpine Meadows, or into the Tahoe City and Rawhide area. One loop starts at Rawhide, goes over to Snowcrest, and then heads back along the bike trail between Alpine Meadows and Tahoe City. Another trail starts at Chamonix, goes around the meadows, and then loops back to the same starting point or down to Ward Canyon Boulevard. Explore the area and see where you end up.

Tahoe Cross-Country Ski Area and Burton Creek State Park

DIFFICULTY Moderate. A variety of trails and loops provide opportunities for all riders, from beginners to experts.

MAP *Tahoe Rim Trail Section 7: Echo Lake to Barker Pass (Map 1)*, page 144

BEST SEASONS Late June–November or until the first major snow. After mild winters with less than average snow, it is possible to access this area by late May.

HIGHLIGHTS A gently rolling open forest makes for great riding on smooth trails. You will find beautiful meadows, spectacular wildflower displays, and several excellent lake views at the top of the climbs. Tahoe XC rents bikes and provides refreshments from their lodge.

HEADS UP! It's easy to get lost in the confusing trail pattern here. This is a busy area—watch out for hikers, dogs, children, horses, and bears.

GETTING THERE From Tahoe City, take CA 28 about 2.5 miles northeast to Fabian Way and turn left. Turn right on Village Road and proceed to the top of the hill, where Village veers right. Quickly turn left on Country Club Drive, and left again into the Tahoe Cross-Country Ski Area parking lot.

BRIEF TRAIL DESCRIPTION From the Nordic center, go up the dirt road, heading west. This area has dozens of miles of trails that go to Tahoe City, Truckee, Northstar, or Brockway Summit. Mount Watson is located at about 8 miles of steady climbing from the Nordic center, where you'll have great lake views. Most trails are easy to moderate and very fun to ride. Look for maps of the trail networks at intersections. Try out the Osprey Trail and the Lakeview Ridge Trail if you can find them. The opportunities for different rides are almost endless. For a detailed description of the Tahoe Rim Trail portion of this trail system, refer to the trail description for Section 1 (page 60).

Flume Trail and Tahoe Rim Trail Loop

DIFFICULTY Strenuous 23-mile round-trip with a lot of climbing. The Flume Trail portion, which is 4.5 miles long, is on the edge of a cliff and may give the acrophobic the heebie-jeebies.

MAP *Tahoe Rim Trail Section 3: Tahoe Meadows to Spooner Summit,* page 87

BEST SEASONS Mid-June–October

HIGHLIGHTS This is one of the most spectacular mountain biking routes in the United States. The views of Lake Tahoe are awe-inspiring, the fall colors can be extraordinary, and most of the trail is smooth and a treat to ride.

HEADS UP! This very popular trail is used by both hikers and bikers and can be quite congested on weekends. Be especially cautious of hikers, and follow the posted bike speed limits.

The 4.5-mile Flume Trail portion of the trail, while well constructed, may be challenging to those who fear heights.

GETTING THERE The trailhead is off of NV 28, about 0.5 mile north of the intersection of NV 28 and US 50. It is located in Lake Tahoe Nevada State

Park at Spooner Lake, about 27 miles from Tahoe City and 14 miles from South Lake Tahoe. A fee is required to park.

BRIEF TRAIL DESCRIPTION From the parking lot, head down a short hill to North Canyon Road, which you follow about 4 miles uphill to the saddle above Marlette Lake. There are maps at several kiosks along the route. A 1-mile descent takes you to a junction next to Marlette Lake. Turn left and follow the road around the west side of the lake to Marlette Lake's dam. To the left of the dam, the Flume Trail begins as a steep singletrack that quickly crosses the lake's outlet creek. For the next 4.5 miles the trail traverses mostly level terrain over the location of the former water flume that ran from Marlette Lake to Carson City. In the late 1800s this flume carried logs to build Virginia City silver mines. The lake views from the Flume Trail are spectacular. Eventually the trail reaches Tunnel Creek Road.

If you would like a shorter ride, turn left and head down this road to NV 28. In the summertime you can pay for a shuttle back to your car. Call 775-298-2501 or go to theflumetrail.com for shuttle information and times.

To continue on the Flume Trail and TRT loop, turn right and head up the steep hill 0.5 mile to the TRT, where you turn right. Follow the trail past Twin Lakes and begin climbing. The TRT heads mostly uphill for 2.4 miles and then mostly downhill for 2.7 miles to a junction at Hobart Road. Turn right on Hobart Road, and soon you will head downhill steeply to your junction next to Marlette Lake. Now you are retracing your route to the saddle above Marlette Lake and then on a long, fun downhill on North Canyon Road back to the trailhead.

Commemorative Emigrant Trail

DIFFICULTY Easy–moderate. For most people who have experience on single-track trails, this is a fun and not-too-difficult ride. It is a special treat for advanced riders looking for an opportunity to ride fast.

MAP USGS *Truckee*

BEST SEASONS Late May–November. The snow on this trail usually melts earlier than that on any other singletrack trail in the North Tahoe and Truckee area. After a mild winter you may be able to ride this trail by mid-April.

HIGHLIGHTS This is a fun ride with gentle ascents and descents through an open forest that strong riders can complete in about 2 hours. While the scattered forest scenery on this trail is pleasant, its great riding conditions are what make it especially enjoyable. Keep your eyes open for deer, which are commonly found along this trail.

HEADS UP! Since in the spring this trail may be the only North Tahoe–area mountain biking trail free of snow, it can be overcrowded, especially on weekends. As the snow melts and other trails become available, the number of riders on the trail drops significantly. In the middle of the summer, this very exposed and dry trail can be quite hot and dusty.

GETTING THERE Take CA 89 about 4.5 miles north from the intersection of I-80 and CA 89 in Truckee. Just past the bridge across Prosser Creek (the first large creek you pass heading north from Truckee), take a right on Hobart Mills Road. The trailhead parking lot is on your right just after you turn.

BRIEF TRAIL DESCRIPTION The trail heads 9 miles north through a recently logged forest, eventually reaching Stampede Reservoir, where you turn around and return the same way. The trail intersects many dirt roads; just follow the well-marked singletrack trail. Along the route you see several meadows and Mount Rose in the distance through the trees.

The final push to Dicks Pass (Section 7, page 143)

Appendix

A Resources

LISTED BELOW ARE public agencies, U.S. Forest Service information centers, and other useful tidbits to help you plan your trip to the Tahoe Rim Trail.

National Forests

EL DORADO NATIONAL FOREST
Supervisor's Office
100 Forni Road
Placerville, CA 95667
530-622-5061; fs.usda.gov/eldorado

HUMBOLDT-TOIYABE
NATIONAL FOREST
Carson Ranger District
1536 S. Carson St.
Carson City, NV 89701
775-882-2766; fs.usda.gov/htnf

LAKE TAHOE BASIN
MANAGEMENT UNIT
35 College Drive
South Lake Tahoe, CA 96150
530-543-2600; fs.usda.gov/ltbmu

TAHOE NATIONAL FOREST
Truckee Ranger District
10811 Stockrest Springs Road
Truckee, CA 96161
530-587-3558; fs.usda.gov/tahoe

Other Agencies

LAKE TAHOE NEVADA STATE PARK
Incline Village, NV
775-831-0494
parks.nv.gov/parks
/lake-tahoe-nevada-state-park-1

TAHOE RIM TRAIL ASSOCIATION
Office:
128 Market St., Ste. 3
Stateline, NV 89449

Mailing address:
P.O. Box 3267
Stateline, NV 89449

775-298-4485; tahoerimtrail.org

TOM HARRISON MAPS
tomharrisonmaps.com

Useful Phone Numbers

EMERGENCY
911

**EL DORADO COUNTY SHERIFF
(SOUTH LAKE TAHOE OFFICE)**
530-573-3000

NEVADA COUNTY SHERIFF
530-265-1471

PLACER COUNTY SHERIFF
530-889-7800

WASHOE COUNTY SHERIFF
775-328-3001

Useful Websites

DAVE'S SIERRA FISHING
davessierrafishing.com

FLUME TRAIL BIKES
theflumetrail.com
Bike rentals and information about
the Flume Trail shuttle

KIRKWOOD
kirkwood.com
Information about Kirkwood Downhill
and Cross-Country ski areas

MOONSHINE INK
moonshineink.com
Truckee and Tahoe's great monthly
news magazine

TAHOE DAILY TRIBUNE
tahoedailytribune.com
Daily news for Tahoe
information about fishing in the
Sierra Nevada

TAHOE RIM TRAIL ASSOCIATION
tahoerimtrail.org
Official website of the Tahoe Rim
Trail Association

TAHOE RIM TRAIL ENDURANCE RUNS
trter.com

TAHOE WEEKLY
thetahoeweekly.com
Up-to-date Tahoe information

TAHOE XC
tahoexc.org
Information about the Tahoe
Cross-Country Ski Area

Appendix

B

Mileages for the Tahoe Rim Trail

THE MILEAGES FOR the distances between points along the Tahoe Rim Trail presented below are based on the cartographic work of the Tahoe Rim Trail Association, Jeffrey P. Schaffer, and Tom Harrison Maps.

Section Mileages (clockwise)		
Location	**Total Miles**	**Miles Between Points**
SECTION 1: Tahoe City to Brockway Summit	19.1	
Painted Rock		8.0
Fiberboard Freeway crossing		9.1
Watson Lake		12.4
Brockway Summit		19.1
SECTION 2: Brockway Summit to Mount Rose	20.3	
Spur trail to viewpoint		1.2 (viewpoint is 1.5)
Road to Martis Peak		4.3
Rock Pile viewpoint		6.8
Wilderness boundary		7.6
Rose Knob Peak and Gray Lake junction		10.0
Gray Lake junction and Mud Lake		11.2
Relay Peak		14.6
Wilderness boundary (dirt road)		15.0
Via road (original TRT):		
Mount Rose Trail junction		16.4
Mount Rose Trailhead		19.6

(continued on next page)

(continued from previous page)

Section Mileages (clockwise)

Location	Total Miles	Miles Between Points
SECTION 2: Brockway Summit to Tahoe Meadows (continued)	20.3	
Via trail and Mount Houghton Ridge:		
Junction with Mount Houghton Trail		15.5
Junction with former TRT and Snow Pond Trail		17.1
Bottom of waterfall and Mount Rose Summit Trail junction		17.7
Mount Rose Trailhead		20.3
SECTION 3: Tahoe Meadows to Spooner Summit	23.1	
Tunnel Creek Road		9.2
Twin Lakes		9.5
Christopher Loop junction		11.6 (viewpoint is 12.8)
Marlette Peak Campground		13.8
Hobart Road		14.3
Marlette Lake via Hobart Road		16.4
Spooner Lake via Hobart Road		21.2
Snow Valley Peak Road		17.2
Snow Valley Peak		17.5
Spooner Summit Trailhead		23.1
SECTION 4: Spooner Summit to Kingsbury Grade	19.4	
South Camp Peak		6.0
Genoa Peak		7.8
Junction with Kingsbury North Access Trail		12.9
Kingsbury North Trailhead via access trail		13.4
Junction with North Kingsbury Loop Trail		15.6
Kingsbury Grade crossing		15.8
Junction with Van Sickle Trail		18.7
Junction with Kingsbury South Trail		19.4
Kingsbury South Trailhead (if stopping at trailhead)		19.9
SECTION 5: Kingsbury Grade to Big Meadow	23.2*	
Mott Canyon Creek		3.6
Monument Pass		5.1
Star Lake		8.8
Freel Peak saddle		10.7

* Add 0.5 mile if coming from the Kingsbury South Trailhead.

Section Mileages (clockwise)

Location	Total Miles	Miles Between Points
SECTION 5: Kingsbury Grade to Big Meadow *(continued)*	23.2	
Armstrong Pass		13.7
Tucker Flat (Saxon Creek Trail)		18.8
Grass Lake junction		21.2
Grass Lake Trailhead (optional)		21.8
Big Meadow Trailhead		23.2
SECTION 6: Big Meadow to Echo Summit	15.7	
Big Meadow		0.7
Dardanelles Lake junction		2.0
Dardanelles Lake		3.4
Round Lake		2.6
PCT and TRT junction		4.9
Showers Lake		7.0
Sayles Canyon Trail		10.5
Bryan Meadow		11.4
Echo Summit		15.7
Echo Lake (if continuing to Section 7)		17.9
SECTION 7: Echo Lake to Barker Pass	32.7**	
Upper Echo Lakes water taxi		2.5
Tamarack Lake		3.6
Lake Aloha		6.0
Junction with Mosquito Pass Trail		7.4
Heather Lake		7.9
Susie Lake		9.0
Glen Alpine Springs Trail junction		9.7
Gilmore Lake		10.7
Dicks Pass		13.6
Junction to Bayview Trail		15.3
Dicks Lake		15.5
Fontanillis Lake		16.0
Middle Velma Lake		17.7
Phipps Peak Trail junction		18.9
Richardson Lake		26.0

** Add 2.2 miles if coming from Echo Summit.

(continued on next page)

(continued from previous page)

Section Mileages (clockwise)

Location	Total Miles	Miles Between Points
SECTION 7: Echo Lake to Barker Pass	32.7**	
Miller Lake jeep road		28.4
Barker Pass		32.7
SECTION 8: Barker Pass to Tahoe City	16.7	
Twin Peaks trail junction		4.8
Twin Peaks on TRT		6.0
Junction of TRT and Stanford Rock Trail		6.3
Ward Creek Road		11.5
Tahoe City		16.7

** Add 2.2 miles if coming from Echo Summit.

Appendix

C

Tim's Top Five Places on the Trail

For Views

DICKS PASS (SECTION 7) Since it is quite a climb to reach the top of Dicks Pass, you'll want to spend some time enjoying the breathtaking views of two huge watersheds and a dozen lakes.

CHRISTOPHER LOOP (SECTIONS 3 AND 4) Located about halfway between Tahoe Meadows and Spooner Summit at the end of a short spur trail, this viewpoint is not easy to reach, but you are rewarded with a view of the entire lake and surrounding mountains (Section 3, page 86). The other great east-shore lake view is from South Camp Peak, halfway between Spooner Summit and Kingsbury Grade (Section 4, page 113).

GRANITE CHIEF WILDERNESS BETWEEN BARKER PASS AND TWIN PEAKS (SECTION 8) Just south of the PCT junction near Twin Peaks, at the end of a long climb, you reach a great open ridge, where you enter Granite Chief Wilderness. Views into the big valley of that wilderness and toward Desolation Wilderness and Lake Tahoe are spectacular. It's a perfect lunch spot.

RELAY PEAK (SECTION 2) The high point of this ridge in the Mount Rose area is referred to as the "Million Dollar Mile" because it affords spectacular 360-degree views. On a clear day you can see the Sierra Buttes and Lassen Peak to the north.

LAKE ALOHA (SECTION 7) On a midsummer day without much wind, gazing up at the Crystal Range while you lounge on a rock with one foot in the water is unbeatable.

To Swim

LAKE ALOHA (SECTION 7) Here is Lake Aloha again. What can I say? If you swim from island to island offshore when the water is warm, you'll swear you have died and gone to heaven.

MIDDLE VELMA LAKE (SECTION 7) This is another great lake for swimming, with numerous islands begging you to jump in and swim to them. If you are northbound on the TRT, it will be more than 80 miles before the next really good swimming lake (and that next lake is colder).

TRUCKEE RIVER AND LAKE TAHOE (INTERSECTION OF SECTIONS 1 AND 8) Even though you cross the river right in the middle of Tahoe City, jump in and float around; it feels great. If you're ready for a break, consider a leisurely raft trip down the Truckee River; contact Mountain Air Sports at 530-583-1111 for more information. Also, the Commons Beach on Lake Tahoe in the center of Tahoe City is about 0.25 mile east of the Truckee River on CA 28. If you are hiking the Tahoe Rim Trail, doesn't it make sense to swim in Lake Tahoe?

STAR LAKE (SECTION 5) Because of its high elevation, the lake can be extremely brisk (OK, it's bone-chillingly cold), but the views are great and Star is the best lake along the east-shore trail. If you hit it when it's warm, it makes for a great swim.

SHOWERS LAKE (SECTION 6) This lake has big, flat granite rocks that go right down to the water's edge, which makes for great swimming au naturel.

To Ride a Bike

PAINTED ROCK (SECTION 1) Between Tahoe City and Brockway Summit, 2 miles in either direction of Painted Rock, is the smoothest, most enjoyable singletrack trail you'll ever ride. The easiest access point is Dollar Hill at the Tahoe Cross-Country Ski Area.

TUNNEL CREEK ROAD TO MARLETTE LAKE (SECTION 3) This portion of trail can be used as part of a loop with the Flume Trail. It includes some tough climbs and some thrilling downhills with spectacular views. Get off your bike to hike up to the view from Herlan Peak (aka Christopher Loop).

PAGE MEADOWS (SECTION 8) The Page Meadows area, which has an extensive network of trails besides the Tahoe Rim Trail, offers some wonderful twists and turns on very ridable terrain. Stay out of the meadow itself until it dries up in late summer or fall.

SPOONER SOUTH TO SOUTH CAMP PEAK (SECTION 4) This section offers great riding over sandy terrain with tremendous views along the way. Either turn around at the peak and enjoy the downhill stretch, or continue to Kingsbury for something a little more challenging and technical.

TAHOE MEADOWS TO TUNNEL CREEK (SECTION 3) Available for use only on even-numbered days, this is probably the most popular mountain biking section on the TRT. After an initial climb, it is mostly downhill, with beautiful sandy conditions and great views. Some parts are pretty technical, but if you go on a summer weekend, the most difficult challenge may be avoiding the crowds.

To Camp

LAKE ALOHA (SECTION 7) Hundreds of great spots are available on this big lake. It will give you privacy when the smaller Desolation Wilderness lakes are crowded.

VELMA, FONTANILLIS, AND DICKS LAKES (SECTION 7) All of these give you the full Desolation Wilderness experience, however crowded they become in mid-summer. Very few campsites are available at Fontanillis.

BARKER PASS (SECTION 8) About 2.5 miles north of Barker Pass is a peaceful little meadow with great views, a stream, and a nice camping spot among the trees.

STAR LAKE (SECTION 5) This lake is beautiful, the campsites have views of both Lake Tahoe and Star Lake, and the next lake is at least 17 miles away. Isn't it time to make camp? If you are feeling energetic, you can hike up to the top of Freel Peak in the morning; it's only 2 miles away.

SHOWERS LAKE (SECTION 6) Showers is a beautiful little lake offering great swimming and fine views. If you go there in the middle of the week, it might even be quiet and peaceful.

Appendix

Ways to Save Lake Tahoe

WE HAVE BEEN BLESSED with a deep-blue alpine lake surrounded by majestic mountains. We must make an effort to preserve this lake and its environment so that future generations can enjoy it as well. The Tahoe Regional Planning Agency has come up with ways to save Lake Tahoe. A few of the best are listed below. These are a good place to start, but don't hesitate to think up your own.

1. **Take the bus. Share a ride. Take a hike. Ride a bike.** When you pick up your car keys, stop to plan the trip you're about to make. Can you run several errands while you're out? Could you save this trip until you need to make another? Is there another way you could get there? Consolidating trips and getting around without driving your car are ways to reduce traffic congestion and protect air quality, and may improve your social skills and your health.

2. **Fill . . . don't spill.** If you fill your tank to the brim, gasoline may spill out and into Lake Tahoe.

3. **Skip a stone and leave the other rocks alone.** Rocks of all sizes and shapes are fish habitat. Fish need rocks to carry out their life cycles. Underwater rock gardens are where they spawn, feed, and hide from predators. By moving or rearranging rocks, you could be destroying valuable habitat.

4. **Don't be a trail blazer.** Erosion from unmaintained dirt roads presents a serious water-quality challenge. Off-highway vehicles, dirt bikes, and hikers all contribute to erosion when they travel off the maintained roads. Kids, stay on the designated roads. Parents, make sure your kids stay on the designated roads.

5. **You can lead a horse to water, but you shouldn't set up camp there.** The less activity there is in a stream environment zone, the better. The law requires that you pitch your tent at least 200 feet from a body of water. That includes lakes, streams, creeks, reservoirs, and rivers.

6. **Garbage in, garbage out.** You could even pick up after a litterbug who went before you.

7. **Finally, teach your children well.**

The above information was provided as a courtesy of the Tahoe Regional Planning Agency. For more information, call them at 775-588-4547 or visit trpa.org. The Tahoe Fund (tahoefund.org) and the League to Save Lake Tahoe (keeptahoeblue.org) also provide information on ways you can help.

Appendix

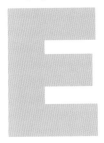

Leave No Trace Principles

THE LEAVE NO TRACE CENTER for Outdoor Ethics promotes the Seven Principles of Leave No Trace. Before heading out to the Tahoe Rim Trail or other outdoor environment, go to lnt.org and find out more information about how you can enjoy nature responsibly.

The Seven Principles

1. Plan ahead and prepare.

2. Travel and camp on durable surfaces.

3. Dispose of waste properly.

4. Leave what you find.

5. Minimize campfire impacts.

6. Respect wildlife.

7. Be considerate of others.

© 1999 by the Leave No Trace Center for Outdoor Ethics: www.lnt.org

Index

A

Aloha Lake Loop via Tamarack Trail, 182–183
Alpenglow Sports, Tahoe City, 42
Alpine Meadows, 65, 67, 169, 170, 171, 185
Alpine Peaks, 164, 170, 171
Alta Morris Lake, 143, 147, 155
altitude. See elevation
amenities at trail–road crossings/communities, 42–45
America Lake, 150
American River Canyon, 141, 146, 181
American robin, 11
amphibians, 13
Anderson Peak, 180
Angora Fire of 2007, 107, 121
animals, 5–10
Applegate's paintbrush, 23
Armstrong Pass, 51, 115, 117, 124–125
aspect, snowpack and, 31
aspen, 16
asters, 23
avalanches, 34

B

backcountry hiking, tips for, 43
backpacking, 41–46. See also camping
    acquiring food along the TRT, 42–45
    bears and, 5–6
    equipment to bring, 45–46
    food, what to carry, 46
bald eagle, 11
Barker Pass, 44, 143, 146–147, 160, 161, 166, 197
    horse trailer parking, 50
Barker Pass to Tahoe City (Section 8), 161–172
    fear of heights and, 39
    map, 162
    mountain biking, 48, 163–164
    side trips along, 170, 171
    trail description, 166–172
Barker Peak, 160, 166
Basque sheepherders' oven, 170
bear canisters, 46
Bear Lake, 160
bears, 5–6
bees, 14
best spots
    for children, 53–57
    for dogs, 57
    for mountain biking, 196–197
Big Meadow, 133–134
    hiking with children, 55
Big Meadow Creek, 133

Big Meadow to Echo Summit (Section 6), 130–142
    map, 131
    mountain biking, 47, 132
    side trips along, 135, 140
    trail description, 133–142
Big Meadow Trailhead, 44, 133
    horse trailer parking, 50
birds, 11–13
black bear, 5–6
Blackwood Canyon, 108, 147, 164, 166, 167
blue grouse, 11, 73
bluebird, 12
bobcat, 7
Boyle, William, 63
Brockway Summit
    hiking with children, 54–55
    horse trailer parking, 49
Brockway Summit to Mount Rose (Section 2), 70–85
    fear of heights and, 38
    map, 71
    mountain biking, 47, 72
    side trips along, 73, 74, 76, 79, 82, 84
    trail description, 73–85
brook trout, 15
brown trout, 15
Bryan Meadow Trail, 140
buckthorn, 24
Burton Creek, 67
Burton Creek State Park, 185–186
bushes, 24–25

C

cabins, renting, 4, 101
California ground squirrel, 9
camping, 41–46
    bears and, 5–6
    in Section 2, 72, 73
    in Section 3, 88–89
    in Section 4, 103
    in Section 5, 121–122
    in Section 6, 134–135, 138, 140
    in Section 7, 150, 154, 157
    in Section 8, 161, 167
    limitations on, 4
    supplies for, 45–46
    Tim's top five places for, 197
    with horses, 51
Canada goose, 11
Carson City, 101
Carson Pass, 126, 177
Carson Range, 106
Castle Peak, 75, 108
Castle Rock Vista, 110–111
catch-and-release fishing, 52, 53
catfish, 177

C *(continued)*

checkermallow, 21
chickaree, 9
children, best places to take, 53–57
chinquapin, 24
chipmunk, 10
Christopher Loop, 86, 97, 195
Cinder Cone, 65
Clark's nutcracker, 11, 79
Clinton, Hillary, 3
clothing
    for backpacking, 45
    for winter hiking/snowshoeing, 35
Commemorative Emigrant Trail, 187
cony (pika), 10
corn lily, 19
cougar, 6–7
cow parsnip, 23
coyote, 7
coyote mint, 22
Cracked Crag, 150
Crag Lake, 178–179
Crag Peak, 159
crimson columbine, 19
Crystal Range, 121, 124, 140, 149, 150, 151, 195
Cutter, Ralph, 52
cutthroat trout, 15
cycling. *See* mountain biking

D

Daggett Pass, 44
daisies, 23
Dardanelles Lake, 53, 55, 135, 139
Dave's Sierra Fishing (website), 190
deep forest pinedrops, 21
deer, 6
dehydration, 33
delphinium, 19–20
Desolation Wilderness, 4, 41, 51, 108, 121, 124, 140, 143, 148, 158
    fishing in, 52
Diamond Peak Ski Area, 93, 94
Dicks Lake, 13, 143, 153, 155–157, 180, 197
Dicks Pass, 37, 143, 152, 153, 156, 195
Dicks Peak, 152, 153, 154, 155, 157
dogs, on trails, 57
Dollar Point, 95
Donner Lake, 79
Donner Party of 1846, 181
Donner Summit, 31, 108
Donner to Squaw Valley, 180–182
Douglas (Sierra) wallflower, 21
Douglas squirrel, 9
drinking water, 4, 38, 42, 43, 88

E

Eagle Creek, 174–175
Eagle Lake, 179, 180
east shore area, fishing in, 53
Echo Chalet, 44, 55, 143
Echo Chalet Store, 146
Echo Lakes area, 143, 145–148
    hiking with children, 55
Echo Peak, 148
Echo Summit, 44
    horse trailer parking, 50
Echo Summit and Echo Lake to Barker Pass (Section 7), 143–160
    map, 144–145
    mountain biking, 48
    regulations/permits, 4, 146
    side trips along, 148, 154, 156, 157, 159
    trail description, 147–160
Eldorado National Forest, 189
elephant's heads, 20
elevation
    snowpack and, 31
    trees and, 18
Ellis Peak, 167
Emerald Bay, 156, 173–175
emergencies
    sheriff phone numbers, 190
    survival kits for, 35
    winter weather risks, avoiding, 34
Emigrant Trail, 181, 187
endurance runs, TRT, 190
equipment, backpack recommendations, 45–46
explorer's gentian, 23

F

Fairway Community Center, 62
fall, hiking in, 37–38
Fallen Leaf Lake, 143, 148, 182
fear of heights, 38–39
Fiberboard Freeway, 63, 66, 67, 68, 69
fireweed, 21
fishing, 51–52
    best spots for, 52–53
    fish species, 15, 51–52
    licenses for, 52
Flagpole Peak, 148
Flume Trail, 96, 101, 186–187
Flume Trail Bikes, 101, 102, 190
flying squirrel, 10
Fontanillis Lake, 13, 155, 157, 158, 180, 197
food
    protecting from bears, 5–6, 46
    when backpacking, 46
Fountain Face/Fountain Place, 124

Freel Peak, 74, 79, 82, 107, 115, 119, 121, 123, 126, 139, 151, 178
Frog Pond. *See* Snow Pond
frostbite, 34

G

Galena Falls, 54, 78, 83
Genoa Peak, 107, 108–109
giardia (waterborne parasite), 38
Gilmore Lake, 142, 153–154
Ginny Lake, 78
golden-mantled ground squirrel, 10
Granite Chief Wilderness, 4, 161, 167, 168, 182, 195
Granlibakken ski area, 63
Grass Lake, 3, 128–129, 153
Grass Lake Creek, 115, 129
Gray Lake, 70, 76, 77, 78, 79
    fishing in, 53
Great Ski Race, 67
ground squirrels, 9–10
Grouse Rock, 170
Grubb viewpoint, 111
A Guide to Winter Preparedness and Survival, 37
guided-hiking program, Tahoe Rim Trail Association, 3
    in winter, 35

H

Half Moon Lake, 143, 147, 153, 154, 155
Hampton, Glenn, 2
Harrison, Tom, 58
Hauserman, Tim, 57, 212
Haypress Meadows, 149
Heather Lake, 143, 150, 151, 152, 183
Heavenly Ski Area Stagecoach parking lot, 50
Heavenly Village, 44
Hell Hole Canyon, 126
Herlan Peak, 86, 97, 196. *See also* Christopher Loop
High Loch Leven Lake, 175–177
hiking
    backcountry, tips for, 43
    drinking water and, 4, 38
    guided hikes. *See* guided-hiking program,
        Tahoe Rim Trail Association
    limitations on, 4
    near horses, 27–28
    seasonal suggestions, 36–38
    trail behavior and, 26–27, 29
horse camping spots, 51
horseback riding, 48–49
    camping spots, 51
    hiking near, 27

trail use and, 27–28
    trailer parking, 49–51
horsemint, 21–22
huckleberry oak, 24
Humboldt-Toiyabe National Forest, 189
hypothermia, 33

I

incense cedar, 16
Incline Lake Trail, 70, 78, 79
Incline Village, 43, 54, 93, 94
insects, 14
Interpretive Trail, Tahoe Meadows, 54

J

Jacks Peak, 108, 152, 154, 155
Jeffrey pine, 16–17
Jobs Sister, 74, 115, 120, 121, 122, 123
junco, 12

K

Keiths Dome, 153
Kings Beach, 43
Kingsbury Grade North and South, horse trailer parking, 50
Kingsbury Grade to Big Meadow (Section 5), 115–129
    fear of heights and, 39
    map, 116
    mountain biking, 47, 117
    side trips along, 121, 123, 124, 125, 128
    trail description, 118–129
Kingsbury Stinger Trail, 110
Kirkwood Downhill and Cross-Country Ski Area, 36, 190
Knight, Lora, 173
kokanee salmon, 15, 52

L

Lahontan cutthroat trout, 53
Lake Aloha, 55, 140, 147, 149–150, 155, 182, 195–196, 197
Lake Forest "island," 95
Lake Genevieve, 159, 179
Lake Lucille, 149
lake (mackinaw) trout, 15
Lake Margery, 149
Lake of the Woods, 55, 149
Lake Tahoe, 65, 66, 68, 75, 78, 86, 89, 94, 97, 98, 100, 106, 108, 125, 160, 186
    geographic setting, 2

L *(continued)*
map, xii
snowpack, 30–32
trail history, 2–3
ways to save, 199–200
Lake Tahoe Basin Management Unit, U.S. Forest
Service, 4, 189
Lake Tahoe Nevada State Park, 4, 189
Lake Tahoe Recreation Map (Harrison), 58
Lake Tahoe's Desolation Wilderness Fishing Guide
(Yesavage), 52
larkspur, 19–20
Lassen Peak, 80, 155, 195
League to Save Lake Tahoe, 2
Leave No Trace principles, xi, 201
legend, for maps, 59
Lewis's monkeyflower, 20
licenses, fishing, 52
Lily Lake, 148
Loch Leven Lakes, 175–177
lodgepole pine, 17
Lower Echo Lake, 55, 145–146, 147–148
horse trailer parking, 50
Lower Twin Lake, 96
lupine, 23

M
mackinaw (lake) trout, 15, 52
Maggies Peaks, 93, 180
mahala mat, 25
manzanita, 24
maps
legend for, 59
Tom Harrison Maps, 58, 189, 191
TRT sections. *See under individually named trail sections*
Mariposa lily, 22
Marlette, Seneca Hope, 100
Marlette Campground, 4, 42, 88
Marlette Lake, 53, 86, 89, 97–101, 186, 187
marmot, 8
marten, 8
Martis Peak, horse trailer parking, 49
Martis Peak Lookout/Fire Lookout, 72, 74
McCloud Falls, 57, 169
McKinney Rubicon OHV Trail, 160
Meeks Bay, 159
Meiss Lake, 53, 137
Meiss Meadows, 51, 53, 130, 138
Meiss Meadows Trail, 134, 135
Meyers, 44, 146
Middle Loch Leven Lake, 175–177

Middle Velma Lake, 143, 144, 155, 157, 158, 179, 180, 196
mileages, on Tahoe Rim Trail, 191–194
Miller Creek, 160
Miller Lake Creek, 143
Mokelumne Wilderness Area, 177
monkeyflower, 20
monkshood, 20
Monsters in the Woods: Backpacking with Children (Hauserman), 57
Monument Pass, 117, 121
Moonshine Ink, 190
Mosquito Pass, 151
mosquitoes, 14
Mott Canyon Creek, 115, 119, 120
Mount Baldy, 74, 76, 79, 94
Mount Houghton, 82
Mount Judah Loop Trail, 181
Mount Price, 150, 155
Mount Rose, 72–73, 78, 79, 80, 82–85, 106, 122, 178
hiking with children, 53
horse trailer parking, 49–50
Mount Rose Campground, 72, 84
Mount Rose Wilderness, 4, 73, 76, 79, 82, 85
Mount Shasta, 80
Mount Tallac, 74, 92, 108, 109, 110, 154, 159, 178
Mount Watson, 68, 185
Mountain Air Sports, 196
mountain biking
Burton Creek State Park, 185–186
Commemorative Emigrant Trail, 187–188
Page Meadows and Ward Canyon, 183–185
rules for, 26, 27
section regulations, summarized, 47–48
Tahoe Cross-Country Ski Area, 185–186
Tim's top five places for, 196–197
tips for, 48, 72, 89–90, 105, 117, 132, 163
TRT loop, 186–187
mountain bluebird, 12
mountain chickadee, 12
mountain hemlock, 17
mountain lion, 6–7
mountain pennyroyal, 22
mountain quail, 12
mountain whitethorn, 24
Mr. Toad's Wild Ride, 117, 127, 128
Mud Lake, 70, 76, 78, 79
fishing in, 53
Muir, John, 1, 18, 46
mule deer, 6
mule-ears, 22

N

national forests, 189
  navigation, in winter, 32–33
North Daggett Loop Trail, 112
north shore area, fishing in, 53

O

165 Mile Club, 3, viii
Ophir Creek, 43, 51, 54, 86
osprey, 12
owls, 12

P

Pacific Crest Trail: Northern California
  (Schaffer), 58, 69
Pacific Crest Trail (PCT), 3, 136–137, 147
  mountain biking and, 47–48
Pacific tree frog, 13
Page Meadows, 36, 161, 163, 170, 171, 172
  hiking with children, 56–57
  mountain biking, 183–185, 196–197
paintbrush, 23
Painted Rock, 196
parking, for horse trailers, 48–51
permits/regulations, 4, 41–42, 177
Phipps Creek, 158
Phipps Pass and Peak, 137, 159, 179
Phipps Pass Trail, 158–159
phone numbers, useful, 190
pika (cony), 10
pines, 16–18, 19
plants, 16–25
ponderosa pine, 17
porcupine, 8
pretty yellow flowers (PYF), 24
prettyface, 22
provisioning, along the TRT, 42–45
Pyramid Peak, 108, 140, 147, 150, 155, 178

Q

quails, 15
quaking aspen, 16

R

Raborn, Shannon, 45
raccoon, 9
rain, 31, 37–38
rainbow trout, 15
Ralston Peak, 149, 182
Rawhide Drive, 171

red fir, 17
Red House Flume Trail, 95, 96
red mountain heather, 24–25
regulations/permits, 4
rein orchis, 20
Relay Peak, xi, 70, 78, 79, 80, 81, 83, 84,
  94, 195
reptiles, 14
resources, 189–190
Richardson Lake, 143, 157, 158, 159–160
Rim to Reno Trail, 72–73, 85
road crossings/communities, along TRT,
  42–45
Robie Equestrian Park, 51
robin, 11
Roller Pass, 181
Rose Knob Peak, viii, 76, 77, 79, 94
Round Lake, 53, 55, 129, 130, 134–135
Round Top, 126, 141, 177, 178
Round Top Lake, 177–178
Rubicon Lake, 159, 179
Rubicon Peak, 108
Rubicon River, 158, 159

S

salmon, 15
Salmon Lake, 177
Saxon Creek Trail, 117, 127
Sayles Canyon Trail, 140
scarlet gilia, 22
scenic views, 73
  Tim's top five places for, 195
Schaffer, Jeffrey P., 58, 191
Schneider Cow Camp, 136, 138, 140
Scott Peak, 171, 185
Sections, of TRT
  #1. *See* Tahoe City to Brockway Summit
  #2. *See* Brockway Summit to Mount Rose
  #3. *See* Tahoe Meadows to Spooner Summit
  #4. *See* Spooner Summit to Kingsbury Grade
  #5. *See* Kingsbury Grade to Big Meadow
  #6. *See* Big Meadow to Echo Summit
  #7. *See* Echo Summit and Echo Lake to
    Barker Pass
  #8. *See* Barker Pass to Tahoe City
sheriffs, phone numbers for, 190
Shirley Canyon, 181
shooting stars, 20–21
Showers Lake, xi, 51, 53, 130, 132, 133, 138–
  140, 153, 196, 197
shrubs, 24–25
Sierra Canyon Trail, 110
Sierra (Douglas) wallflower, 21
Sierra Trout Guide (Cutter), 52

S *(continued)*

64 Acres parking lot, 49, 163, 165, 172
Slab Cliffs, 80
Slide Mountain, 85, 91
snakes, 14
snow geese, 11
Snow Pond, 54, 81, 83
Snow Valley Peak, 74, 86, 88–89, 97, 98, 99, 100, 101, 106
snowbush, 24
snowpack
avalanches and, 34
average, 58
factors influencing, 30–32
snowplant, 22–23
snowshoeing
clothing for, 35
guided hikes in winter, 35
locations for, 36
South Camp Peak, 103, 105, 107, 108
South Shore area, fishing in, 53
Spooner Lake, 53, 86, 88, 90, 101, 102, 103
Spooner Summit, 44
horse trailer parking, 50
Spooner Summit to Kingsbury Grade (Section 4), 103–114
map, 104
mountain biking, 47, 105
side trips along, 109, 110, 112, 113
trail description, 106–114
spring, hiking in, 36–37
squaw carpet, 25
Squaw Valley, 65, 180–182
squirrels, 10
Stanford Rock, 164, 169
Star Lake, 51, 115, 121–123, 128, 196
Star Lake to High Meadows Trail, 122
Steel, Morgan, xi
Steller's jay, 13
Stony Ridge, 108
Stony Ridge Lake, 159, 179
sugar pine, 18
summer, hiking in, 37–38
sunburn, in winter, 34
survival kit, for winter weather, 35
Susie Lake, 143, 147, 151–155, 183
swimming spots, 88, 90, 100, 115, 121, 130, 133, 134, 135, 137, 138, 143, 148, 150, 152, 157, 161, 162, 165, 172, 175, 178, 179, 180
Tim's top five places, 196

T

Tahoe City, 42
horse trailer parking, 49
Tahoe City to Brockway Summit (Section 1), 60–69
map, 61
mountain biking, 47
side trips along, 63, 65, 66, 68
trail description, 62–69
Tahoe Cross-Country Ski Area, 37, 67, 185, 196
Tahoe Daily Tribune, 190
Tahoe Meadows, 35, 36, 91, 102
hiking with children, 53–54, 84
horse trailer parking, 49–50
mountain biking, 72
Tahoe Meadows to Spooner Summit (Section 3), 86–102
map, 87
mountain biking, 47, 89–90
regulations/permits, 4
shorter alternative routes, 102
side trips along, 91, 96, 97, 100, 101
trail description, 91–102
Tahoe National Forest, 189
Tahoe Nordic Search and Rescue Team (NSAR), 37
Tahoe region, flora and fauna of, 5–25
Tahoe Regional Planning Agency, 2
ways to save Lake Tahoe, 199–200
Tahoe Rim Trail Association (TRTA), x–xi, 3–4, 59
guided-hiking program, 3, 35
mileages and, 191
165 Mile Club, viii, 3
resources, 189, 190
Tahoe Rim Trail Fund, 2, 3
Tahoe Rim Trail (TRT)
best spots for kids, 53–57
favorite places on. *See* Tim's top five places
geographic setting, 2
history of, 2–3
introduction to, 1–2
mileages for, 191–194
overview map, xii
permits/regulations, 4
resources, 189–190
road crossings/communities along, 42–46
seasonal suggestions, 36–38
snow and, 30–32
Tim's top five places on, 195–197
unnerving spots along, 38–39
Tahoe Rim Trail (TRT) Sections
#1. *See* Tahoe City to Brockway Summit
#2. *See* Brockway Summit to Mount Rose
#3. *See* Tahoe Meadows to Spooner Summit
#4. *See* Spooner Summit to Kingsbury Grade

#5. *See* Kingsbury Grade to Big Meadow
#6. *See* Big Meadow to Echo Summit
#7. *See* Echo Summit and Echo Lake to Barker Pass
#8. *See* Barker Pass to Tahoe City
maps. *See under individually named trail sections*
Tahoe Sierra (Schaffer), 58
Tahoe XC, 37, 190
Tahoe-Yosemite Trail (TYT), 137, 143, 159
Tallant Lakes, 137
Tamarack Lake, 143, 148
Tamarack Peak, 84
Taylor Creek Visitor Center, 4
Tevis Cup 100-mile horse ride, 51
thimbleberry, 25
thunderstorms, 37–38
tiger (alpine) lily, 21
Tim's Knob, 156
Tim's top five places
    for camping, 197
    for mountain biking, 196–197
    for scenic views, 195
    for swimming, 196
Tinker Knob, 181–182
tobacco brush, 25
toiletries, when backpacking, 45
trailers, horse, where to park, 49–51
Tramway Market, 44
trees, 16–19
    elevation and, 18
Triangle Lake, 148
Triangle Lake Trail, 182
trout, 15
Truckee River, 52, 60, 75, 161, 163, 165, 172, 196
Truckee River Access parking lot.
    See 64 Acres parking lot
Truckee River Canyon, 60, 64, 140
Tunnel Creek Cafe, 101
Tunnel Creek Road, 90, 92, 95, 96, 97
Twin Lakes, 53, 86, 90, 96
Twin Peaks, xi, 74, 93, 108, 155, 161, 164, 168, 169, 170

U

Upper Echo Lake, 55, 143, 148
Upper Loch Leven Lake, 175–177
Upper Price Lake, 91
Upper Truckee River, 53, 130, 137, 140, 141
Upper Velma Lake, 143, 157
U.S. Forest Service (USFS).
    See Lake Tahoe Basin Management Unit, U.S. Forest Service

V

Van Sickle Trail, 44, 113, 118, xi
Velma Lakes Loop, 179–180, 197
Vikingsholm Castle, 173, 174–175
Virginia City, 66, 101, 186
visible trails, lacking in winter, 32–33

W

The Wall, 66
Ward Canyon, 51, 57, 164, 169, 183–185
    hiking with children, 57
Ward Creek, 57, 164, 169, 170
Ward Creek Boulevard, 44–45, 57, 163–165, 170, 194
Washoe Lake, 80, 93, 94, 95
wasps, 14
water
    for horses, 48–49, 51
    potable, for humans. *See* drinking water
water taxi, Echo Lakes, 55, 143, 148
Watson Creek, 69
Watson Lake, 51, 53, 60, 69
weasel, 8
weather, winter precautions, 30–34
websites, useful, 190
The Wendell and Inez Robie Foundation, 51
western fence lizard, 14
western flying squirrel, 10
western gray squirrel, 10
western rim area, fishing in, 52
western (Sierra) juniper, 18
Western States Trail, 66, 70, 78
western tanager, 13
western white pine, 18, 120
western yellow pine, 17
white fir, 19
whitebark pine, 19
wildflowers, 19–24
Willits, Sonja, 27
wind, snow and, 31–32
Winnemucca Lake, 177–178
winter
    precautions in, 30–35
    snowpack in, 30–32
    trail suggestions, 36–37

Y

yellow jackets, 14
Yesavage, Jerome, 52

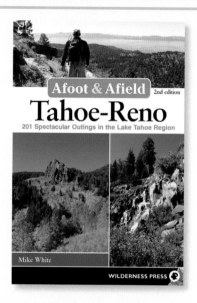

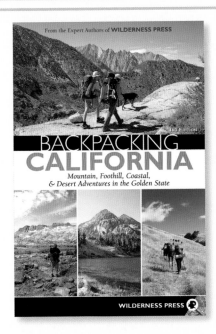

About the Author

TIM HAUSERMAN has been a resident of North Lake Tahoe since 1960. He has hiked and biked in the area for many years and has been a guide for Tahoe

Trips and Trails (a private excursion company) and the Tahoe Rim Trail Association. A member of the Tahoe Rim Trail Board of Directors from 1998 to 2007, he became the 11th member of the Tahoe Rim Trail 165 Mile Club in 1999. His other books include *Monsters in the Woods: Backpacking with Children, Gertrude's Tahoe Adventure's in Time* (a children's book), and *Cross-Country Skiing in the Sierra Nevada*. He also writes for a variety of local and regional publications. Tim lives on the west shore of Lake Tahoe, where he likes to hike, bike, cross-country ski, kayak, and canoe.